Kultobjekt
Designobjekt
Fahrrad

Cult Object
Design Object
Bicycle

Kultobjekt
Designobjekt
Fahrrad

Cult Object
Design Object
Bicycle

Die Neue Sammlung – The Design Museum
Verlag der Buchhandlung Walther und Franz König

Inhalt

Contents

Angelika Nollert

Das Rad
neu erfinden

Das Rad wurde im 5. Jahrtausend vor Christus erfunden, nachweisbar als Drehscheibe für die Keramikherstellung. Erste Hinweise für die Nutzung eines Rades zum Transport von Dingen datieren um 4.000 vor Christus. Vor diesem Hintergrund erscheint die Erfindung des Fahrrads im Jahre 1817 zunächst als eine relativ späte Entwicklung.

Aber es ist eine Entwicklung der damaligen komplexen Zeit: des 18. Jahrhunderts als Jahrhundert der Topografie mit seinen Aufzeichnungen und seriellen Abbildungen von Städten und Landschaften, der Epoche der Aufklärung, die dem Bürger mehr Rechte zubilligte, und schließlich des Zeitalters der Romantik, die die Sehnsucht nach der Natur und fremden Ländern postulierte sowie den Reiseroman entdeckte. Die Reiseliteratur erhielt mit dem 1832 erschienenen ersten Baedeker ein neues Gesicht. Es war eine Zeit, die von den letzten großen Entdeckungsreisen geprägt war und gleichzeitig einen schnell wachsenden technischen Fortschritt generierte.

Mit dem Fahrrad wurde der Wunsch nach Beschleunigung und Erweiterung des menschlichen Aktionskreises mittels einer durch ein Werkzeug oder Maschine gestützten Fortbewegung aus eigener Muskelkraft nun zum ersten Mal funktionstüchtig auf der Erde umgesetzt. Diese Erfindung kann trotz ihrer Weltbedeutung somit als bodenständig gelten.

Als Konzept einer individuellen Mobilität durch die eigene menschliche Kraft steht das muskelbetriebene Veloziped als Besonderheit zwischen den Erfindungen der dampfbetriebenen Eisenbahn (1804) und des motorisierten Automobils (1886).

Am 12. Juni 1817 konnte der deutsche Forstbeamte und Erfinder Karl Friedrich Drais der Öffentlichkeit seine erste lenkbare und zweirädrige Laufmaschine vorstellen. Er hatte vier Jahre zuvor bereits einen tretmühlengetriebenen „Wagen ohne Pferde" entwickelt. Jedoch war die vom Schlittschuhlaufen abgeleitete Bewegung des Fahrradlaufens und damit das Prinzip der dynamischen Bewegung das Entscheidende. Seine Laufmaschine oder Draisine, die durch abwechselndes Abstoßen mit den Beinen angetrieben wurde, gilt heute als das Ur-Fahrrad. Erst 50 Jahre später, 1868, wurde das kettengetriebene Fahrrad entwickelt, was eine deutlich weniger anstrengende Fortbewegung mit Pedalen ermöglichte.

Wenige Jahre später, 1873, veröffentlichte der sich für visionäre Fahrgeräte begeisternde Schriftsteller Jules Verne seinen Roman „Reise um die Erde in 80 Tagen". Hiervon inspiriert fuhr 1895 Heinrich Horstmann als erster Deutscher mit dem Fahrrad um die Welt und publizierte „Meine Radreise um die Erde

Angelika Nollert

Reinventing the wheel

The wheel was invented in the 5th millennium BCE – there is evidence of it being used in making pottery. First indications of a wheel being used to transport things date from 4,000 BCE. Against this background, the invention of the bicycle in 1817 initially seems to be a relatively late development.

However, it is a development during a highly complex era: the 18th century as the century of topography with its mappings and serial illustrations of cities and landscapes, the epoch of the Enlightenment, which accorded citizens greater rights, and finally the Age of Romanticism, which first elaborated on the yearning for nature and foreign countries and discovered travel fiction. Travel literature was given a new face in 1832 with the appearance of the first Baedeker guidebook. It was a period in history that was shaped by the last major voyages of discovery and at the same time set in motion technological progress at an ever-faster pace.

The bicycle was the first functional realization on earth of the wish to accelerate and expand the radius of human activity by means of locomotion driven by human power alone and relying on a tool or a machine. The invention can, for all its international significance, thus be regarded as very down-to-earth.

As a concept for personal mobility using one's own power, muscle-driven velocipedes remained quite unique, wedged between the inventions of steam-driven railway locomotives (1804) and motorized automobiles (1886).

On June 12, 1817, German forest official and inventor Karl Friedrich Drais presented his first steerable and two-wheel 'running machine' to the public. Four years earlier, he had already developed a "cart without horses" driven by a treadmill; however, the motion of running with the bicycle derived from ice skaters and thus the principle of dynamic movement was the key advance in the new invention. His 'running machine' or 'Draisine', propelled by pushing off alternately with one leg and then the other, is today considered the ur-bicycle.

The chain-driven bicycle was not developed for another 50 years, namely in 1868, and enabled a far less strenuous form of locomotion using pedals.

A few years later, in 1873, author Jules Verne who was an enthusiast of visionary vehicles, brought out his novel "Round the world in 80 days". Inspired by it, in 1895 Heinrich Horstmann was the first German to circumnavigate the globe by bicycle, publishing his account as "Meine Radreise um die Erde vom 2. Mai 1895 bis 16. August 1897". Thomas Stevens was first round the world by bike, in 1884. Ten years later Annie Londonderry had departed from Boston by bicycle to travel round the world. The new vehicle's potential seemed endless.

vom 2. Mai 1895 bis 16. August 1897". Die erste Weltreise auf dem Fahrrad hatte der Brite Thomas Stevens bereits 1884 unternommen. Ihm folgte 1894 Annie Londonderry aus den USA, die als erste Frau mit dem Fahrrad die Erde umrundete. Das Potenzial dieses Fahrzeugs erschien grenzenlos.

Schon früh gab es bekannte und bekennende Fahrradfahrer*innen wie die Künstlerin und Schriftstellerin Colette, den Künstler Lyonel Feininger, den Physiker Albert Einstein oder den Schriftsteller Ernest Hemingway. Ihnen allen war gemeinsam, dass sie das Fahrradfahren als Akt der Freude, der Freiheit und des befreiten Denkens begriffen. Seit seiner Erfindung ist das Fahrrad ein Kulminationspunkt von gesellschaftlicher und politischer Bedeutung, von Zukunftsvisionen, als Motiv in Literatur und Kunst, und es ist bis heute von hohem sozialen und kulturellen Interesse. Diese Erfolgsgeschichte des Fahrrads scheint kein zeitliches Limit zu besitzen. Heute gibt es etwa eine Milliarde Fahrräder auf der Welt und in Deutschland rund 81 Millionen.

Das Fahrrad ist vor allem aber auch ein Thema der Gestaltung. Seit Beginn hat das Design eines Fahrrads die technischen Innovationen umgesetzt oder sie sogar erst möglich gemacht. Und seit Beginn hat die Gestaltung eines Fahrrads auch die Art und Weise beeinflusst, wer wie wohin fährt.

Lange hatten Frauen es schwer, Fahrrad zu fahren. Die Mode mit Korsett und langen Röcken bis in die 10er-Jahre des 20. Jahrhunderts sowie die seinerzeitige Etikette waren Hindernisse. Eine Befreiung brachte 1889 das „Lady's Rover Safety Bicycle", ein Damenrad, das auf das Oberrrohr verzichtete und damit einen niedrigen Einstieg bot. Mit dem Rad wurde die Eigenständigkeit der Frauen erhöht, indem sie sich auch alleine im Freien bewegen und aufhalten können. In Saudi-Arabien ist den Frauen erst seit 2013 das Fahren mit dem Fahrrad erlaubt.

Das Potenzial der Frauenemanzipation durch das Fahrrad hat hingegen nicht dazu geführt, dass es viele Designerinnen in diesem Bereich gibt. Deutlich mehrheitlich ist das Fahrraddesign noch immer männlich besetzt.

Das Fahrrad ist vielfach auch ein Symbol der Demokratisierung. Denn mit dem Fahrrad können sich viele Menschen unabhängig von Einkommen und Beruf weiträumig bewegen und sich an dritten Orten in Gleichheit begegnen.

Seit den 90er-Jahren des letzten Jahrhunderts gibt es die Fahrradbewegung Critical-Mass. „Massen" an Fahrradfahrer*innen treffen sich zu bestimmten Zeiten, um in einem Korso die Autostraßen für sich zu beanspruchen. Die Critical-Mass-Bewegung sieht das Fahrrad als Möglichkeit, das Automobil neu zu überdenken. Sie möchte zum aktiven Einsatz von Fahrrädern auffordern, um öffentliche und soziale Räume neu zu definieren und zu nutzen.

Jahrzehntelang wurde eine Stadt rund um das Auto gebaut. Autos dominierten den Straßenverkehr und damit die Stadtplanung. Heute hat ein Umdenken stattgefunden. Die Stadt will sicherer werden für den Menschen, will grün werden für ein gutes Klima, will den Lärm reduzieren, mehr Platz schaffen und die Aufenthaltsqualität verbessern. Die neuen nachhaltigen Mobilitätskonzepte fördern daher die Mikromobilität von Fahrrädern.

Die Beliebtheit des Fahrrades liegt auch an seiner funktionalen Vielfalt. Heute scheint es für jeden Bedarf ein Fahrrad zu geben. Neben Damen-, Herren-

There were famous, self-confessed cyclists such as artist and journalist Colette, artist Lyonel Feininger, physicist Albert Einstein or author Ernest Hemingway. They all shared the feeling that bicycling was an act of joy, of freedom, of liberated thought.

Ever since its invention, the bicycle has been a culmination point of social and political significance, of future visions, a theme in literature and art, and to this day of great social and cultural interest. The bicycle's success story can seemingly go on forever. Today, there are about 1 billion bicycles world-wide and about 81 millions in Germany.

The bicycle's popularity stems also from its functional diversity. The bicycle is above all also a theme for design. Since the very beginning, the design of a bicycle has realized technical innovations or even made them possible in the first place. And since the early days, the design of a bicycle has also influenced the way who cycles where and how.

For a long time, cycling was difficult for women. The fashion of corsets and long skirts that prevailed until the 1910s as well as the etiquette of the day were inhibiting obstacles. Liberation came in 1889 in the form of the "Lady's Rover Safety bicycle", a bicycle for women that dispensed with the top tube and thus lowered the step-over entry point. The bicycle increased women's independence, they were able to move further on their own outside and spend time there. In Saudi Arabia, women have only been permitted to ride bicycles since 2013.

The potential for women's liberation afforded by the bicycle has not, however, led to many female designers being active in this field. The clear majority of bicycle designers are men.

In many cases and places, the bicycle is a symbol of democratization. Because bicycles enable many people, irrespective of their incomes or professions, to move around widely and meet as equals at a third place.

The bicycle movement "Critical Mass" has been in existence since the 1990s. "Masses" of cyclists meet at a pre-arranged time in order to ride together and with the safety of numbers lay claim to roads that are otherwise used mainly by cars. The "Critical Mass" movement considers bicycles a means of rethinking automobiles. It calls on people to actively use bicycles in order to rethink and re-use public and social spaces.

For decades, cities were built around automobiles. Autos dominate road traffic and thus urban planning. Today, people have started to think differently. Cities seek to be safer for people, to be green, to improve the (ambient) climate, to reduce noise levels, create more space, and improve the quality of leisure time spent in them. The new sustainable mobility concepts therefore foster the micro-mobility provided by bicycles.

Today, there seems to be a special bicycle for every need. Alongside women's, men's, and children's bikes, there are bikes for older people and gender-neutral bikes. There are city-bikes, racing bikes, mountain bikes, tricycles, and cargo bikes. The materials used to build bicycles range from steel, aluminum, plastic, carbon, or wood to bamboo. A bicycle made of paper has also been developed. The key thing is for a bicycle to be light and stable, aerodynamic, and

und Kinderrädern gibt es alters- und genderübergreifende Fahrräder. Es gibt Citybikes, Rennräder und Mountainbikes, Dreiräder und Lastenräder. Die Materialien der Räder variieren zwischen Stahl, Aluminium, Kunststoff, Karbon, Holz und Bambus. Auch ein Rad aus Papier wurde bereits entwickelt. Ein Fahrrad sollte dabei leicht und stabil sein, aerodynamisch und komfortabel. Aus der Perspektive des Designs sollte es zusätzlich zur Funktionalität eine klare Formensprache, stimmige Elemente und eine innovative Rahmengeometrie besitzen.

In den letzten Jahren hat die Fahrradproduktion einen Boom verzeichnet. Die Klimakrise, die zunehmende Work-Life-Balance und das verstärkte Leben im Freien in Zeiten der Pandemie sind sicher begünstigende Faktoren ebenso wie die Gesundheit und das wachsende Bedürfnis nach körperlicher Ertüchtigung. Aber vor allem erscheinen immer mehr Bikes heute „cooler" als viele Autos, respektive die Bikefahrer*innen sportlicher als ihre Autokolleg*innen. Mit dem Kauf eines Fahrrads werden gleichzeitig Narrative und Emotionen erworben.

Hinzu kommt die Hinwendung zur Individualisierung. Diese ist vor allem durch eine Differenzierung über das Design möglich, denn die großen Radhersteller verfügen gleichermaßen über ein großes technisches Wissen. Fahrräder werden auf ihre Fahrer*innen zugeschnitten, die einzelnen Elemente werden über einen Konfigurator ausgewählt und dann customized zusammengesetzt.

Das Fahrrad hat sich zu einem hochpreisigen Statussymbol entwickelt, es ist zu einem Kultobjekt geworden.

Die Ausstellung in der Neuen Sammlung widmet sich genau diesem Thema: das Fahrrad als Kultobjekt und Designobjekt. 70 internationale Fahrräder aus über 200 Jahren werden präsentiert, die genau diese Werte spiegeln. Es sind Fahrräder, die sich durch ihr besonderes Design derart auszeichnen, dass sie zum Kult geworden sind.

Es gilt an dieser Stelle Dank zu sagen. Ein großer Dank geht an den Kurator Josef Straßer für Konzeption und Realisierung von Ausstellung und Katalog. Ihm ist es zu verdanken, dass sich so viele außerordentlich und innovativ gestaltete Fahrräder begegnen und so den Ausstellungsraum in eine Bike-Arena verwandeln.

Wir danken den Leihgeber*innen Reiner Balke, Monika Bock, Stephan Dornhofer, Dirk Eger, Adrien Elmiger, Heinz Fingerhut, Sebastian Fischer, Sebastian Jacobi sowie Eva Mayer. Insbesondere möchten wir uns bei dem Deutschen Fahrradmuseum, namentlich Ivan Sojc und Stefanie Faust für die vielen Leihgaben und die wunderbare Kooperation bedanken.

Wir danken PIN. Freunde der Pinakothek der Moderne für ihre großzügige Förderung. Und wir freuen uns, dass die Publikation erneut im Verlag der Buchhandlung Walther und Franz König erscheinen kann. Für die grafische Umsetzung danken wir Petra Lüer vom Grafikbüro wigel.

„Das Leben ist wie Fahrrad fahren, um die Balance zu halten, musst du in Bewegung bleiben", lautet ein Zitat von Albert Einstein. Die Fahrräder in der Ausstellung stehen still. Nur so können sie ihre gestalterischen Qualitäten offenbaren. Dafür bleiben die Besucher*innen in Bewegung.

comfortable. From the perspective of design, in addition to the functionality, a bicycle has to have a clear formal language, coherent elements, and an innovative frame geometry.

In recent years, bicycle production has boomed. The Climate Crisis, the increasing emphasis on a work-life balance and a stronger focus on outdoor life during the pandemic are no doubt factors here, as are health and the growing need for physical fitness. That said, first and foremost an increasing number of today's bicycles are "cooler" than many autos and/or the cyclists are more sporting than their car-driving colleagues. When you purchase a bicycle today, you also buy a narrative and emotions.

Then there's the turn to customization. This is possible above all thanks to differentiation through design, as the major bicycle manufacturers also possess a great deal of technological knowhow. Today, bicycles are custom-fitted to the cyclist, the individual elements selected by a configurator and then assembled.

The bicycle has emerged as a high-end status symbol and simultaneously evolved into a cult object.

The exhibition at Die Neue Sammlung foregrounds precisely this theme: the bicycle as cult object and design object alike. A total of 70 international bicycles straddling over 200 years of history will be on show, each of which reflects exactly these values. These are bicycles that became cult items precisely by virtue of their special design.

I would like at this juncture to offer a word of thanks. I am most grateful to curator Josef Straßer for devising and realizing the exhibition and publication concept. Thanks to him, the exhibition space boasts so many extraordinary and innovatively designed bicycles, transforming it into a veritable bike arena.

I would also like to thank the lenders Reiner Balke, Monika Bock, Stephan Dornhofer, Dirk Eger, Adrien Elmiger, Heinz Fingerhut, Sebastian Fischer, Sebastian Jacobi as well as Eva Mayer. We are especially grateful to Deutsches Fahrradmuseum, and specifically to Ivan Sojc and Stefanie Faust for the many exhibits they have lent us and for the marvelous cooperation.

Our thanks likewise go to PIN. Freunde der Pinakothek der Moderne for their generous support. And we are delighted that this book is again being brought out by Verlag der Buchhandlung Walther und Franz König. Our thanks go to Petra Lüer of Grafikbüro wigel for the graphic design.

"Life is like riding a bicycle. To keep your balance you must keep moving," Albert Einstein once said. However, the bicycles in the exhibit do not move. Only in this way can they reveal their design qualities. The visitors for their part keep moving.

Josef
Straßer

Zur Geschichte des Fahrraddesigns

In den Überblickswerken zur Designgeschichte kommt das Thema Fahrrad kaum vor und wenn, dann nur am Rande. Das Automobil dagegen ist aus diesen Publikationen nicht wegzudenken. Das erstaunt doch etwas, denn das Fahrrad gilt als der Vater des Automobils (und die Kutsche als Mutter), das Fahrrad ist um einige Jahrzehnte älter, das Fahrrad ist das weltweit am weitesten verbreitete Verkehrsmittel, das Fahrrad ist das effizienteste mit Muskelkraft zu bewegende Gefährt, mit dem Fahrrad begann der Individualverkehr – und heute gehört es zu den wichtigsten Antworten auf unsere Mobilitätskrise.

Seit einigen Jahren erlebt das Fahrrad einen regelrechten Boom. Die Verkaufszahlen schnellen enorm in die Höhe, vor allem bei den Rädern mit Elektroantrieb. In Deutschland bemühen sich die Städte darum, fahrradgerecht zu werden, bauen Fahrradstraßen und Fahrradschnellwege. Hier gibt es viel aufzuholen, denn in anderen europäischen Städten ist man häufig weiter.

Aber woran liegt die Vernachlässigung des Fahrrads in der Designgeschichte? In den letzten Jahren gab es einige Fahrrad-Ausstellungen, allerdings meist von Technikmuseen und weniger von Designmuseen organisiert. Handelt es sich doch mehr um ein Thema der Technik- als der Designgeschichte, eine Geschichte der technischen Erfindungen und Entwicklungen? Oder liegt es daran, dass die Designgeschichte sich noch in den Anfängen befindet und das Thema Design erst in den letzten Jahrzehnten zunehmend an Bedeutung gewann, dass der Begriff Design sich über die Jahrzehnte so gewandelt hat, sich so schwer definieren lässt bzw. von so vielen Interessen vereinnahmt wird?

Ohne eine Antwort auf all die Fragen geben zu können, soll doch an dieser Stelle der Versuch gestartet werden, das Fahrrad als designgeschichtlich relevantes Objekt zu betrachten. Deshalb wurde auch bei der Auswahl der einzelnen Objekte der Fokus auf das Design und weniger auf die Technologie gelegt, obwohl sich beide gegenseitig bedingen.

Funktion und Form gehen Hand in Hand und damit auch die im Lauf der Jahrzehnte immer stärkere Ausdifferenzierung in die unterschiedlichen Typen von Fahrrädern: Reiserad, Rennrad, Stadtrad, Klapp- oder Faltrad, Liegerad, Mountainbike, BMX-Fahrrad, Trekkingrad, Gravelbike, E-Bike etc. Nicht alle Typen, vor allem die jüngeren, konnten in diesem Kontext berücksichtigt werden, um den Aspekt des Fahrrad-Designs zu veranschaulichen. Auch ein Blick auf das Design der einzelnen Komponenten wäre sicherlich aufschlussreich, doch könnte man diesem Thema eine eigene Ausstellung widmen.

Josef Straßer

On the History of Bicycle Design

In the surveys of design history there is as little as no mention of bicycles, and if there is, then only as a marginal phenomenon. By contrast, such publications are inconceivable without descriptions of automobiles. This is surprising, if only because the bicycle is considered the father of the automobile (the coach was its mother), the bicycle is several decades older, the bicycle is the means of transport most widespread the world over, the bicycle is the most efficient vehicle powered by the muscles, the bicycle marked the beginning of personal means of transport – and today the bicycle is one of the most important answers to our mobility crisis.

For some years now there has been a veritable boom in cycling. Sales figures have rocketed, above all for bicycles with electric drives. In Germany, cities are busy trying to do justice to bicycles, building bicycle streets and fast-track cycle paths. And they have a lot of ground to make up, as in other European cities things have often progressed significantly further.

What, then, are the reasons for the bicycle being so neglected by and in design history? In recent years there have been a few bicycle exhibitions, albeit mainly organized by technology museums rather than design museums. Is it more a topic for technological than design history after all, namely a history of technological inventions and developments? Or is the reason that design history is still in its infancy and the topic of design only gained greater importance in recent decades, and that the concept of design has itself changed down through the decades in such a way that it is hard to define it and/or it has been appropriated by so many different interest groups?

Without being able to offer answers to all these questions, at this point an attempt will be made to view the bicycle as an object of relevance to design history. For this reason, when selecting the individual objects, the focus has been on the design and less on the technology, although the one determines the other and vice versa.

Function and form go hand in glove. And as a result, over the decades there has been ever greater differentiation between different types of bicycles: randonneurs, racing bikes, city bikes, folding bikes, recumbent bikes, mountain bikes, BMX bikes, trekking bikes, gravel bikes, e-bikes, etc. It was not possible to consider all these types, especially the more recent additions, when it came to visualizing bicycle design. A glance at the design of the individual components would no doubt also be revealing, but that is a topic for an exhibition in its own right.

Die Anfänge

Mythen und Legenden
Ganz am Anfang steht natürlich die Frage, wer die Idee hatte, ein allein auf menschliche Muskelkraft basierendes Fortbewegungsmittel zu entwickeln. Wer hat das Fahrrad erfunden?

Leonardo da Vinci wäre hierfür ein würdiger Kandidat. 1974 fand man in seinem Codex Atlanticus[1], eine Ansammlung von losen Blättern, auf der Rückseite eines Manuskripts eine kleine Zeichnung mit einem fahrradähnlichen Gefährt: zwei gleichgroße Räder mit je acht Speichen, eine Gabel mit Lenkstange, Pedale, eine Kette und ein Sattel. Durch die starre Lenkstange scheint eine Lenkung unmöglich.

Die Zeichnung wurde bald einem Schüler Leonardos zugeordnet, danach infrage gestellt und schließlich als Fälschung des späten 20. Jahrhunderts identifiziert.[2] Aber wie dem auch sei, ohne funktionierende Lenkung wäre das Gefährt (Abb. 1) ohnehin nicht fahrtauglich gewesen.

Das Prinzip zweier hintereinander angeordneter, mit einer Stange etc. verbundener Räder taucht Jahrhunderte später wieder auf, darunter die nicht lenkbaren Nürnberger Laufmaschinen oder die Célérifères des Grafen Mede de Sivrac. Neben diesen durchaus ernst zu nehmenden Fahrrad-Vorläufern im Europa des 18. Jahrhunderts führen wesentlich ältere Spuren nach China und Japan.[3]

Die Laufmaschine von Karl Friedrich Drais
01   054   Doch heute gilt Mannheim als Geburtsort des Fahrrads, auch wenn das dort entwickelte Gefährt mit unseren Vorstellungen vom Fahrrad noch nicht ganz übereinstimmt: Es handelt sich um ein einspuriges, lenkbares Fahrzeug mit zwei hintereinander laufenden Rädern, besser vielleicht als Laufmaschine zu bezeichnen. Erfinder dieses Gefährts war Karl Friedrich Drais, der seine Laufmaschine im Jahr 1817 erstmals der Öffentlichkeit vorführte.[4] Er hatte für ursprünglich nicht-lenkbare Laufräder eine Lenkvorrichtung gebaut, eine sogenannte Drehschemel-Lenkung, sowie ein Balancierbrett für die Unterarme. Damit blieben diese frei zum Lenken und das Gleichgewicht konnte leichter gehalten werden, während sich der Fahrer mit den Füßen vom Boden abstieß, um vorwärtszukommen. Balancieren auf zwei Rädern stellte damals die bahnbrechende Neuerung dar.

Wie ausgeklügelt die von dem Mannheimer Stellmacher Johann Frey nach den Entwürfen von Drais gefertigte Maschine war, zeigt sich an zahlreichen Details: extrem leichte Speichenräder mit 27 Zoll Durchmesser, schmierbare Messingbüchsen der Naben zur Reibungsreduzierung, gepolstertes Balancierbrett, Vorderrad mit ca. 15 cm Nachlauf, damit sich dieses immer wieder in Fahrtrichtung einstellte, die Leitstange konnte nach vorne umgeschlagen werden, um die Laufmaschine am Berg hinter sich herzuziehen. Später kam noch ein höhenverstellbarer Sitz hinzu. All diese funktionalen Elemente lassen sich auch unter dem Aspekt der Gestaltung betrachten. Hinzu kommt die für die Anfänge des Designs, aber auch heute noch geltende Prämisse der Arbeitsteilung, die

The Early Days

Myths and legends

The question that must be asked at the very beginning is of course: Who had the idea of dreaming up a means of locomotion that relied solely on the power of human muscles? Who, in other words, invented the bicycle?

Leonardo da Vinci would be a worthy candidate. In 1974, in his Codex Atlanticus,[1] a collection of loose sheets, on the back of a manuscript a small drawing was found with a bicycle-like machine: two equal-sized wheels, each with eight spokes, forks with handlebars, pedals, a chain, and a saddle. The fixed handlebars suggest that it was not possible to steer it.

The drawing was soon attributed to a student of da Vinci's, this was soon doubted, and it eventually identified as a late 20th-century forgery.[2] Be that as it may, without a functioning steering system it would not have been possible to drive the vehicle (fig. 1) anyway.

The principle of two wheels positioned one behind the other, connected by a rod, etc., crops up again centuries later, among them the non-steering Nuremberg running machines or the Célérifère created by Comte Mede de Sivrac. Alongside these precursors in 18th-century Europe, all worthy of serious consideration, there are far older signs of ideas for bicycles in China and Japan.[3]

Karl Friedrich Drais' "Running Machine"

Today, Mannheim is considered the birthplace of the bicycle, even if the vehicle in question does not yet completely accord with our notions of the bicycle: It was a vehicle with two wheels in a single line the one behind the other, and it could be steered, but is possibly best described as a 'running machine' or 'running bicycle.' The device was invented by Karl Friedrich Drais, who in 1817 presented his running machine to the public for the first time.[4] He had constructed a steering appliance for running bicycles that could originally not be steered, so-called turntable steering, as well as a balancing board for the lower arms. As a result, the latter remained free to steer the vehicle and it was easier for the runner to keep his balance when pushing off from the ground with his feet in order to propel himself forwards. Back then, balancing on two wheels was a pioneering novelty.

Countless details reveal just how ingenious the machine was, which Mannheim-based cartwright Johann Frey made to the designs Drais provided. The vehicle had extremely light 27-inch spoked wheels, greasable brass hub bearings to reduce friction, an upholstered balancing board, a front wheel with a lag of some 15 cm so that it always readjusted to the direction of travel, and the steering rod could be flipped forward to act as a handle for pulling the machine behind you when going uphill. Later, a height-adjustable seat was added. All these functional elements can also be viewed from the point of view of design. Then there is the notion of a division of labor, something still valid today, whereby the design work was kept separate from the manufacture. In this regard, Drais could be termed one of the very first designers.

Abb. 1   01   054
Holzmodell von
Giovanni Sacchi nach
angeblicher Zeichnung
von Leonardo da Vinci,
ca. 1985
Fig. 1
Wooden model by
Giovanni Sacchi based
on an alleged drawing by
Leonardo da Vinci,
c. 1985

die Trennung von Entwurf und Herstellung beinhaltet. In diesem Sinne könnte Drais als einer der ersten Designer bezeichnet werden.

Die weitere Entwicklung im 19. Jahrhundert

Der nächste Schritt in der Entwicklung des Fahrrads bestand darin, Kurbeln am Vorderrad anzubringen. Wer zuerst auf diese Idee kam, gehört zu den vieldiskutierten Fragen der Fahrradgeschichte.[5] Kurbeln für standfeste Gefährte, also drei- oder vierrädrige Fahrzeuge, gab es schon Anfang des 19. Jahrhunderts, aber die Umsetzung der Idee, sich auf zwei Rädern mithilfe einer Kurbel und gleichzeitigem Balancieren fortzubewegen, erfolgte erst Jahrzehnte später. In den frühen 1860er-Jahren begann der auf Kutschenteile spezialisierte Pariser Schmied Pierre Michaux zusammen mit seinem Sohn, Zweiräder mit einem Tretkurbelantrieb am Vorderrad zu bauen. Er war jedoch nicht der Einzige. Erste Berichte über diese Neuerung erschienen 1866. Nach 1867 gab es allein in Frankreich über 150 Hersteller, wobei die meisten bereits vorhandene Modelle einfach nachbauten.[6] Große Gedanken über das Aussehen dieser Fahrzeuge scheint man sich, abgesehen von Michaux, nicht gemacht zu haben.

Erst mit Eugène Meyer hat sich in dieser Hinsicht etwas geändert, denn seine Tretkurbelräder erregten durch ihre Eleganz die Aufmerksamkeit der Leute. Jedes Detail seiner Räder war nicht nur funktional durchdacht, sondern auch ästhetisch gestaltet. Allein die Naben aus Messing oder die Form seiner gegossenen Bronzepedale setzten sich in ihrem Aussehen von den zeitgenössischen Beispielen ab. Meyer gehörte sicherlich zu den innovativsten Fahrradbauern seiner Zeit. Er erfand die Zugspeichen und war Wegbereiter, wenn nicht sogar Erfinder des Hochrads.[7] Er verwendete wohl als einer der Ersten Eisenrohre für seine Konstruktionen, griff er doch auf die Gasleitungsrohre der Straßenbeleuchtung zurück. Meyer entwickelte Stahlfelgen für Hartgummireifen.[8]

Mit dem Hochrad der darauffolgenden Jahre kam man nicht nur gestalterisch in eine Sackgasse. Um schneller fahren zu können, vergrößerte man die Vorderräder mit der festmontierten Kurbel. Damit wurde nicht nur das Aufsteigen auf diese hohen Räder schwieriger, sondern auch die Gefahr, kopfüber nach vorne zu stürzen und sich schwer zu verletzen.

Bald darauf setzten die ersten Versuche ein, das Hochrad sicherer zu machen. Dazu gehörte die Idee, Antrieb und Lenkung auf beide Räder zu verteilen. Beim Hochrad wurde mit dem großen Antriebsrad gelenkt. Ein weiterer Schritt bestand darin, ein umgekehrtes Hochrad zu bauen, bei dem sich das kleine – nun lenkbare – Rad vorne befand, sodass man nicht mehr kopfüber nach vorne kippen konnte.

Der Amerikaner Leonard B. Gaylor war zwar nicht der Erste, der auf diese Idee kam, aber er war derjenige, der sie mit seinem Eagle gestalterisch am besten umsetzte. Die Fertigung dieses Sicherheitshochrads begann 1889 zu einem Zeitpunkt, als sich die Geschichte des Hochrads bereits dem Ende zuneigte.

Rund zehn Jahre zuvor hatte sich Josef Erlach aus Kärnten mit seinem aus überwiegend geschraubten Winkelprofilen bestehenden Gefährt eine

02 058

04 066

03 062

Further developments in the 19th century

The next step in the development of the bicycle consisted of attaching cranks to the front wheel. Who first had the idea is one of the most debated issues in bicycle history.[5] Cranks for sturdy vehicles, such as tricycles or four-wheelers, existed as far back as the early 19th century, but the idea of locomotion on two wheels by means of a crank and balancing at the same time was not realized until decades later. In the early 1860s Parisian blacksmith Pierre Michaux, a specialist in coach sections, together with his son set about building two-wheelers with a foot crank on the front wheel. He was not the only one. Initial reports on this innovative vehicle emerged in 1866. And after 1867 in France alone there were over 150 manufacturers, although most of them simply copied existing models.[6] It would not seem as if much thought was given to the appearance of these vehicles, apart from Michaux.

02 058

Things did not change in this regard until Eugène Meyer appeared on the scene, as his pedal crank bicycles attracted great attention on account of their elegance. Each detail of his bikes was not only thought through in functional terms, but also aesthetically crafted. In terms of appearance, the brass hubs or the shape of his cast bronze pedals already stood out from other contemporary examples. Meyer was without doubt one of the most innovative bicycle makers of his day. He invented pulling spokes and was a trailblazer if not actually the inventor of the penny-farthing.[7] He was evidently one of the first to make use of iron tubes for his constructions, relying in this context on gas piping from streetlights. Meyer also developed steel wheel rims for solid rubber tires.[8]

In subsequent years, in the form of the penny-farthing, developments hit a dead end, and not just in design terms. In order to be able to cycle faster, the front wheel with the fixed crank shafts was made larger. This made getting onto the bike harder and also increased the danger of falling forwards and sustaining serious injuries.

Soon, efforts were being made to make the penny-farthing safer. This included the idea of dividing the drive system and the steering up between the two wheels. In penny-farthings, it is the large drive wheel that is steered. A next step was to build an inverted penny-farthing, where the small wheel, which was now steered, was at the front, meaning one could no longer fall head over heels forwards.

04 066

American Leonard B. Gaylor was admittedly not the first person to have this idea, but he was the one who with his Eagle came up with the best design solution. His safety bicycle went into production in 1889 – at a time when the history of the penny-farthing was already coming to an end.

03 062

About ten years earlier, Josef Erlach from Carinthia in Austria had devised a different solution with his vehicle made of riveted and screwed angle profiles. He placed the point of gravity between the wheels so that the rider could touch the ground with his feet, which was not possible with a penny-farthing. Moreover, he constructed a pushrod drive, and by shifting the position of the pushrod, the cyclist had two gears from which to choose.

andere Lösung überlegt. Er legte den Schwerpunkt zwischen die Räder, sodass der Fahrer oder die Fahrerin im Gegensatz zum Hochrad mit den Füßen den Boden berühren konnte. Zudem konstruierte er einen Schubstangenantrieb und konnte so über das Verstellen der Schubstange mit zwei Gängen fahren.

Der indirekte Hinterrad-Antrieb über Ketten, Riemen, Wellen etc. sollte gegen Ende des Jahrhunderts zusammen mit weiteren technischen Errungenschaften wie Freilauf, Luftreifen, Federungen die Entwicklung des Fahrrads vorantreiben.

Das moderne Fahrrad und seine Materialien

Seit den 1880er-Jahren setzten sich langsam die Sicherheitsniederfahrräder, die „Safeties" durch. Damit waren die Grundlagen für das moderne Fahrrad mit seinen zwei annähernd gleichgroßen Rädern geschaffen. Die Rahmenformen variierten zunächst noch erheblich, doch kristallisierten sich allmählich zwei Grundtypen heraus, der Kreuzrahmen und der Diamantrahmen. Die Oberhand gewann Letzterer. Der aus zwei Dreiecken bestehende Rahmen verkörpert die ideale Vereinigung von Stabilität und Gewicht. Sattelrohr und Tretlagergehäuse dienen dabei als verbindende Elemente. Bis heute prägt diese Rahmenform unser Bild vom Fahrrad.

Andere Rahmenformen tauchten zwar immer wieder einmal auf, doch erlangte keine von ihnen eine so große Bedeutung wie der Diamantrahmen. Der Rahmen im Allgemeinen ist es, der viel Spielraum für die Gestaltung bietet, zugleich jedoch durch die Überlegungen bezüglich Funktionalität, Umsetzbarkeit und Kosten diese Freiräume wieder einengt.

Abgesehen von zahlreichen Experimenten, der Erfindung des Luftreifens (Dunlop 1888), den technologischen Neuerungen bei den Komponenten (Schaltung, Bremsen, Federung etc.) und Antrieben gab es zunächst nur wenige Veränderungen, gerade, was das Design betraf. Am deutlichsten lässt sich die Entwicklung bei den verwendeten Materialien und den damit verbundenen Herstellungstechniken ablesen. Mit dem Aufkommen von Kunststoff, Karbon bzw. Kompositwerkstoffen eröffneten sich den Designern und Designerinnen grundlegend neue Gestaltungsmöglichkeiten. Doch auch die traditionellen Materialien wie Holz oder Metall (Stahl, Aluminium etc.) boten sich immer wieder für neue Herausforderungen an, denen mit ungewöhnlichen Einfällen begegnet wurde.

Holz

01   054
Die Laufmaschine von Drais bestand nicht nur deshalb aus Holz, weil dieses Material leicht verfügbar war, sondern auch, weil Drais Gewicht einsparen wollte. Nur mit dem jahrelang abgelagerten Eschenholz war es möglich, ein so leichtes Gefährt zu bauen. Auch die Räder bestanden aus Holz. Sie waren lediglich mit Eisenbändern beschlagen.

Für die weitere Entwicklung spielte dann geschmiedetes Eisen eine wichtige Rolle. Abgelöst wurde dieses Material durch Stahl. Als sich die Entwicklung

Toward the end of the 19th century the indirect back-wheel drive using chains, belts, or shafts, etc., along with other technical achievements such as the freewheel, pneumatic tires, and shock absorbing systems, was to advance the further development of the bicycle.

The Materials for Modern Bicycles

From the 1880s onwards, the low safety bicycles gradually started to win the day. This laid the foundations for modern bicycles with their two approximately equal-sized wheels. Initially, frame shapes differed significantly, yet over time two basic shapes slowly but surely evolved: the cross frame and the diamond frame. The latter emerged victorious. Consisting of two triangles, the diamond frame embodies the ideal combination of stability and weight. The saddle tube and the bottom bracket shell serve as the connecting elements. To this day, this frame shape defines our notion of what a bicycle is.

Other frame shapes repeatedly pop up over time, but none of them ever achieved the same significance as the diamond frame. In general, it is the frame that offers much scope for design, and yet at the same time constrains that freedom by involving factors such as functionality, realizability, and costs.

If we ignore the countless experiments with and technological innovations for components (gears, brakes, shock absorbing springs, etc.) and drive systems, pneumatic tyres (Dunlop 1888), there were initially few changes that impacted precisely on bicycle design. This trend can be most clearly seen when it comes to the materials used and the related manufacturing techniques. With the emergence of plastic, carbon and/or composite materials, designers suddenly had fundamentally new opportunities at their fingertips. Yet the traditional materials such as wood or metal (steel, aluminum, etc.) repeatedly posed new issues for which designers conjured up unusual solutions.

Wood

01 054

Drais' "Running Machine" was not just made of wood because the material was readily available, but also because Drais wanted to keep his invention's weight down. It was only using ash wood that had been left to dry for several years that such a lightweight vehicle could be built. The wheels were likewise made of wood, although they were shod with iron bands.

Forged iron played an important role in further advances in bicycles. Frame-builders subsequently switched to steel. In the mid-1890s, steel frame technology was reaching its peak, and yet suddenly bicycles made of wood or bamboo came back onto the scene. London's Bamboo Cycle Company Ltd. ran ads in 1895 stating that its bamboo bicycles were "better than steel" and "preferred by the nobility."[9]

Different techniques were developed to connect the individual bamboo tubes and thus assemble the frame – ranging from slotted, screwed, or clamped, to glued. The steel muffs were the central element used to connect

der Stahlrahmentechnologie Mitte der 1890er-Jahre auf dem Höhepunkt befand, tauchten plötzlich wieder Räder aus Holz bzw. aus Bambus auf. Die Londoner Bamboo Cycle Company Ltd. warb 1895 damit, dass ihre Bambusräder „besser als Stahl" und vom „Adel favorisiert" seien.[9]

Für die Verbindung der einzelnen Bambusrohre und damit für den Aufbau des Rahmens wurden unterschiedliche Techniken eingesetzt, die von gesteckt, geschraubt und geklemmt bis geklebt reichten. Zentrales Element waren dabei die Stahlmuffen, die die einzelnen Bambusrohre verbanden. An ihnen und an den anderen Metallteilen zeigten sich die gestalterischen Vorstellungen der einzelnen Hersteller, wie etwa bei Grundner & Lemisch deutlich zu erkennen ist. Das gleiche Phänomen war auch bei den Holzfahrrädern zu beobachten, obwohl hier manchmal auch auf andere Technologien zurückgegriffen wurde. Bei dem Old Hickory beispielsweise bestehen die einzelnen Streben aus laminiertem Holz, das ohne Fügung über die Ecken gebogen und verleimt wurde.

Rund vierzig Jahre später bauten die Fratelli Vianzone ihre Rahmen ebenfalls aus gebogenem Holz. Für sie war es die Rohstoffknappheit, die sie auf die bewährte Bugholztechnik zurückgreifen ließ, mit der sie bereits Erfahrungen durch die Herstellung von Radfelgen, Skiern und anderen Produkten hatten. Wie bei den ersten Stühlen aus gebogenem Holz – man denke an Michael Thonet – führte diese Verarbeitungstechnik zu neuen gestalterischen Lösungen, die in diesem Fall durch die gerundeten Übergänge geprägt wurden.

Das Interesse an Fahrrädern aus Holz oder Bambus ist in den letzten Jahrzehnten wieder deutlich gestiegen; denn gerade, was den Nachhaltigkeitsaspekt betrifft, hat das Material Holz durchaus seine Vorteile. Unter den zahlreichen Entwürfen der jüngsten Zeit, seien es die Räder von My Esel (Abb. 2), von My Boo oder anderen Herstellern, ragt das Fahrrad der französischen Designerin Paule Guérin und ihres Partners Till Breitfuss aufgrund der gestalterischen Qualität heraus.

10   090

09   086

20   132

Abb. 2
Christoph Fraundorfer /
Heinz Mayrhofer,
Fahrrad Tour, My Esel GmbH,
Österreich, 2017/21
Fig. 2 Christoph Fraundorfer /
Heinz Mayrhofer,
Fahrrad Tour, My Esel GmbH,
Austria, 2017/21

Stahl

In der Frühzeit des Fahrrads spielte neben Holz vor allem Eisen eine zentrale Rolle. Doch Eisen war schwer und man wollte die Gefährte eigentlich leichter machen. Aus diesem Grund setzte man zunehmend auf Rohre, anfangs Wasser- und Gasleitungsrohre, später auch Stahlrohre. Mit den Kostensenkungen und Fortschritten bei der Stahlherstellung, etwa der Entwicklung von kalt gezogenen, nahtlosen Rohren (u. a. von Mannesmann, Reynolds oder Columbus), setzte sich dieses Material durch. Parallel zu den immer besseren, leichteren und günstigeren Rohren aus Stahl entstanden immer anspruchsvoller gepresste Stahlkomponenten, etwa Kurbelgehäuse, Gabelköpfe, Rahmenmuffen, Kettenräder, Ritzel und Pedale.[10] Zu einem Rahmen verbinden ließen sich die einzelnen Stahlteile durch neue bzw. weiterentwickelte Techniken wie Löten oder Schweißen.

Mit diesem Material und seinen Verarbeitungstechniken eröffneten sich den Designern die verschiedensten Möglichkeiten für die Gestaltung von Fahrrädern. Für die unterschiedlichen Fahrradtypen, seien es die Alltagsräder, die Herren-, Damen- oder Kinderräder, seien es die Sport- und Rennräder,

10 090

09 086

20 132

the individual bamboo tubes. The muffs and other metal parts often reveal the particular manufacturer's design ideas, as can be clearly seen, for example, with Grundner & Lemisch. The same phenomenon is to be observed with wooden bicycles, although in this instance the makers sometimes resorted to other technologies. For the Old Hickory, for example, the individual struts are made of laminated wood glued without seams and bent round the corners.

About 40 years later, Fratelli Vianzone built a frame made of bentwood. They were prompted to rely on the tried-and-true bentwood technology by a lack of raw materials and they already had gained a lot of know-how using the method to make wheel rims, skis, and other products. As with the first chairs made of bentwood, this processing technology gave rise to new design solutions that in this case took the shape of rounded transitions.

The interest in bicycles made of wood or bamboo has grown considerably in recent years; for precisely in terms of sustainability, wood has clear advantages as a material. Among the countless designs in the immediate past, be it the bicycles by My Esel (fig. 2), My Boo or other makers, the one masterminded by French designer Paule Guérin and her partner Till Breitfuss stands out for its exceptional design quality.

Steel

In the early days of the bicycle, alongside wood it was iron that played the central role. Iron was, however, heavy, and producers were seeking to make the vehicles lighter. For this reason, increasingly tubes were used – initially water and gas pipes, later steel pipes. As steelmaking costs fell and the industry made technological advances, such as the development of cold drawn, seamless pipes (among others by Mannesmann, Reynolds or Columbus), it was steel that gradually won the day. Parallel to the ever improving, lighter, and more cost-effective steel tubing came pressed-steel components of an ever-better quality, such as crankcases, fork heads, frame muffs, chain rings, cogs and pedals.[10] The individual steel parts could be combined to form a frame using new or advanced methods such as soldering or welding.

Steel and the different methods available for working it afforded designers all manner of scope for designing bicycles. A kind of canon of frame types evolved – and it remained almost unchanged down through the decades – for the different bicycle types, be they everyday bikes, men's, women's or children's bikes, or sports or racing bikes. Advances in technology and in the design of bicycles centered on achieving greater comfort, reducing weight, increasing possible speeds, and delivering more stability and safety.

What is, however, less known is the impact the bicycle has on Modernist furniture design: One anecdote would have it that Marcel Breuer was inspired at the Bauhaus in Dessau to develop the first tubular-steel chairs when studying the bent tubular-steel handlebars of his bicycle.[11] As a cabinetmaker, Breuer had no experience whatsoever in using tubular steel. With the assistance of locksmiths from the neighboring Junkers airplane factory he succeeded in bending the tubular steel such that he was able to build furniture with it. In this way, the

entwickelte sich eine Art Kanon an Rahmenformen, der über die Jahrzehnte fast unverändert blieb. Die Bestrebungen nach mehr Komfort, nach geringerem Gewicht und nach höherer Geschwindigkeit, nach mehr Stabilität und Sicherheit bildeten die Basis für das Fortschreiten der Technik und des Designs bei den Fahrrädern.

Wenig bekannt ist jedoch, welche Bedeutung das Fahrrad für das Möbeldesign der Moderne hatte: Der Erzählung nach wurde Marcel Breuer am Dessauer Bauhaus vom gebogenen Stahlrohrlenker seines Fahrrads angeregt, die ersten Stahlrohrstühle zu entwickeln.[11] Als Tischler hatte Breuer keine Erfahrung im Umgang mit Stahlrohr. Mithilfe der Schlosser bei der benachbarten Junkers Flugzeugwerft gelang es ihm, das Stahlrohr so zu biegen, dass er damit seine Möbel bauen konnte. Auf diese Weise entstand der Sessel B 3, der später als Wassily-Sessel Berühmtheit erlangte. Ende der 1920er-Jahre entwarfen Marcel Breuer, Ludwig Mies van der Rohe und Mart Stam die ersten Freischwingerstühle aus Stahlrohr und revolutionierten so das Möbeldesign. Bis zu diesem Zeitpunkt hatte Stahlrohr noch keinen Eingang in den privaten Wohnbereich gefunden. Kurz danach wurde mit Aluminium ein anderes Metall für den Möbelbau entdeckt.

Stahlrohr ist bis heute das dominierende Material im Fahrradbau. Bei den Rennrädern erfolgte gegen Ende der 1980er-Jahre eine allmähliche Verdrängung des Stahls durch Karbon. Gerade, wenn es um Geschwindigkeit geht, spielt die Aerodynamik eine große Rolle, das Gewicht dagegen weniger. Das Interesse an Fahrrad-Aerodynamik stieg seit der Mitte der 1970er-Jahre kontinuierlich an. Nun wurden erste stromlinienförmige Komponenten wie Sattelstützen und Pedale sowie strömungsgünstige Rohre entwickelt. Nach den Erfolgen der aerodynamisch geformten Räder bei den Olympischen Spielen 1984 war dieses Thema aus dem Radrennsport nicht mehr wegzudenken.

Neben der Optimierung von Lenkern, Helmen, Schuhüberzügen, Kleidung und allem, was nur in irgendeiner Weise den Windwiderstand senken konnte, waren es natürlich die Laufräder und Rahmen, aber auch die Haltung der Fahrer und Fahrerinnen.

Obwohl einige Studien gezeigt haben, dass klassische Rundprofilrahmen auch gute aerodynamische Eigenschaften aufweisen, arbeitete man weiter mit ovalen oder tropfenförmigen Querschnitten bei den Rohren. Zu den Höhepunkten der aerodynamischen Stahlrohrräder zählt zweifellos das Bottecchia Air. Aber auch bei anderen Rennrad-Gestaltern und -Herstellern führten die Bemühungen um die Verbesserung des Windwiderstandes zu bemerkenswerten Lösungen, wie das Cinelli Laser oder das Textima belegen.

50   242

39   202
42   210

Aluminium

Mit Aluminium als Rahmenmaterial für Fahrräder hatte man bereits Ende des 19. Jahrhunderts experimentiert. Aluminium ist wesentlich leichter als Stahl, besitzt aber auch eine geringere Steifigkeit und Ermüdungsbeständigkeit. Daher waren Aluminiumrahmen den Stahlrahmen unterlegen, auch wenn durch sie das Gewicht reduziert werden konnte. Aluminiumlegierungen wie

B 3 armchair was born, later becoming famous as the Wassily armchair. At the end of the 1920s, Marcel Breuer, Ludwig Mies van der Rohe and Mart Stam designed the first cantilever-base chairs made of tubular steel and in so doing revolutionized furniture design. Up until then, tubular steel had not played any part in private living rooms. Only a little later, aluminum was discovered by furniture makers as another metal they could use.

To this day, tubular steel remains the predominant material in bicycle making. At the end of the 1980s, in the case of racing bikes, steel was gradually replaced by carbon. Precisely when speed was the objective, aerodynamics played a major role and less the bike's weight. Interest in bicycle aerodynamics grew steadily as of the mid-1970s. The very first streamlined components such as saddle pins and pedals as well as aerodynamic tubes started to be developed. After the success of aerodynamically shaped bicycles at the Los Angeles Olympics in 1984, the subject became a firm feature in bicycle racing.

Alongside the optimization of handlebars, helmets, overshoes, clothing, and anything and everything that could in some way lower wind resistance, it was of course the wheels and the frames that came into focus, as did the cyclist's position on the bike.

50 242

Although some studies had shown that classical round profile frames also possess good aerodynamic properties, the buffs continued to experiment with oval or teardrop-shaped cross sections for the tubes. The Bottecchia Air is without a doubt exemplary among aerodynamic tubular-steel bikes. That said, in their efforts to improve wind resistance other racing bike designers and manufacturers came up with remarkable ideas, such as the Cinelli Laser or the Textima.

39 202
42 210

Aluminum

People had experimented with using aluminum as a material for bicycle frames back in the late 19th century. Aluminum is far lighter than steel but exhibits less rigidity and resistance to fatigue. For that reason, aluminum frames were inferior to their steel counterparts even if they were lighter in weight. Aluminum alloys such as Duralumin improved the material's properties considerably as regards rigidity and hardness.

The 1930s marked a turning point in the aluminum industry as documented by the extensive use in automobiles, railways, aircraft and ships. As the "metal of Modernism" it was becoming increasingly important and was being ever more frequently used to make furniture – once again it was Marcel Breuer who was one of the pioneers in architecture and in industrial design.[12] The one or other bicycle maker also opted for aluminum: in Italy, for example, Fratelli Vianzone; in France, Pierre Caminade, who usedoctagonal aluminum tubes, or Nicola Barra.

15 110

As a light metal aluminum, and above all Duralumin, was one of the key materials in the aircraft industry – if only because of its low weight. After the end of World War II, occasionally aircraft aluminum ended up being used for bicycles. Frenchman Reyé Bardet constructed a noteworthy bicycle frame

21 136

Duralumin(ium) verbesserten die Eigenschaften dieses Material in Sachen Festigkeit und Härte erheblich.

Die 1930er-Jahre bedeuteten für die Aluminiumindustrie einen ersten Höhepunkt, wie der extensive Einsatz bei Automobilen, Eisenbahnen, Flugzeugen und Schiffen belegt. Als „Metall der Moderne" erlangte Aluminium zunehmend Bedeutung, fand im Möbelbau – wieder war hier Marcel Breuer einer der Pioniere –, in der Architektur und im Industriedesign immer häufiger Verwendung.[12] Auch vereinzelte Fahrradhersteller setzten auf Aluminium: in Italien beispielsweise Fratelli Vianzone, in Frankreich Pierre Caminade mit seinen achteckigen Aluminiumrohren oder Nicola Barra.

15 110

Das Leichtmetall Aluminium, vor allem Duraluminium, gehörte aufgrund seines geringen Gewichts zu den wichtigsten Materialien der Flugzeugindustrie. Nach dem Ende des Zweiten Weltkriegs verwendete man gelegentlich nicht mehr benötigtes Flugzeugaluminium für Fahrräder. Der Franzose Reyé Bardet konstruierte einen bemerkenswerten Fahrradrahmen aus gelochten und genieteten Profilen, der durch seine Gestaltung auffällt und zugleich als ein frühes Beispiel für das Recycling (Wiederverwertung) von wertvollen Rohstoffen gesehen werden kann.

21 136

Einen etwas anderen Weg beschritten die Ingenieure von Mitsubishi in Japan. Da sie nach Kriegsende keine Flugzeuge mehr entwickeln und bauen durften, verlegten sie sich auf das Fahrraddesign. Für ihr Dujee-Rad verwendeten sie nicht nur das bei ihnen vorhandene Material Aluminium, sondern verarbeiteten es auch wie im Flugzeugbau, indem sie die Rahmenbestandteile vernieteten. Dennoch blieben Fahrräder aus Aluminium in der Nachkriegszeit zunächst eher eine Ausnahme. Das Problem war nach wie vor die Verbindung der Aluminiumrohre, die geklemmt, gekeilt, genietet oder geschraubt wurden. Und mit dieser Verbindungstechnik ergaben sich keine wesentlichen Vorteile gegenüber den Stahlrahmen.

22 140

Das Schweißen von Aluminium war kompliziert, und nur wenige Spezialisten beherrschten diese Technik. Zwar stellte Nicola Barra bereits 1936 den ersten geschweißten Aluminiumrahmen vor, doch Eingang in die Serienfertigung fand diese Technik erst wesentlich später. In Deutschland war es der Campingmöbelhersteller Heinz Kettler, dem es aufgrund seiner Erfahrungen bei der Möbelproduktion gelang, Ende der 1970er-Jahre geschweißte Aluminiumrahmen auf den Markt zu bringen, die preislich mit den Konkurrenten aus Asien mithalten konnten. In den USA leisteten Unternehmen wie Cannondale und Klein Pionierarbeit in diesem Bereich, in England Raleigh.

Das gegenüber dem Stahl schlechtere Ermüdungsverhalten von Aluminium wirkte sich auch auf die Gestaltung aus. So versuchte man etwa, die notwendigen dickeren Rohrdurchmesser zu vermeiden, indem man, wie etwa beim Kettler 2600, das leicht schräg geführte und in die Sattelstrebe übergehende Oberrohr durch zwei dünnere Doppelrohre ersetzte.

33 182

Bei den Rennrädern waren es in den 1970er- und 1980er-Jahren vor allem Alan in Italien und Vitus in Frankreich (Abb. 3), die mit ihren perfekt gestalteten Aluminiumrahmen Akzente setzten. Besonders hervorzuheben ist in

22   140

Abb. 3
Alumnium Rennrad,
Rahmen Vitus,
Frankreich, ca. 1982
Fig. 3
Aluminum racing bike,
Vitus frame,
France, c. 1982

from leftover perforated and riveted profiles – it has a striking design and can also be considered an early example of recycling valuable raw materials.

The engineers at Mitsubishi in Japan took a slightly different approach. Since they were no longer allowed to develop or build aircraft after the end of the War, they simply reinvented themselves as bicycle designers. For their Dujee bicycle they not only used the aluminum material they still had on hand, but processed it the same way as in aircraft construction, simply riveting the frame components together.

Nevertheless, bicycle frames made of aluminum essentially remained an exception in the post-War period. The problem remained the connections between the aluminum tubes, that had to be clamped, wedged, riveted or screwed together. And these connection methods offered no real advantages over steel frames.

Welding aluminum was complicated and only a very few experts had mastered the relevant methods. While Nicola Barra had presented the very first welded aluminum frame as early as 1936, the process was not adopted for mass manufacture until much later. In Germany, it was camping furniture maker Heinz Kettler who at the end of the 1970s succeeded in marketing welded aluminum frames made on the back of the company's experience in furniture production and able to hold their own against the cheap competition from Asia. In the USA it was companies such as Cannondale and Klein that blazed the trail in this regard, and in the UK Raleigh. The designs were constrained by the fact that aluminum fatigued faster than steel. Thus, efforts were made to avoid having to opt for larger tube diameters, for example in the case of the Kettler 2600, by replacing the upper tube with two thinner tubes.

In the field of racing bikes, in the 1970s and 1980s it was above all Alan in Italy and Vitus in France (fig. 3) who set the stage, with perfectly designed aluminum frames. Especially worthy of mention in this context is, however, André Sablière, whose muff-free aluminum cycles are among the highlights in the art of frame-building.

As early as 1949, Hermann Klaue took a completely different approach to using aluminum as a material in bicycle building. In order to solve the problem of connecting the individual parts and also be able to build as lightweight a bicycle as possible, Klaue devised a frame cast as a single piece. He had to factor various parameters into the process, first and foremost stability and/or torsion rigidity, something he achieved by including in the casting flat reinforcements in the corners at the transitions from the saddle and top tubes to the diagonal central tube. The frame was hollow in order on the one hand to spare materials and save weight and, on the other, to hold the gear cables. By choosing a cross frame, it also had a low entry point, meaning it could be used by both sexes.

44   218   diesem Kontext jedoch André Sablière, dessen muffenlose Aluminiumräder zu den Höhepunkten der Rahmenbaukunst zählen.

Einen völlig anderen Ansatz im Umgang mit dem Material Aluminium im Fahrradbereich lieferte Hermann Klaue bereits 1949. Um das Problem mit den Verbindungen der einzelnen Teile zu lösen und um ein möglichst leichtes Fahrrad bauen zu können, entwarf er einen Rahmen, der in einem Stück gegossen 24   148   wurde. Dafür musste er verschiedene Parameter berücksichtigen, in erster Linie natürlich die Stabilität bzw. Verwindungssteifheit, die er durch die flachen, mitgegossenen Verstärkungen in den Ecken der Übergänge von Sattel- und Steuerrohr zum diagonalen Zentralrohr erreichte. Der Rahmen war innen hohl, um einerseits Material und Gewicht zu sparen und um andererseits den Zug für die Schaltung aufnehmen zu können. Durch die Entscheidung für einen Kreuzrahmen hatte das Fahrrad einen niedrigen Einstieg, sodass es von beiden Geschlechtern benutzt werden konnte.

Magnesium und Titan

Andere Leichtmetalle wie Magnesium oder Titan spielten im Fahrradbau eine untergeordnete Rolle, wenngleich damit einige bemerkenswerte Entwürfe umgesetzt wurden. Dazu gehören beispielweise die gegossenen Magne48   232   siumrahmen des englischen Luftfahrt- und Automobilingenieurs Frank Kirk, die in den 1980er-Jahren weltweit großes Aufsehen erregten.

Magnesium ist etwa ein Drittel leichter als Aluminium und gehört somit zu den leichtesten Baumetallen. Die etwas geringere Steifigkeit wurde durch die entsprechende Gestaltung des Rahmens ausgeglichen. Im Gegensatz zu dem ebenfalls gegossenen Rahmen des Hermann-Klaue-Rads handelt es sich hier nicht um einen Hohlguss. Der Rahmen war trotz der Aussparungen im Oberrohr und den Aussteifungsstreben relativ schwer und die Züge mussten außen verlegt werden. Das Druckgussverfahren bot jedoch den Vorteil, dass innerhalb kürzester Zeit – Kirk sprach von acht Sekunden – ein einzelner Rahmen produziert werden konnte. Obwohl das Material kostengünstig und in der Gewinnung umweltfreundlich war und auch recycelt werden konnte, blieb der wirtschaftliche Erfolg aus. Das lag weniger am Design als an anderen Faktoren.[13]

Auch das Titan sollte sich als Grundmaterial für den Fahrradbau trotz seines geringen Gewichts nicht durchsetzen. Titan ist rund 50 Prozent leichter als Stahl und weist eine ähnliche Zugfestigkeit auf, war seinerzeit aber erheblich teurer und nur begrenzt verfügbar. Titanrahmen wird aufgrund des im Vergleich zu Stahl geringeren Elastizitätsmoduls ein flexibles und weiches Fahrverhalten nachgesagt.[14]

Die ersten Titanrahmen produzierte die englische Firma Speedwell ab 1972. Größere Stückzahlen stellte wenig später Teledyne in den USA her. In Deutschland war es Anfang der 1970er-Jahre der Mannheimer Konstrukteur 31   174   und Rahmenbauer Fritz Fleck, der Renn- und Bahnräder aus den Titanrohren der Firma Steinzeug in Friedrichsfeld fertigte. Nachdem ein erster Prototyp bei einem Rennen durch Flattern bei extrem hoher Geschwindigkeit zu Bruch ging, setzte Fleck entsprechende Verstärkungen an den gefährdeten Stellen im Bereich

Magnesium and titanium

Other light metals such as magnesium or titanium played but a subordinate role in bicycle making, although a few quite noteworthy designs were realized using them. These include, for example, the cast magnesium frames created by British aerospace and automobile engineer Frank Kirk, which caused a real stir worldwide in the 1980s.

Magnesium is about one third lighter than aluminum and is thus one of the lightest construction materials. While it possesses slightly less rigidity, Kirk offset this by designing the frame accordingly. In contrast to the likewise cast frame of Hermann Klaue's invention, Kirk's cast was not hollow. Despite the perforations in the upper tube and the reinforcing struts, the frame was relatively heavy, and the cables had to be placed on the outside. However, die-casting as a process had the advantage that a single frame could be produced very quickly: Kirk reckoned with eight seconds a frame. Although the material is cost effective and recyclable and its extraction environmentally friendly, the frame was not a commercial success. This can be attributed less to the design and more to other factors.[13]

Titanium, for all its lightness, likewise did not gain sway in bicycle construction. Titanium is roughly 50 percent lighter than steel and exhibits a similar tensile strength, but at the time it was considerably more expensive and not easy to come by. Given their lower elastic modulus compared to steel, titanium frames were said to offer a more flexible and softer ride.[14]

Speedwell, a British company, produced the first titanium frames in 1972. Soon after, Teledyne in the USA manufactured them in larger numbers. In Germany, in the early 1970s Mannheim-based engineer and frame-builder Fritz Fleck manufactured racing and track bicycles from titanium tubes supplied by the firm Steinzeug in Friedrichsfeld. A first prototype broke during a race owing to shimmy at an extremely high speed, and Fleck then inserted corresponding reinforcements at the points at risk in the top tube and the bottom bracket. The reinforcements were perforated to reduce weight, and gave the classical diamond frame a unique look.

Plastic

After World War II, fiberglass-reinforced plastic (FRP) revolutionized furniture design. In the United States, organically shaped seat shells started to be made from the material. From 1960 onwards, one of the very first plastic bicycles was made there – the brand was named Spacelander (fig. 4). It was designed by British automobile engineer Benjamin Bowden as early as 1946 and featured a hollow monocoque frame made using complementary metal-pressed parts or plastic molding parts that were "attached to each other along the central section of the frame."[15] Yet after the construction of a prototype made of aluminum with an electric shaft drive for an exhibition at the Victoria and Albert Museum, for a decade no further progress was made. Only after Bowden moved to the USA did he manage to have a total of 522 plastic bicycles built according to his design.

48 232

31 174

des Steuerrohrs und des Tretlagers ein. Die aus Gewichtsgründen gelochten Verstärkungen verleihen dem klassischen Diamantrahmen sein charakteristisches Aussehen.

Kunststoff

Glasfaserverstärkter Kunststoff (GFK) revolutionierte nach dem Zweiten Weltkrieg das Möbeldesign. In den USA entstanden die ersten organisch geformten Sitzschalen aus diesem Material. Ab 1960 wurde dort unter dem Namen Spacelander (Abb. 4) auch eines der frühesten Fahrräder aus Kunststoff produziert. Entworfen hatte es der britische Automobilingenieur Benjamin Bowden bereits 1946: ein hohler Monocoque-Rahmen aus komplementären Metallpressteilen oder Kunststoffformteilen, die „entlang der mittleren Ebene des Rahmens aneinander befestigt" waren.[15] Doch nach dem Bau eines Prototypen aus Aluminium mit elektrischem Wellenantrieb für eine Ausstellung im Victoria & Albert Museum ging es mehr als ein Jahrzehnt nicht weiter. Erst nach Bowdens Übersiedelung in die USA gelang es ihm, 522 Exemplare seines Kunststofffahrrads herstellen zu lassen.

In der Folgezeit wurde Kunststoff meist für Verkleidungen verwendet, da es als strukturelles Material zu schwach war. Ende der 1970er-Jahre gestaltete Luigi Colani die aerodynamisch-biomorphe Form seines Fahrrads aus diesem Material. Allerdings beschränkte er sich dabei auf das Oberrohr.

35   190

Dagegen bestand das Itera-Fahrrad komplett aus Kunststoff (Glasfaserverstärktes Polyamid). Die Planungen dafür begannen bereits 1973 mit Beteiligung von Bayer, SKF (Svenska Kullagerfabriken) und der KTH (Kungliga Tekniska Högskolan) in Stockholm. 1980 konnte der erste Prototyp vorgestellt werden, 1982 begann der Verkauf dieses Fahrrads, bei dem nicht nur der Rahmen, sondern auch alle anderen Teile inklusive der Nabenaufnahmen, Speichen und Felgen aus Kunststoff bestanden – nur Klingel, Schloss und Kette waren aus Metall.

37   198

40 Jahre später werden wieder Fahrradrahmen aus Kunststoff, diesmal aus Polycarbonat, hergestellt, aber nicht gegossen, sondern gedruckt. Als Grundmaterial dient hierfür recyceltes Polycarbonat, das selbst wieder recycelt werden kann. Hier vereinen sich Umweltfreundlichkeit und Nachhaltigkeit mit modernster Herstellungstechnologie. Der stabile, transparente Rahmen lässt sich durch diese Form der Produktion zudem individuell an die Nutzer und Nutzerinnen anpassen.

70   316

Karbon

Karbon oder Kohlenstofffasern sind wesentlich älter, als man denkt: Schon 1881 erhielt Thomas Alva Edison ein Patent auf seine Kohlenstofffaserglühlampe mit Glühfäden aus pyrolisierten Bambusfasern. Die eigentliche Entwicklung setzte jedoch erst Ende der 1950er- und Anfang der 1960er-Jahre ein. Zu den Vorreitern gehörte hier das Royal Aircraft Establishment in Farnborough, dessen Ingenieure 1963 erstmals Verfahren zur Entwicklung hochfester Kohlenstofffasern realisierten.[16]

35 190

37 198

In subsequent years, plastic tended to be used for fairings, because it was too weak as a structural material. In the late 1970s Luigi Colani designed the aerodynamic-biomorphic shape of his bicycles using plastic. However, he restricted it to the upper tube.

By contrast, the Itera bicycle was made completely of plastic (fiberglass-reinforced polyamide). Planning had started back in 1973 with the involvement of Bayer, SKF (Svenska Kullagerfabriken) and KTH Royal Institute of Technology in Stockholm. In 1980 the first prototype was launched, and two years later sales commenced, whereby not just the frame but also all the other parts including the hub dropouts, spokes and wheel rims were made of plastic – only the bell, the lock and the chain were metal.

70 316

Not until 40 years later were bicycle frames once again made of plastic, this time polycarbonate; however, they were not cast in a mold, but instead printed. The basic material used was recycled polycarbonate which could itself be recycled again. Here, environmental friendliness and sustainability were combined with ultra-modern manufacturing technology. The stable, transparent frame can be customized to the individual user's preferences thanks to this manufacturing method.

Abb. 4
Benjamin Bowden,
Kunststoff-Fahrrad
Spacelander, USA,
1946/60
Fig. 4
Benjamin Bowden,
Spacelander plastic bicycle,
USA, 1946/60

Carbon

Carbon or carbon fibers are far older than one might think; indeed, Thomas Alva Edison was awarded a patent back in 1881 for his carbon fiber bulb with filaments made of pyrolized bamboo fiber. Development of the material did not really set in until the late 1950s and early 1960s. Among the pioneers was the Royal Aircraft Establishment in Farnborough, UK, where in 1963 engineers for the first time succeeded in inventing a method for developing high-strength carbon fibers.[16]

Experiments with carbon in bicycle making commenced in the 1970s. For example, Exxon Graftek, a company founded in 1975 in South Plainfield, NJ, clad aluminum tubes in carbon matting in order to make optimal use of the properties of both materials. The individual tubes were glued with metal muffs in order to create the frames.[17]

The use of pure carbon tubing first gained sway the following decade, above all in racing bikes, where the focus was on low weight and great stability and rigidity. Prime examples were the Peugeot PY10FC, the Vitus Carbone 9 and the Alan Record Carbonico. In 1986, LOOK built the first frame from carbon (with Kevlar), its KG 86, and Greg LeMond won the Tour de France riding it.

In all these bicycles, carbon tubes took the place of metal tubes. Aluminum or other metal muffs served as the connecting elements. The carbon tubes were glued in place, and on occasion the glue started to give, which did not really contribute to the safety of such bicycles. Carbon did not yet play a strong role in bicycle design, as formally speaking it was simply utilized as a substitute for other materials.

All of that changed completely with the development of so-called monocoque carbon frames, which required no muffs and thus not only created the

Mit Karbon im Fahrradbau experimentierte man bereits in den 1970er-Jahren: Beispielsweise ummantelte die 1975 in South Plainfield, NJ, gegründete Firma Exxon Graftek Aluminiumrohre mit Kohlefasermatten, um die Eigenschaften der beiden Materialien optimal zu nutzen. Für den Aufbau der Rahmen verklebte man die einzelnen Rohre mit Metallmuffen.[17]

Durchzusetzen begann sich die Verwendung von reinen Karbonrohren erst im folgenden Jahrzehnt, vor allem bei den Rennrädern, bei denen es auf geringes Gewicht und große Festigkeit bzw. Steifigkeit ankam, etwa mit dem Peugeot PY10FC, dem Vitus Carbone 9 oder dem Alan Record Carbonico. 1986 stellte LOOK mit dem KG 86 den ersten Rahmen aus diesem Material (in Verbindung mit Kevlar) vor, mit dem Greg LeMond die Tour de France gewann.

Bei all diesen Fahrrädern ersetzten Karbonrohre die Metallrohre des Rahmens. Alu- oder andere Metallmuffen dienten dabei als Verbindungselemente. Die eingeklebten Karbonrohre begannen sich gelegentlich zu lockern, was nicht unbedingt zur Sicherheit dieser Räder beitrug. Für die Gestaltung der Räder spielte Karbon noch keine tragende Rolle, da es formal lediglich als Substitut für andere Materialien Verwendung fand.

Das änderte sich erst grundlegend mit der Entwicklung von Karbonrahmen in Schalenbauweise, den sogenannten Monocoque-Rahmen, die ohne Metallmuffen auskommen und nicht nur die Möglichkeit boten, alle Kabel und Züge ins Innere der Rahmen zu verlegen, sondern den Designern und Designerinnen insgesamt sehr viel größere Freiräume ließen.

Der Engländer Mike Burrows hatte zwar schon 1982/83 einen ersten Karbon-Monocoque-Rahmen entwickelt, doch erst 1985 fertigte er aus diesem Material auch komplette Räder. Ein Jahr später entstand eine Version mit einseitig aufgehängter Vordergabel. Mit dem von Burrows für den Rennwagen-Hersteller Lotus entworfenen Rad Lotus 108 gewann Chris Boardman die 4000-m-Einerverfolgung bei den Olympischen Spielen von 1992 in Barcelona. Dieses Rad von Mike Burrows gilt heute als Ikone unter den Karbonrennrädern. Mit dem Lotus 110, einer Weiterentwicklung des Herstellers als Straßenrennrad, errang Boardman 1996 den Stundenweltrekord.

In Italien baute Marco Bonfanti mit seinem C4 Aero 1986 seinen ersten Karbonrahmen, der im darauffolgenden Jahr vom Team Bianchi im Giro d'Italia eingesetzt wurde.

Die ersten in größerer Serie produzierten reinen Karbonrahmen brachte das amerikanische Unternehmen Cycle Composites (Kestrel) bereits 1987 mit dem von Brent J. Trimble entworfenen Modell 4000 auf den Markt, andere Unternehmen folgten rasch.

In Westdeutschland entwickelte der Stuttgarter Designer Michael Conrad ab 1984 einen Monocoque-Rahmen aus Karbon, der nicht nur durch das Material, sondern auch durch die Form einen etwas anderen Weg einschlug, indem er einen Kreuzrahmen mit einer Art Oberrohr versah und auf die Kettenstreben verzichtete.

Blieben es im Westen zunächst vor allem Experimente einzelner Designer, so setzte man in der ehemaligen DDR gerade beim Sport auf staatliche

54   254

49   236

43   214

opportunity to place all the cables inside the frame, but also gave the designers far greater scope overall.

In 1982-3, British bicycle designer Mike Burrows developed the first carbon monocoque frame, but it wasn't until 1985 that he made complete bicycles from the material. One year later, a version was rolled out with a single-sided fork for the front wheel. Riding a Lotus 108 bicycle, designed by Burrows for racing car manufacturer Lotus, Chris Boardman won the 4,000m individual pursuit at the 1992 Summer Olympics in Barcelona. Mike Burrows' bicycle has been considered an icon of carbon racing bikes ever since. In 1996 Boardman rode the Lotus 110, which the manufacturer then developed for road race time trialing, to set the world hour record.

In Italy, Marco Bonfanti built his first carbon frame, the C4 Aero, in 1986 and it was used the following year by Bianchi in the Giro d'Italia.

The first mass produced carbon frames were brought out by US company Cycle Composites (Kestrel) in 1987, when it marketed Brent J. Trimble's model 4000; other companies swiftly followed suit.

In West Germany, as of 1984 Stuttgart-based designer Michael Conrad built monocoque carbon frames where not only the material stood out, but also the slightly new shape; he gave a cross frame an upper tube of sorts and got by without a chain stay.

While in the West developments were mainly driven by experiments by individual designers, in what was then East Germany sports were able to rely on government support.

In 1963, Institut für Forschung und Entwicklung von Sportgeräten (FES), the institute for research and development of sports equipment, was founded as the development section for sports equipment at the research division of the sports university DHfK (Deutsche Hochschule für Körperkultur und Sport). Its objective was to develop customized sports equipment for East German athletes to enable them to train and compete at an international level. From 1970 onwards, Institut FES also focused on cycling sports.[18] Alongside FES it was above all VEB Kombinat Textilmaschinenbau Karl-Marx-Stadt that sought to make East German cyclists competitive internationally, producing handmade special bicycles, albeit without transitioning from steel frames to carbon ones.

As of 1984, the first self-supporting disc wheel made of carbon was built there, and in 1987 the first carbon-fiber-reinforced bike frame. In 1988, Institut FES's trailblazing invention was crowned by the East German team winning gold in the 100 km team time trial at the Seoul Olympic Games. In 1992, the Institut FES bicycles also won gold (Team time trial) at the Barcelona Games.

In the 1990s, a growing number of manufacturers brought carbon bicycles to market. Specifically in professional cycle racing, this especially lightweight, easily molded and very rigid material has predominated ever since. Companies such as C4, Simplon, Trek, BST, and Giant produced particularly comfortable frames that clearly showed that as a material carbon offered designers greater scope than traditional materials such as steel or aluminum. Thus, Burrows

Unterstützung. 1963 wurde als Entwicklungsabteilung für Sportgeräte der Forschungsstelle der DHfK (Deutsche Hochschule für Körperkultur und Sport) das Institut für Forschung und Entwicklung von Sportgeräten (FES) gegründet, dessen Ziel es war, für die Leistungssportler und Leistungssportlerinnen der DDR individuell angepasste Sportgeräte für Training und Wettkampf von internationalem Niveau zu entwickeln. Seit 1970 widmete man sich dort auch dem Fahrradsport.[18] Neben FES war es vor allem das VEB Kombinat Textilmaschinenbau Karl-Marx-Stadt, das mit den handgefertigten Spezialrädern den DDR-Radsport konkurrenzfähig halten wollte, allerdings nicht den Schritt vom Stahlrahmen zum Karbonrahmen mitging.

Bei FES entstand 1984 das erste selbsttragende Scheibenlaufrad aus Karbon und ab 1987 der erste karbonfaserverstärkte Fahrradrahmen. 1988 wurde die bahnbrechende Entwicklung des Instituts FES durch die olympische Goldmedaille im 100-km-Mannschaftszeitfahren in Seoul gekrönt. 1992 folgte mit der Goldmedaille im Mannschaftszeitfahren in Barcelona die nächste Auszeichnung eines FES-Fahrrads.

In den 1990er-Jahren drängten immer mehr Hersteller von Karbon-Fahrrädern auf den Markt. Gerade im Bereich des professionellen Rennsports dominiert dieses besonders leichte, gut formbare und sehr feste Material die Produktion bis heute. Unternehmen wie C4, Simplon, Trek, BST oder Giant fertigten besonders komfortable Rahmen, die deutlich zeigen, dass das Material Karbon dem Designer größere Freiheiten bei der Gestaltung ließ als die traditionellen Materialien Stahl oder Aluminium. So entwickelte Mike Burrows für die taiwanesische Firma Giant mit den MCR- oder später TCR-Modellen Fahrräder, deren Gestaltung auch auf die Minimierung der Herstellungskosten abzielte.

Die Überlegenheit dieses Kompositmaterials – neben Karbon finden auch Aramid- oder Glasfasern Verwendung – begann sich auch bei anderen Fahrradtypen durchzusetzen, bei Mountainbikes ist es heute nahezu zum Standardmaterial geworden, aber auch bei vielen anderen Fahrradtypen wird es eingesetzt.

Dass auch nach der Jahrtausendwende dieses Material für Designer eine große Rolle spielt, belegen die Modelle Biolove von Ross Lovegrove oder Coren des Münchners Christian Zanzotti, das die UBC GmbH nur in geringer Stückzahl fertigte und das 2012 bei der Vorstellung auf der ISPO-Bike zu den teuersten Fahrrädern zählte.

Falträder und andere Fahrradtypen

Die Idee, Fahrräder zum Zerteilen, Klappen, Falten oder Stecken zu bauen, führt in die Frühzeit der Fahrradgeschichte zurück und hängt eng mit den Vorstellungen zusammen, die Mitnahme in anderen Transportmitteln (z. B. Bahn) und die Unterbringung auf engem Raum zu erleichtern. Bereits 1878 entwickelte William Henry Grout aus London ein zerlegbares Hochrad.[19] In den Jahren danach gab es zahlreiche Versuche, die Dimensionen der Fahrräder zu verringern.

developed bicycles for Taiwanese corporation Giant – such as the MCR or later the TCR models – which were also designed to minimize production costs.

57 268

The superiority of the composite material (alongside carbon, aramid or fiberglass are used) started to make inroads into other bicycle types, too. Today, it is more or less a standard material for mountain bikes, but is also utilized for all manner of other bicycle types.

56 262
59 266

Even after the turn of the millennium the material continued to attract designers, as can be seen from Biolove (the model was the brainchild of Ross Lovegrove), or the Coren, dreamed up by Munich-based Christian Zanzotti and produced by UBC GmbH in a very small number. It was among the most expensive on show when it was presented at the 2012 ISPO Bike.

65 296
66 300

Folding bikes and other types of bicycle

The idea of building bicycles that can be taken apart, folded, or slotted together goes back to the early days of bicycle history and is closely intertwined with notions of taking a bike along on other means of transport (such as a train) and being able to store it more easily in a confined space. London-based William Henry Grout devised a penny-farthing that could be taken apart as early as 1878.[19] In the years that followed there were countless attempts to reduce the bicycle's size. Among others, it was the military who tinkered with the idea; it was hoped that using folding bikes would offer strategic advantages. Before the 19th century was out, all manner of models had been created that were then taken further in the decades that followed.

In the context of the parachute regiments that were assembled after World War I, some thought went into deploying folding bicycles to enable soldiers to swiftly leave the landing site. The BSA Airborne is the best-known military folding bike. Its simple and functional folding mechanism was so convincing that even after the end of World War II the bicycle was still being rolled out and in the early 1980s it morphed into a sleek lifestyle item courtesy of the Trussardi fashion company.

19 126

40 130

Less lifestyle and more technology midwifed BMW's Super-Tech 1997 mountain bike. Not only does it feature the Telelever system developed for motorcycles (when you brake the front end does not drop, meaning there is less danger of going over the front wheel), but it also boasted full suspension despite being a folding mountain bike.

60 276

Another method for making bicycles handier and easier to transport was to opt for smaller wheels, frequently in combination with dividable or foldable frames. Since cycling comfort suffered owing to the smaller wheel diameters, special solutions were devised such as widening the wheels or focusing on suspension systems.

In this context, it was Alex Moulton who with his ideas took things that decisive step forwards in 1960. Not only did he develop an entirely new frame geometry, but also a special suspension system for his bikes.

26 154
38 158

Hier war es unter anderem das Militär, das sich durch den Einsatz klappbarer Fahrräder strategische Vorteile erhoffte. Noch Ende des 19. Jahrhunderts entstanden die verschiedensten Modelle, die in den folgenden Jahrzehnten weiterentwickelt wurden.

Auch bei den in den Zwischenkriegsjahren aufgestellten Fallschirmjäger-Regimentern dachte man an den Einsatz von Klapprädern, damit sich die Soldaten schnell von ihren Landeplätzen entfernen konnten. Mit dem BSA Airborne entstand eines der bekanntesten militärischen Klappräder, dessen ebenso einfacher wie funktionaler Klappmechanismus so überzeugte, dass man dieses Fahrrad nach dem Ende des Zweiten Weltkriegs für den Zivilverkauf anbot, bevor es schließlich Anfang der 1980er-Jahre von der Modefirma Trussardi zum schicken Lifestyleobjekt umfunktioniert wurde.

Weniger für Lifestyle als für Technik steht das 1997 entstandene SuperTech Mountainbike von BMW. Nicht nur übernahm man mit dem Telelever-System eine aus dem Motorradbereich kommende Technik – das Fahrrad taucht beim Bremsen nicht nach vorne ab und vermindert so die Gefahr des Überschlags –, man konnte damit ein vollgefedertes und zugleich klappbares Mountainbike ausstatten.

Eine andere Möglichkeit, Fahrräder handlicher und leichter transportierbar zu machen, bestand im Einsatz von kleineren Laufrädern, häufig in Verbindung mit teilbaren, klapp- oder faltbaren Rahmen. Da unter der Verkleinerung des Raddurchmessers der Fahrkomfort litt, sann man hier auf entsprechende Lösungen, indem man die Reifen verbreiterte oder sich auf die Federungssysteme konzentrierte.

In diesem Kontext war es Alex Moulton, der 1960 mit seinen Ideen einen entscheidenden Schritt voranging. Er entwickelte nicht nur eine völlig neue Rahmengeometrie, sondern auch eine spezielle Federung für seine Räder.

Fahrräder mit Federungen gab es bereits lange zuvor, etwa bei den Rahmenkonstruktionen von Adolf Bareuther oder Praga (Abb. 5), hier in Verbindung mit einer gefederten Gabel, oder bei zahlreichen weiteren Gefährten, ganz abgesehen natürlich von den gefederten Sätteln. Doch waren diese Fahrräder gewöhnlich mit normalgroßen 28-Zoll-Laufrädern ausgestattet.

Alex Moulton jedoch verband beides, kleine Laufräder und eine spezielle Federung. Da ihm sein Fahrrad immer noch zu groß war, gestaltete er zwei Jahre später auch einen entsprechenden Steckmechanismus, um sein Rad in zwei Teile zerlegen zu können.

Andere Entwerfer und Hersteller folgten seinem Vorbild. Union Rijwielfabriek etwa brachte mit dem Strano ein kompaktes Fahrrad auf den Markt, dessen kleines Vorderrad in Verbindung mit der Untersitzlenkung die Dimensionen extrem reduzierte. Das Fahrrad war ganze 120 cm lang. Hinzu kam der abnehmbare Lenker, der die Unterbringung im Kofferraum deutlich erleichterte.

Bei der Gestaltung des Duemila ging es nicht nur um den Klappmechanismus, sondern um das Fahrrad als Ganzes, von der ungewöhnlichen Rahmenform, der klappbaren Sattelstütze über die Gepäckträger, das integrierte Licht und die Schutzbleche bis hin zur Farbgebung.

Abb. 5.
Gefedertes
Fahrrad
Praga, 1928,
Centrala Praga,
Tschechoslowakei,
1928
Fig. 5
Praga suspension
bicycle, 1928,
Centrala Praga,
Czechoslovakia,
1928

19   126

40   130

60   276

26   154
38   158

16   114

26   154

27   160

28   164

16 114 Bicycles featuring suspension had already long existed, for example the frames designed by Adolf Bareuther and <u>Praga</u> (fig. 5) featured them (in connection with suspension forks) and there were countless other vehicles, not to mention all the saddles that had springs. That said, these bicycles tended to have normal sized 28-inch wheels.

By contrast, Alex Moulton combined both – small wheels and a special suspension system. Since he felt the bicycle was still too large, two years later he developed a corresponding pin mechanism in order to be able to divide it

26 154 into two parts.

Other designers and manufacturers followed his example. Union

27 160 Rijwielfabriek launched a compact bicycle (<u>Strano</u>) on the market which had extremely reduced dimensions thanks to a small front wheel and handlebars positioned under the seat. The bicycle was a mere 120 cm in length. Added to which, the handlebars could be removed, making it far easier to store the bike in a car trunk.

28 164 The design of the <u>Duemila</u> hinged not only on the folding mechanism, but on the bicycle as a whole, from the unusual frame shape and folding saddle pin to the pannier, the integrated lights and the mudguards, not to forget the way color was used.

61 280 Richard Sapper's <u>Zoombike</u> is doubtless one of the highlights in the history of folding bicycles. After devoting years to developing the idea, he produced a bike where every detail had been thought through and aligned to the latest production technologies used in the aerospace industry and in automobile design.

46 226
47 230 <u>Strida</u> with its triangular frame geometry was the product of Marc Sanders' final-year university project in 1985. The project has since been posted on the Internet so that all the steps in his deliberations on creating the design can now be followed.

In the 1970s, at a time when bicycles were falling into disrepute as the quality of manufacturing had clearly deteriorated and the market was flooded

32 178 with cheap mass-produced bicycles, the <u>Five Rams</u> appeared in China. The central idea underpinning the design was to devise a bike that could grow along with the child, a bicycle with a wheelbase that could be changed by moving the back section with the seat and drive along a horizontal central tube. The height of the saddle and handlebars could be adjusted so that the bicycle could be smoothly adapted to the swiftly growing child.

Bicycles for children and youths have existed since the beginning of bicycle making. This applies to the running machines, the front-wheel pedal crank varieties, and even the penny-farthings.[20] It nevertheless took until well into the 20th century for the bicycle industry to bring halfway decent children's bikes to market. Things were somewhat different as regards bicycles for adolescents: In their case, it was the youths themselves who made changes to existing

29 168 models and thus launched a new trend, initially in the United States, and later
30 172 in Europe and above all in Germany – with the so-called <u>Bonanza</u> or chopper bikes which now still enjoy an almost legendary cult status.

61 280   Zu den Höhepunkten in der Geschichte der Falträder zählt zweifellos das Zoombike von Richard Sapper. Nach jahrelanger Arbeit entstand hier ein Rad, bei dem jedes Detail durchdacht und auf die neuesten Produktionstechniken aus den Bereichen der Raumfahrttechnik und der Automobilgestaltung abgestimmt war.

46 226
47 230   Aus der Diplomarbeit Marc Sanders' von 1985 ging das Strida mit seiner dreieckigen Rahmengeometrie hervor. Hier lässt sich durch die Veröffentlichung der Diplomarbeit im Internet jede Überlegung, jeder Schritt des Designers nachvollziehen.

32 178   In den 1970er-Jahren, in einer Zeit, als das Fahrrad in Verruf geriet, da die Fertigungsqualität deutlich abnahm und der Markt mit preiswerten Massenrädern überflutet wurde, entstand in China das Five Rams. Der zentrale Entwurfsgedanke bestand darin, ein mitwachsendes Fahrrad zu konzipieren, ein Fahrrad, dessen Radstand durch das Verschieben des hinteren Teils mit Sitz und Antrieb entlang eines horizontalen Zentralrohres verändert werden konnte. Sattel und Lenker waren höhenverstellbar, sodass sich dieses Rad stufenlos der sich rasch verändernden Körpergröße eines Kindes anpassen ließ.

Kinder- und Jugendfahrräder gab es von Beginn der Fahrradentwicklung an. Das gilt für Laufmaschinen und Vorderrad-Tretkurbelräder bis hin zu Hochrädern.[20] Dennoch dauerte es bis weit in das späte 20. Jahrhundert hinein, bis die Fahrradindustrie einigermaßen brauchbare Kinderäder auf den Markt brachte. Bei den Jugendrädern verhielt es sich etwas anders. Hier waren es die Jugendlichen selbst, die durch das eigenständige Verändern von vorhandenen Modellen einen Trend schufen, der von den Fahrradherstellern aufgegriffen

29 168
30 172   wurde, zuerst in den USA und ein wenig später auch in Europa und vor allem in Deutschland mit den sogenannten Bonanzarädern, deren Kultstatus teilweise heute noch legendär ist.

Dennoch sind die Bonanzaräder in Sachen Kultstatus nicht mit den Rennrädern zu vergleichen. Obwohl sich in diesem Bereich die Rahmengeometrie über Jahrzehnte kaum verändert hat und die Bedeutung der Aerodynamik erst in den 1970er-Jahren allmählich erforscht wurde, ist das Interesse an den Rennrädern aus Stahl nicht nur ungebrochen, sondern scheint kontinuierlich zuzunehmen. Es sind vor allem die Straßenrennräder der 1970er- und 1980er-Jahre, die diesen Kultstatus erlangten, befördert durch die Tour de France und den Giro d'Italia und die Namen berühmter Fahrer wie Fausto Coppi, Eddy Merckx, Francesco Moser, später Chris Boardman oder Greg LeMond, um nur wenige zu nennen.

Geschwindigkeit und Rekorde trugen zur Legendenbildung bei, mehr noch bei den Straßenrennen als bei den Bahnrennen, obwohl auch da die Sekundenbruchteile den Unterschied ausmachten. Um schneller zu sein, entwickelte man ständig neue Formen und Technologien, wie etwa die Liegefahrräder, deren Luftwiderstand erheblich geringer ist als bei klassischen Rennrädern. Interessanterweise hatte der Stromlinien-Pionier Paul Jaray bereits 1919 ein niedriges

12 098   Sesselrad (für die Hesperus Werke) entworfen, das die Vorteile dieses Fahrradtypus aufzeigte.

However, in terms of cult status, chopper bikes still lag well behind racing bikes. Although hardly anything about racing bikes has changed in decades and although the importance of aerodynamics did not start being explored more thoroughly until the 1970s, interest in steel-frame racing bikes not only remains intact but would seem to constantly be on the rise. It is above all the road racing bikes of the 1970s and 1980s that now have such a cult status – an interest fueled by the Tour de France and the Giro d'Italia and the names of famous riders such as Fausto Coppi, Eddy Merckx, Francesco Moser, and later Chris Boardman or Greg LeMond, to name but a few.

Speeds and records have fanned the legend, more in the case of road races than track races, although even there fractions of a second can make all the difference. In order to be faster, new shapes and technologies are forever being invented, such as recumbent bicycles, where the drag is far lower than with classic racing bikes. Interestingly, streamlining-pioneer Paul Jaray designed a low-rider bike as long ago as 1919 that demonstrated the advantages of this type of bicycle.

12   098

It was not always the fastest bicycles that won the day, as bicycle racing is regulated by various bodies that in part define the parameters for the construction of bicycles. Founded in 1900 in Switzerland, the Union Cycliste Internationale (UCI) is among the best known but also one of the most restrictive organizations in this context. How meaningful some of their rules are may be a moot point, but what is certain is that as a result some developments were blocked or had to be changed – and not always to the advantage of progress and design.

62   284

Where the rules were less rigid, new things arose, for example for triathlon, as can be seen from Softride's RocketWing. In other areas, new bicycle types evolved, too; one need only think of BMX bikes or mountain bikes. Moreover, the industry itself repeatedly devised new types, such as the gravel bikes that have been on the market since about 2015.

The cycling boom of recent years has also led to various changes in city and leisure-time bikes, randonneurs and freight bikes. However, the greatest upheaval in the history of cycling has been the introduction of electric bicycles, the e-bike or pedelec. Here, again, the roots can be traced back to the 19th century. For example, the likes of Frenchman Louis-Guillaume Perreaux developed bicycles back around 1870 with steam or electric drives.[21] Nevertheless, we had to wait almost 150 years until e-bikes became generally acceptable. After the tentative new beginnings in the 1980s, countless years passed until the e-bike boom set in – and it is definitely ongoing. The reasons related to both technology and design. Indeed, on the one hand, since 2005 new and lighter lithium batteries and the development of new engines have improved e-bikes' range and considerably reduced their weight. On the other, design has helped boost acceptance levels and make e-bikes more "chic", for example by classical geometric frame shapes (fig. 6).[22]

68   308

This can be seen in particular in the case of bicycles where industrial designers took up the baton. Without doubt, Nick Foley and his team's Jump

Nicht immer konnten sich die schnellsten Räder durchsetzen, war und ist doch der Radsport durch viele Gremien geregelt, die zum Teil auch die Bestimmungen für die Konstruktion von Fahrrädern aufstellen. Die 1900 in der Schweiz gegründete Union Cycliste Internationale (UCI) gehört zu den bekanntesten, aber auch zu den restriktivsten Organisationen in diesem Kontext. Wie sinnvoll manche ihrer Regeln sind, sei dahingestellt, sicher ist jedoch, dass dadurch auch Entwicklungen verhindert wurden oder verändert werden mussten und das nicht immer zum Vorteil für den Fortschritt und das Design.

62   284

Dort, wo die Regeln weniger streng waren, entstand Neues, etwa für den Triathlon, wie bei dem RocketWing von Softride zu sehen ist. Auch in anderen Bereichen entwickelten sich neue Fahrradtypen, wenn man nur an die BMX-Fahrräder oder die Mountainbikes denkt. Zudem schafft sich die Industrie immer wieder neue Typen, wie die sogenannten Gravelbikes, die seit etwa 2015 auf dem Markt sind.

Aber auch bei den Stadt- und Freizeiträdern, den Touren- und Lastenrädern veränderte sich mit dem Fahrradboom der letzten Jahre einiges. Doch die größte Umwälzung in der Geschichte des Fahrrads brachte das Elektrofahrrad, das E-Bike oder Pedelec. Auch hier reichen die Ursprünge bis ins 19. Jahrhundert zurück. So hatte etwa bereits um 1870 der Franzose Louis-Guillaume Perreaux Fahrräder mit Dampf- und Elektroantrieb entworfen.[21] Dennoch dauerte es fast 150 Jahre, bis das E-Bike salonfähig wurde. Nach den zaghaften Neuanfängen in den 1980er-Jahren vergingen noch etliche Jahre, bis der bis heute ungebrochene E-Bike-Boom einsetzte. Die Gründe dafür lagen sowohl im Technologie- wie auch im Designbereich. Einerseits konnten ab 2005 durch den Einsatz der neuen und leichteren Lithium-Akkus und der Entwicklung neuer Motoren die Reichweite verbessert und das Gewicht erheblich reduziert werden, andererseits gelang es durch das Design, die Akzeptanz zu erhöhen und das E-Bike „schicker" zu machen[22], etwa durch klassisch geometrische Rahmenformen (Abb. 6).

Abb. 6.
Ties Carlier / Taco Carlier,
Elektrofahrrad Van Moof S3,
Niederlande, 2019/20
Fig. 6
Ties Carlier / Taco Carlier,
Van Moof S3 electric bicycle,
Netherlands, 2019/20

68   308

Besonders deutlich zeigt sich das an den Rädern, bei denen sich Industriedesigner des Themas annahmen. Sicherlich bietet hier das Jump-E-Bike von Nick Foley und seinem Team ein besonders prägnantes Beispiel dafür. Zugleich handelt es sich aber auch um einen Sonderfall, da dieses Fahrrad als Sharing-Modell konzipiert, gestaltet und produziert wurde. Sich die Nutzung von Fahrrädern zu teilen bzw. Fahrräder zu verleihen, hat ihren Ursprung im personalisierten Verleih beispielsweise von Unternehmen wie Call a bike, das später von der Deutschen Bahn übernommen wurde, entwickelte sich jedoch in den letzten Jahrzehnten rasant weiter, unterstützt von der zunehmenden Digitalisierung unserer Lebenswelt.

Für das Design von Leihfahrrädern gelten andere Prämissen als für gewöhnliche Stadträder. Hier stehen Robustheit hinsichtlich Witterung und Dauereinsatz sowie die Anpassung an die unterschiedlichen Benutzer und Benutzerinnen, was Geschlecht, Größe und Gewicht betrifft, im Vordergrund. Wie rasant die Entwicklung in diesem Bereich verläuft, zeigt sich allein schon am Wechsel der Bezahlsysteme, an der Appsteuerung oder daran, dass die

e-bike is an especially striking example. That said, it is a special case, as the bicycle in question was conceived, designed and manufactured as a sharing model. Sharing the use of bicycles or hiring bicycles has its origins in personalized hiring, such as by Call a bike now owned by Deutsche Bahn, a trend that has really taken off in recent decades, supported by the increasing digitization of our lifeworld.

The design criteria for share/hire bikes are unlike those for normal city bikes. The emphasis is on robustness with regard to weather and continous use and adjustability to different users in terms of gender, body size, and weight. Just how quickly developments are ongoing in this segment can be seen from the change in payment systems, from the App-controlled systems and from the way fixed bike collection points are swiftly being abandoned with a view to making use more comfortable to the hirer. The example of the e-bike designed by Christian Zanzotti for Vässla highlights the latest developments in this segment.

69   312

This indicates just how much potential there is for bicycle design today and also points to the future, in which precisely with e-bikes users can expect to see the deployment of more digital technologies. This is where the design unites both the design of the hardware, the bicycle and its components, with the software – and thus differs fundamentally from the traditional bicycle assembly of yore.

The designers

Last but not least, the question arises as to who the people behind the designs were, who moved the development of bicycles forward with their ideas and thus also helped shape bicycle design history. In the early days of bicycle history the concept of the designer did not yet exist, which makes it somewhat difficult to even talk about designers during the bicycle's infancy.

Karl Friedrich Drais studied Mathematics, Physics and Architecture – as his insufficient knowledge of Latin prevented him from studying Law. He then entered the Forestry Service. He was essentially overqualified for the job and therefore used his free time to invent things. His university studies meant he had an understanding of mechanical functions. After creating a piano recorder he dedicated himself to devising a four-wheel driving machine to be moved solely by muscle power. The "Running Machine" was more or less a logical consequence of his preoccupation with locomotive machines.

The subsequent protagonists of bicycle history had all sorts of different education backgrounds or their inventions, which they then patented, tended to be the result of a knowledge of the trades. Initially, they were mainly craftsmen from the realm of metalworking, i.e., locksmiths or blacksmiths (Pierre Michaux, Josef Erlach, Mikael Pedersen) or mechanics (Eugène Meyer, Leonard B. Gaylor, Franz Grundner). The classical frame-builders likewise usually had such a background (Pierre Caminade, Jacques Schulz, and later Fritz Fleck, André Sablière, etc.).

Abkehr von festen Stationen, die auf die Bequemlichkeit der Nutzer und Nutzerinnen zielt, zu dominieren beginnt. Das Beispiel des von Christian Zanzotti für Vässla entworfenen E-Bikes belegt die neuesten Entwicklungen in diesem Bereich.

69 312

Damit wird das Potenzial des aktuellen Fahrraddesigns aufgezeigt und gleichzeitig auf die Zukunft verwiesen, in der gerade bei den E-Bikes durch den Einsatz digitaler Techniken noch einiges für die Benutzer und Benutzerinnen zu erwarten sein wird. An diesem Punkt vereinigt das Design die Gestaltung der Hardware, des Fahrrads und seiner Komponenten mit der Software und unterscheidet sich damit grundsätzlich vom traditionellen Fahrradbau der Zeit zuvor.

Die Designer

Zu guter Letzt stellt sich die Frage, wer die Menschen waren, die hinter den Entwürfen stecken, die die Entwicklung des Fahrrads mit ihren Ideen vorangetrieben und damit auch die Designgeschichte des Fahrrads mitbestimmt haben. Den Begriff des Designers gab es in der Frühzeit der Fahrradgeschichte noch gar nicht. Im deutschen Sprachraum etablierte sich das Wort Design erst nach 1945. Deshalb ist es schwierig, in der Frühzeit überhaupt von Designern zu sprechen.

Karl Friedrich Drais studierte Mathematik, Physik und Baukunst, für Jura reichten seine Lateinkenntnisse nicht aus. Danach trat er in den Forstdienst ein. Dafür war er eigentlich überqualifiziert und nutzte deshalb seine freie Zeit für Erfindungen. Durch sein Studium brachte er auch das Verständnis für mechanische Funktionsweisen auf. Nach einem Klavierrekorder widmete er sich einer vierrädrigen Fahrmaschine, die allein mit Muskelkraft angetrieben werden sollte. Die Laufmaschine entstand mehr oder weniger als logische Konsequenz seiner Beschäftigung mit Maschinen zur Fortbewegung.

Die nachfolgenden Protagonisten der Fahrradgeschichte hatten ganz unterschiedliche Ausbildungen oder kamen über das Handwerk zu ihren Erfindungen, die sie sich meist auch patentieren ließen. Zunächst waren es vor allem Handwerker aus dem Metallbereich, Schlosser oder Schmiede (Pierre Michaux, Josef Erlach, Mikael Pedersen) sowie Mechaniker (Eugène Meyer, Leonard B. Gaylor, Franz Grundner). Auch die klassischen Rahmenbauer hatten meist einen derartigen Hintergrund (Pierre Caminade, Jacques Schulz, später Fritz Fleck, André Sablière u. a.).

Wichtige Impulse für den Fahrradbau und das Fahrraddesign lieferten Ingenieure und Konstrukteure aus dem Luftfahrt- oder Automobilsektor: Paul Jaray arbeitete nach seinem Maschinenbaustudium zunächst als Chefkonstrukteur im Flugzeugbau Friedrichshafen und anschließend bei den dortigen Zeppelinwerken, wo er im Bereich der Aerodynamik forschte. Seine bahnbrechenden Erkenntnisse beeinflussten die Luftfahrt und den Automobilbau. Der promovierte Ingenieur Hermann Klaue hatte im Rahmen seiner Doktorarbeit die Vollscheibenbremse entwickelt. Er beschäftige sich vor allem mit Fahrzeugtechnik,

Engineers and construction engineers from the aerospace and automobile sectors contributed key ideas to bicycle-making and cycle design. After studying Mechanical Engineering, Paul Jaray, for example, initially worked as the chief construction engineer at Flugzeugbau Friedrichshafen and subsequently at the Zeppelin factories there, where he conducted research in the field of aerodynamics. His pioneering findings influenced both aircraft and automobile construction. Hermann Klaue had a PhD in Engineering and as part of his doctoral thesis developed the multi disc brake. He concerned himself primarily with vehicle technology; his ideas helped advance bicycle making and he submitted some 800 patents in the course of his life. The engineers at Mitsubishi who had built military aircraft during World War II subsequently devoted themselves to building bicycles. As did at a later point in time the engineers at aircraft makers Antonov in the Ukraine. The designer of the Cavallo, Hans Günter Bals, is a mechanical and aircraft engineer. Frank Kirk trained in aerospace engineering and worked in automobile manufacturing when he started focusing on designing bicycles. Alex Moulton studied Mechanical Sciences, worked for the Bristol Aircraft Company in engine development, and later for the British Motor Corporation and for Dunlop on the idea of rubber suspension systems. Mike Burrows, one of the most highly regarded of the bicycle designers, occupies a slightly unique position in this regard as he was self-taught.

With the exception of Jean Prouvé, who having trained as a metal-smith and then embarked on a career as an architect and designer, and who launched his own bicycle design as early as 1941 (fig. 7), only at a relatively late point in time did designers in today's sense engage with bicycle manufacturing. Luigi Colani, one of the best-known designers, originally studied Sculpting and Painting before turning his attention to aerodynamics and vehicle building. By contrast, Michael Conrad, a graduate of Ulm School of Design, Richard Sapper, Odo Klose, Giorgetto Giugiaro, Marc Newson, Ross Lovegrove, Marc Sanders, Nick Foley, Paule Guérin and Christian Zanzotti are among the classical industrial designers who have masterminded bicycles. We have them to thank for the fact that modern bicycle design has repeatedly received new stimuli. Their ideas and experiences with other products and manufacturing methods proved highly advantageous to the bicycle industry, for example bringing the latest metalworking techniques to bear for bicycle design – Marc Newson, Richard Sapper and Michael Conrad all bear mentioning in this regard. The development of today's e-bikes with all their functional complexity in combination with digital applications for the controls, safety, and use involve tasks and requirements that go far beyond the traditional understanding of bicycle making, as is demonstrated by the examples by Nick Foley or Christian Zanzotti presented here.

Abb. 7
Jean Prouvé, Fahrrad,
Frankreich, ca. 1941
Fig. 7
Jean Prouvé, bicycle,
France, c. 1941

brachte den Fahrradbau mit seinen Ideen voran und reichte rund 800 Patente ein. Die Ingenieure von Mitsubishi, die im Zweiten Weltkrieg Kampfflugzeuge konstruiert hatten, widmeten sich dem Fahrradbau. Ebenso später die Ingenieure des Flugzeugbauers Antonov in der Ukraine. Auch der Gestalter des Cavallo, Hans Günter Bals, ist ein Maschinen- und Flugzeugbauingenieur. Frank Kirk hatte eine Ausbildung als Luft- und Raumfahrtingenieur und arbeitete im Automobilbau, als er sich dem Fahrraddesign zuwandte. Alex Moulton studierte Mechanical Sciences, arbeitete bei den Bristol-Flugzeugwerken in der Motorenentwicklung, später für die British Motor Corporation und für Dunlop an der Idee der Gummifederung. Eine gewisse Sonderstellung nimmt Mike Burrows ein, der sich als Autodidakt zu einem der renommiertesten Fahrraddesigner entwickelte.

Abgesehen von Jean Prouvé, der nach seiner Ausbildung zum Kunstschmied als Architekt und Designer Karriere machte und der bereits 1941 sein Fahrrad (Abb. 7) vorstellte, beschäftigten sich die Designer im heutigen Sinne erst relativ spät mit dem Fahrrad.

Luigi Colani hatte ursprünglich angefangen, Bildhauerei und Malerei zu studieren, bevor er sich der Aerodynamik und dem Fahrzeugbau widmete. Klassische Industriedesigner sind dagegen Michael Conrad, Absolvent der HfG Ulm, Richard Sapper, Odo Klose, Giorgetto Giugiaro, Marc Newson, Ross Lovegrove, Marc Sanders, Nick Foley, Paule Guérin oder Christian Zanzotti.

Ihnen ist es zu verdanken, dass das moderne Fahrraddesign immer wieder neue Impulse erhielt. Ihre Ideen und Erfahrungen mit anderen Produkten und Herstellungstechniken erwiesen sich auch im Fahrradbereich als vorteilhaft, etwa wenn neueste Materialverarbeitungstechniken wie bei Marc Newson, Richard Sapper oder Michael Conrad für das Fahrraddesign erschlossen wurden. Die Entwicklung der aktuellen E-Bikes mit ihrer funktionalen Komplexität in Kombination mit digitalen Anwendungen für die Steuerung, Sicherheit und Nutzung ist mit Aufgaben und Anforderungen verbunden, die weit über das traditionelle Verständnis vom Fahrradbau hinausgehen, wie die hier vorgestellten Beispiele von Nick Foley oder Christian Zanzotti aufzeigen.

1   Codex Atlanticus, fol. 133 verso, Mailand, Biblioteca Ambrosiana.
2   Hans-Erhard Lessing: The Leonardo da Vinci Bicycle Hoax. In: Cycle Publishing, 1997. https://www.cyclepublishing.com/history/leonardo%20da%20vinci%20bicycle.html (15.09.2022).
3   Hans-Erhard Lessing u. Tony Hadland, Evolution des Fahrrads. Berlin/Heidelberg 2021 (Übersetzung der englischen Edition: Tony Hadland and Hans-Erhard Lessing, Bicycle Design. An Illustrated History. Cambridge, Massachusetts 2014), 1–7.
4   Hans-Erhard Lessing, Wie Karl Drais das Fahrrad erfand. Karlsruhe 2018.
5   Vgl. Lessing/Hadland 2021 (wie Anm. 3), 41–62.
6   Vgl. Lessing/Hadland 2021 (wie Anm. 3), 41 ff., 63.
7   Vgl. Lessing/Hadland 2021 (wie Anm. 3), 41 f., 93–94.

8   Vgl. Jacques Seray, Deux Roues. La véritable Histoire du Vélo. Millau 1988, 101–102.
9   Vgl. Lessing/Hadland 2021 (wie Anm. 3), 173.
10   Vgl. Lessing/Hadland 2021 (wie Anm. 3), 170.
11   Otakar Máčel, Marcel Breuer – „Erfinder der Stahlrohrmöbel", in: [Kat. Ausst.] Marcel Breuer. Design und Architektur. Vitra Design Museum. Weil am Rhein 2003, 56.
12   Vgl. Sarah Nichols, Aluminum by Design. Carnegie Museum of Art, Pittsburgh, New York 2000, 34–35.
13   http://cozybeehive.blogspot.com/2009/01/8-second-bicycle.html (20.07.2022).
14   Vgl. Lessing/Hadland 2021 (wie Anm. 3), 375.
15   Zitiert nach Lessing/Hadland 2021 (wie Anm. 3), 175.
16   https://en.wikipedia.org/wiki/Royal_Aircraft_Establishment#cite_note-9 (17.09.2022).

17   http://www.classicrendezvous.com/USA/Graftek.htm (17.09.2022).
18   https://fes-sport.de/chronik.htm (17.09.2022).
19   Vgl. Lessing/Hadland 2021 (wie Anm. 3), 429.
20   Vgl. Volker Briese, Children's Corner. Die Geschichte des Kinderrads, in: Michael Bollschweiler, Michael Mertins, Gerhard Renda (Hrsg.), Rückenwind. Ein Streifzug durch die Fahrradgeschichte. Bielefeld 2011, 24–29.
21   Vgl. Lessing/Hadland 2021 (wie Anm. 3), 83.
22   Vgl. den E-Bike-Artikel bei Wikipedia, https://de.wikipedia.org/wiki/E-Bike (17.09.2022).

1   Codex Atlanticus, fol. 133 verso, Milan, Biblioteca Ambrosiana.
2   Hans-Erhard Lessing: The Leonardo da Vinci Bicycle Hoax. In: Cycle Publishing, 1997. https://www.cyclepublishing.com/history/leonardo%20da%20vinci%20bicycle.html (last retrieved Sept. 17, 2022).
3   Hans-Erhard Lessing/Tony Hadland, Evolution des Fahrrads. Berlin/Heidelberg 2021 (english edition: Tony Hadland and Hans-Erhard Lessing, Bicycle Design. An Illustrated History. Cambridge, Massachusetts 2014), 1–7.
4   Hans-Erhard Lessing, Wie Karl Drais das Fahrrad erfand. Karlsruhe 2018.
5   Cf. Lessing & Hadland 2021 (see note 3), 41–62.
6   Cf. Lessing & Hadland 2021 (see note 3), 41, 63.
7   Cf. Lessing & Hadland 2021 (see note 3), 41 pp, 93–4.

8   Cf. Jacques Seray, Deux Roues. La véritable Histoire du Vélo, (Millau, 1988), 101–2.
9   Cf. Lessing & Hadland (see note 3), 173.
10 Cf. Lessing & Hadland (see note 3), 170.
11 Otakar Máčel, "Marcel Breuer – 'Erfinder der Stahlrohrmöbel,'" in: exh. cat. Marcel Breuer. Design und Architektur. (Vitra Design Museum, Weil am Rhein, 2003), 56.
12 Cf. Sarah Nichols, Aluminum by Design. Carnegie Museum of Art, Pittsburgh, New York 2000, 34–35.
13 http://cozybeehive.blogspot.com/2009/01/8-second-bicycle.html (last retrieved July 20, 2022).
14 Cf. Lessing & Hadland (see note 3), p. 375.
15 Quoted from Lessing & Hadland (see note 3), 175.
16 https://en.wikipedia.org/wiki/Royal_Aircraft_Establishment#cite_note-9 (last retrieved Sept. 17, 2022).

17 http://www.classicrendezvous.com/USA/Graftek.htm (last retrieved Sept. 17, 2022).
18 https://fes-sport.de/chronik.htm (last retrieved Sept. 17, 2022).
19 Cf. Lessing & Hadland (see note 3), 429.
20 Cf. Volker Briese, "Children's Corner. Die Geschichte des Kinderrads," in: Michael Bollschweiler, Michael Mertins & Gerhard Renda (eds.), Rückenwind. Ein Streifzug durch die Fahrradgeschichte, (Bielefeld, 2011), 24–9.
21 Cf. Lessing & Hadland (see note 3), 83.
22 See the article on e-bikes on Wikipedia, https://en.wikipedia.org/wiki/Pedelec (last retrieved Sept. 17, 2022).

Die Auserwählten
70 Fahrräder zwischen Kult und Design

The Bicycle Selection
70 Bikes Straddling Cult and Design

Johann Frey
Mannheim, DE

Die Erfindung des Fahrrads ist mit dem Namen des badischen Forstbeamten Karl Drais (1785–1851) verbunden. Er hatte für ursprünglich nicht-lenkbare Laufräder eine Lenkvorrichtung gebaut, eine sogenannte Drehschemel-Lenkung, sowie ein Balancierbrett für die Unterarme. Damit blieben diese frei zum Lenken und das Gleichgewicht konnte leichter gehalten werden. Wie ausgeklügelt die von dem Mannheimer Stellmacher Johann Frey auf Anweisung von Drais gefertigte Maschine war, zeigt sich an zahlreichen Details: extrem leichte Speichenräder mit 27 Zoll Durchmesser, schmierbare Messingbüchsen der Naben zur Reibungsreduzierung, gepolstertes Balancierbrett, Vorderrad mit ca. 15 cm Nachlauf, damit sich dieses immer wieder in Fahrtrichtung einstellte, die Leitstange konnte nach vorne umgeschlagen werden, um die Laufmaschine am Berg hinter sich herzuziehen. Später kam noch ein höhenverstellbarer Sitz hinzu.

Seine erste dokumentierte Fahrt mit dem Laufrad von Mannheim in Richtung Schwetzingen fand am 12. Juni 1817 statt. In einer Stunde legte er acht englische Meilen zurück, also etwa vier Poststunden Weg, und erreichte dabei eine Durchschnittsgeschwindigkeit von 14 oder gar 15 km/h. Damit zeigte Drais auf, dass man mit eigener Muskelkraft schneller sein konnte als mit der von Pferden gezogenen Postkutsche.

The invention of the bicycle is linked with the name of forest official Karl Drais (1785–1851) from southwest Germany. He built a steering device for what were originally non-steerable running machines, a so-called turntable steering system, as well as a balancing board for the lower arms. In this way, the rider could use his arms to steer and could more readily keep his balance. The ingenuity of the machine made by Mannheim-based cartwright Johann Frey at Drais' instruction can be seen from the countless details: extremely light 27-inch spoked wheels, greasable brass bearings for the hubs to reduce friction, upholstered balancing board, front wheel with a c. 15-cm lag so that it always righted itself into the direction of travel, and a steering stick that could be flipped over forwards in order to be able to pull the running machine uphill behind one. Later, a height-adjustable seat was added.

Drais' first documented trip with the running machine from Mannheim in the direction of Schwetzingen took place on June 12, 1817. He needed an hour to cover the eight English miles, meaning a distance of some four post hours, achieving an average speed of 14 or even 15 km/h. Drais thus demonstrated that people could move faster powered only by their muscles than a horse-drawn post coach.

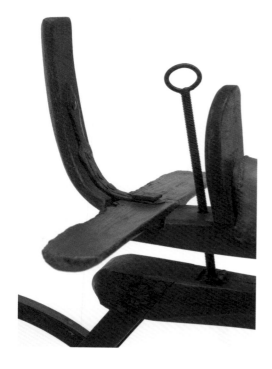

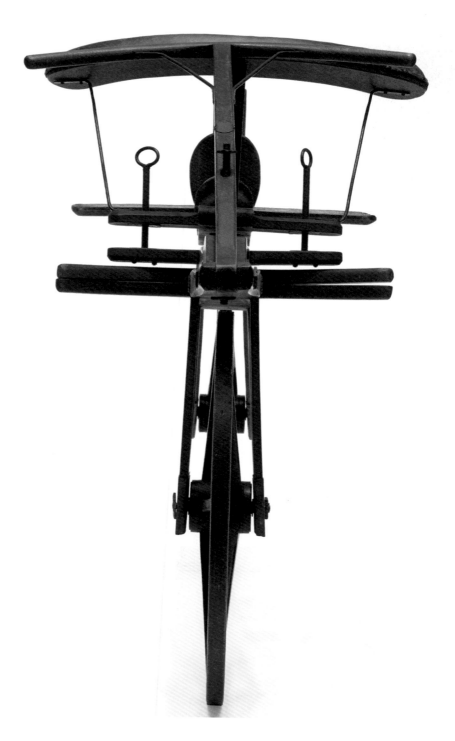

„Wenn man nachher in dem Schuss ist und aus Versehen die Balance etwas verloren hat, kann man sich selbst gewöhnlich mit den Füßen helfen, oder durch das Leiten, wenn man ein bisschen gegen die Richtung leitet, auf welche der Schwerpunkt des Ganzen sich neigte."[1]

"If one ... has inadvertently lost balance, one can help oneself by using the feet or by steering. Specifically, one steers a bit towards the direction to which the point of gravity of the whole tips over."

Karl Drais 1820

Eugène Meyer & Cie
Paris, FR

Der im Elsass geborene Pariser Mechaniker Eugène Meyer (1844–1907) gilt als Erfinder des Zugspeichenrads und des Hochrads. Sein hier vorgestelltes Tretkurbelrad – direkter Vorderradantrieb mithilfe von Kurbeln und Pedalen – wird als „Übergangsmodell" zum Hochrad angesehen. Der große Durchmesser des Vorderrads, die Gummireifen, die Stahlzugspeichen und die Steighilfe sind typische Merkmale der späteren Velozipede. Meyer war für die bemerkenswerte Gestaltung und die mechanische Präzision seiner Konstruktionen berühmt, wie hier anhand der Naben oder Pedale zu erkennen ist. Um seine Räder bekannter zu machen, nahm Meyer selbst an Radrennen teil.

Alsace-born mechanic Eugène Meyer (1844–1907) is considered the inventor of the wire wheel and the penny-farthing, also known as the high wheel or "ordinary." The version of the latter on show here (direct front wheel drive using a crankshaft and pedals) is viewed as the transition model to the penny-farthing proper. The large diameter of the front wheel, the rubber tires, the steel-tensioned wire spokes, and the mounting assistance are all typical features of the later velocipedes. Meyer was renowned for the remarkable design and the mechanical precision of his constructions, as can be seen here from the hub and the pedals. Meyer himself took part in bicycle races to make his inventions better known.

„Herr E. Meyer zeigte uns Stahl[speichen]räder von extremer Eleganz und Leichtigkeit sowie die Velozipede, in denen er sie einsetzt. Es ist kaum vorstellbar, dass es etwas Brillanteres und Leichteres als diese polierten Maschinen gibt."[2]

"Mr. E. Meyer showed us steel[spoke] wheels of exceptional elegance and lightness as well as the velocipedes he used them with. Something more brilliant or lighter than these polished machines is hardly conceivable."

Le Vélocipède Illustré 1869

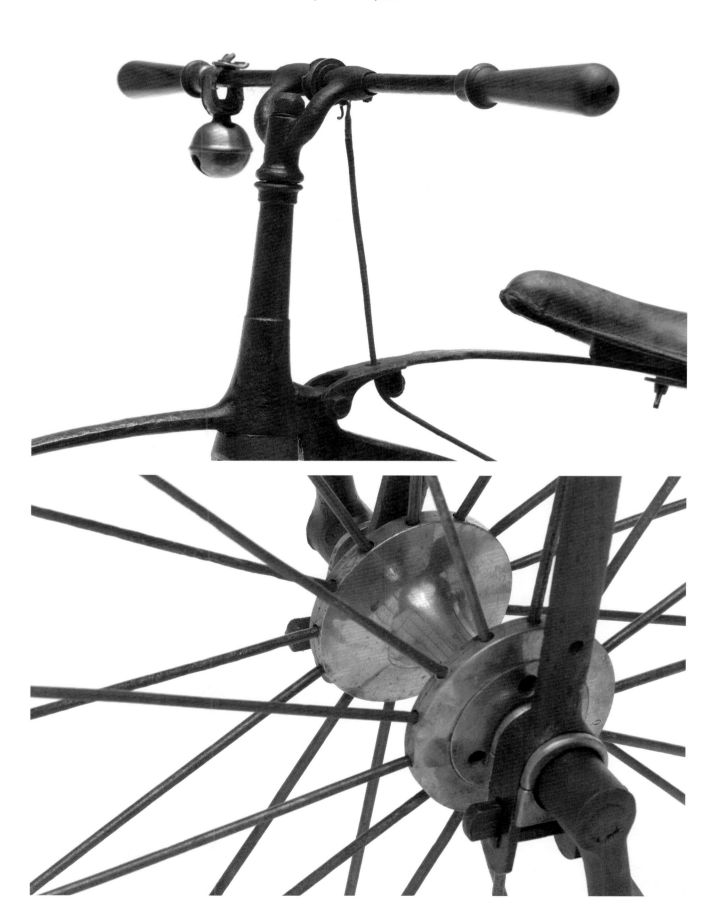

Sicherheitsniederrad c.1880
Low-wheel safety bicycle

Valentin Wiegele
Korpitsch / Villach, AT, c. 1887/88

Der Kärntner Schlosser und Erfinder Josef Erlach (1830–1885) erhielt 1878 ein Patent für seine drei- und zweirädrigen Fahrräder, die er aus geschmiedetem Eisen fertigte.

Bei diesem frühen Sicherheitsniederrad besteht der dreieckige Hauptrahmen aus genieteten und geschraubten Winkelprofilen. Der Schwerpunkt liegt zwischen den Rädern, sodass der Fahrer im Gegensatz zum Hochrad mit den Füßen den Boden berühren konnte.

Auf den Markt kamen Erlachs zweirädrige Fahrräder 1880. Sie waren nach dem gleichen Prinzip wie seine Dreiräder mit einem Schubstangenantrieb konstruiert und konnten über das Verstellen der Schubstange mit zwei Gängen gefahren werden.

Nach Erlachs Tod übernahm sein Werkmeister Valentin Wiegele (†1921) den Betrieb und setzte die Fertigung der Entwürfe Erlachs fort, die er in manchen Details wie Bremsen mit Bremshebel statt Handrolle, in der Sattelkonstruktion und den Rädern modifizierte.

In 1878, Carinthian locksmith and inventor Josef Erlach (1830–1885) was awarded a patent for his bicycles and tricycles that he made from forged iron. This early safety bicycle featured a triangular main frame made of riveted and screwed angled profiles. The point of gravity was located between the wheels so that the cyclist, unlike the ones atop a penny-farthing, was able to touch the ground with his feet.

Erlach's two-wheel bicycles were launched on the market in 1880. They were built according to the same principle as his tricycles and used a slide-bar drive, whereby the drive bar could be shifted, allowing the cyclist two different gear ratios.

After Erlach's death the master locksmith in his workshop, Valentin Wiegele (†1921), took over operations. He continued to manufacture Erlach's designs, modifying the saddle structure, wheels and certain details, such as using brakes with brake levers rather than hand rolls.

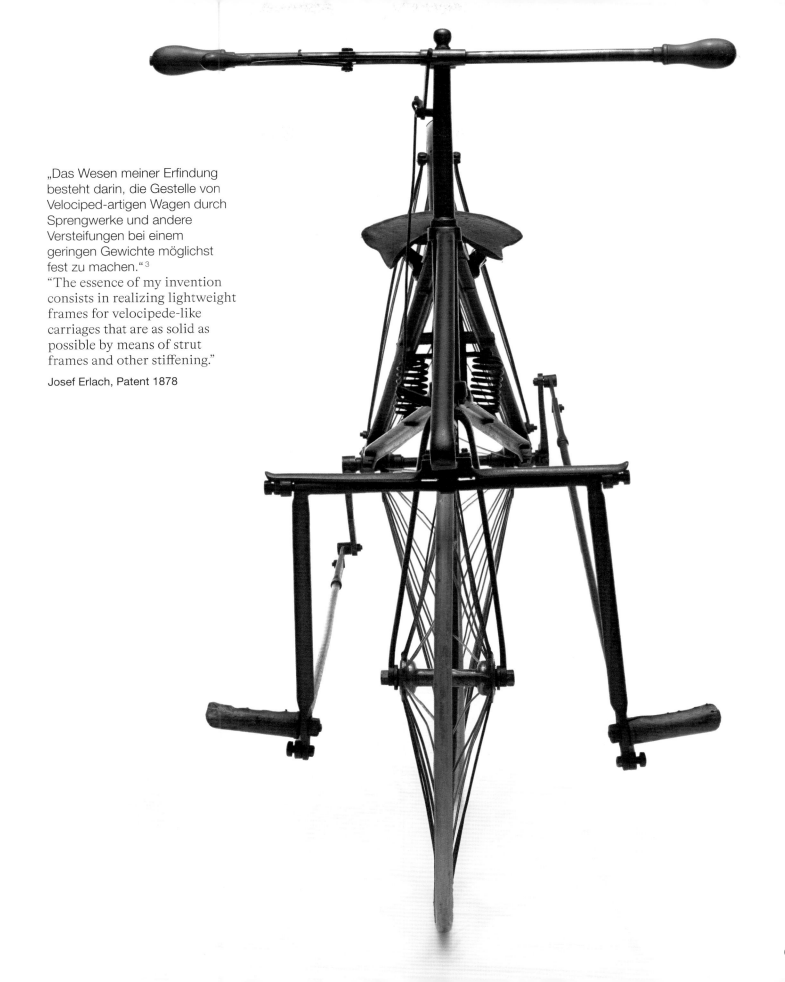

„Das Wesen meiner Erfindung
besteht darin, die Gestelle von
Velociped-artigen Wagen durch
Sprengwerke und andere
Versteifungen bei einem
geringen Gewichte möglichst
fest zu machen."[3]
"The essence of my invention
consists in realizing lightweight
frames for velocipede-like
carriages that are as solid as
possible by means of strut
frames and other stiffening."

Josef Erlach, Patent 1878

Eagle Bicycle Manufacturing Company
Stamford, USA

Leonard B. Gaylor (1857–1931), vielseitiger Erfinder und Gründer des Unternehmens, ließ sich am 19. April 1887 sein Sicherheitshochrad patentieren (No 361280), bei dem das kleine Rad vorne statt hinten angebracht war. Dadurch konnte der Fahrer das Gleichgewicht besser halten und Stürze kopfüber vermeiden.

Mit dieser einfachen, wenn auch entscheidenden Veränderung gegenüber dem Aufbau eines klassischen Hochrads, eines „Ordinary", gingen auch funktional und gestalterisch wichtige Verbesserungen einher: Antrieb und Lenkung erfolgten nicht mehr allein über das große Hauptrad, sondern wurden getrennt. Außerdem ersetzte Gaylor das gekrümmte Verbindungsrohr zwischen den beiden Rädern durch ein gerades, über zwei Streben mit dem Kurbelgehäuse verbundenes Steuerrohr.

Die geraden Rohre und Streben – lediglich das Flacheisen mit dem aufliegenden Sattel sowie die Gabel mit dem kleinen Vorderrad waren gekrümmt – prägen maßgeblich die schlichte Gestaltung.

Die Fertigung dieses Sicherheitshochrads begann 1889 zu einem Zeitpunkt, als sich die Geschichte des Hochrads bereits dem Ende zuneigte.

Leonard B. Gaylor (1857–1931), a versatile inventor and the founder of the company, had his safety penny-farthing patented on April 19, 1887 (patent no. 361280). The novelty was that the farthing wheel was at the front rather than the back. As a result, the cyclist could keep his balance better and avoid crashing head over heels.

This simple, albeit decisive change compared to the classic high wheel, or "ordinary," also included key functional and design improvements: The drive and steering were no longer restricted solely to the large penny wheel, but were now separated. Moreover, Gaylor replaced the bent connecting tube between the two wheels by a straight steering tube that was linked to the crank case by two struts. The straight tubes and struts (only the flat iron with the saddle on it as well as the forks for the small farthing wheel were bent) are the key characteristic of the simple design.

This safety penny-farthing went into production in 1889, at a time when the high wheel was already nearly outdated.

„Unser Ziel bei der Konstruktion des ‚Eagle' ist es, ein Rad zu bauen, das alle Vorteile des ‚Ordinary' in sich vereint, ihm an Geschwindigkeit, Leichtgängigkeit und anmutigem Aussehen gleichkommt oder es übertrifft." [4]

"Our aim in constructing the Eagle is to produce a wheel which will embrace every advantage of the 'Ordinary', that will equal or excel it in speed, in ease of running and in graceful appearance."

Eagle Bicycles 1891

Neckarsulmer Strick-maschinen-Fabrik AG

Sicherheitsniederrad
Low-wheel safety bicycle

c. 1888/89

Neckarsulmer Strickmaschinen-
Fabrik AG, später NSU AG
Neckarsulm, DE

Neckarsulmer Strick-maschinen-Fabrik AG · Sicherheitsniederrad · c. 1888/89 · Low-wheel safety bicycle

Ab 1886 begann das Unternehmen unter dem neuen Direktor Gottlob Banzhaf (1858–1930), neben Strickmaschinen auch Fahrräder zu produzieren, zunächst Hochräder und ab 1888 auch Niederräder. Griff man anfangs noch auf englische Fahrradteile zurück, begann man später, Pedale, Naben, Tretlager etc. selbst zu fertigen. 1897 erfolgte die Umbenennung in Neckarsulmer Fahrradwerke A.G.

Das aufwendig gearbeitete Kreuzrahmen-Sicherheitsrad ist nicht nur mit den eigens entwickelten und patentierten Pedalen ausgestattet, sondern auch mit einem besonderen Kettenspann-Mechanismus, der über das Umklappen des Tretlagers funktioniert, sowie mit einem eigenwilligen Lenker, in dessen Schaftrohr die Stoßbremse untergebracht ist. Bei längeren Bergfahrten konnte diese schleifend eingestellt werden.

From 1886 onwards the company, under its new director Gottlob Banzhaf (1858–1930), started building bicycles in addition to its knitting machines. Initially it made penny-farthings, but as of 1888 safety bicycles, too. While to begin with the company relied on British bicycle parts, later it started manufacturing its own pedals, hubs, bottom bracket bearings, etc. In 1897 the company was renamed Neckarsulmer Fahrradwerke A.G.

The elaborately worked cross-frame safety bicycle came with not only purpose-developed and patented pedals, but also a special chain-tensioning mechanism (it functioned by flipping the bottom bracket round) and an original handlebar, the shaft of which accommodated a spoon brake. For longer trips in mountainous terrain, the plunger could be set to a rub.

Manufacture Française d'Armes et
Cycles de Saint-Étienne, FR

Aus dem 1885 von Étienne Mimard und Pierre Blachon erworbenen, später in Manufrance umbenannten Unternehmen entwickelte sich nicht nur die größte französische Waffen- und Fahrradfabrik, sondern auch das erste und bekannteste Versandhaus Frankreichs. Ab 1888 wurden unter der Marke Hirondelle (Schwalbe) die ersten Fahrräder produziert. Die Société l'Hirondelle war kurz zuvor übernommen worden.

Mit dem Modell Superbe entstand eine der ungewöhnlichsten Rahmenformen in der Geschichte des Fahrraddesigns. Das halbmondförmig gebogene Rahmenrohr sollte für zusätzliche Federung sorgen, ebenso der spiralförmig eingedrehte Lenker. Das Superbe gehörte zu den luxuriösesten Modellen des Herstellers und wurde von 1889 bis 1893 gebaut. Die frühen Modelle besaßen noch Radialspeichen und eine Achsschenkellenkung.

Rahmenform und Lenker weisen deutliche Ähnlichkeiten mit dem von Gormully & Jeffery produzierten Modell American Rambler von 1888 auf. Möglicherweise geht der Entwurf des Superbe auf die Brüder Pierre und Claudius Gauthier zurück, deren Unternehmen sich ebenfalls in Saint-Étienne befand, die anfangs vor allem Räder anderer Hersteller kopierten und die angeblich die ersten Modelle für die Manufacture Française d'Armes geliefert haben sollen.

This company, acquired in 1885 by Étienne Mimard and Pierre Blachon and later renamed Manufrance, evolved not only into France's largest armaments and bicycle factory, but also into France's first and best-known mail order corporation. From 1888 onwards the first bicycles were produced under the Hirondelle (swallow) brand. Société l'Hirondelle had been taken over a short time earlier.

With the Superbe model, the company introduced one of the most unusual frame shapes in the history of bicycle design. The crescent-moon-shaped curved frame tube was intended to deliver additional suspension, as was the hinged handlebar shaft. The Superbe was among the company's most luxurious models and was built from 1889 to 1893. Early models still had radial spokes and a pivot-head steering.

The frame shape and handlebars have clear similarities to the 1888 American Rambler manufactured by Gormully & Jeffery. The Superbe may have been designed by brothers Pierre and Claudius Gauthier, whose firm was also located in Saint-Étienne and initially mainly copied bicycles made by other companies and ostensibly supplied Manufacture Française d'Armes' first models.

07

A. G. Spalding & Bros.

Sicherheitsniederrad   c. 1893
Low-wheel safety bicycle

A. G. Spalding & Bros.
Chicago, New York, Philadelphia, USA

Der amerikanische Baseballspieler Albert Goodwill Spalding (1850–1915) gründete unter seinem Namen 1876 ein bis heute existierendes Sportartikelunternehmen. 1893 erwarb der ehemalige Sportler und geschäftstüchtige Fabrikant die Lamb Knitting Machine Company in Chicopee Falls, Massachusetts, die bereits seit 1890 Fahrräder für sein Unternehmen produzierte. Damit baute Spalding diesen Bereich weiter aus und stieg zu einem der größten Fahrradhersteller der USA auf. 1899 wurde die Fahrradsparte verkauft.

Die Fahrräder von Spalding gehörten nicht nur zu den klassischen frühen Sicherheitsniederrädern, sondern konnten durch die hohen Stückzahlen auch preiswert angeboten werden, sodass sie auch für weniger betuchte Fahrer und Fahrerinnen erschwinglich waren.

Zudem zeichnet sich dieses Fahrrad durch seine schlichte Gestaltung und sein geringes Gewicht (11 kg) aus, das durch den leichten Stahlbau mit den konischen Rohren in Kombination mit Holzfelgen und entsprechenden Komponenten (Sattel, Pedale etc.) zustande kommt. Eine weitere Besonderheit sind die speziellen Kettenspanner und die geringe Speichenanzahl.

American baseball player Albert Goodwill Spalding (1850–1915) founded the eponymous sports goods company in 1876 – it exists to this day. In 1893, the former athlete and enterprising factory owner acquired the Lamb Knitting Machine Company in Chicopee Falls, Massachusetts, which had already been producing bicycles for his company since 1890. In this way, Spalding expanded operations in the segment further and emerged as one of the largest bicycle makers in the United States. It sold off its bicycle division in 1899.

Spalding bicycles were not only among the classic early safety bicycles, but could be sold at an affordable price as they were produced in large numbers. This made them accessible to less well-off cyclists.

At the same time, the bicycle stood out for its plain design and low weight (11 kg), which resulted from the lightweight steel construction with conical tubes combined with wooden wheel rims and corresponding components (saddle, pedals, etc.). Other special features are the chain tensioners and the low number of spokes.

„Die Perfektionierung des
mechanisch Machbaren."
"The Perfection of Mechanical Skill".

Katalogblatt / catalog page 1896

Dursley-Pedersen Cycle Co., Ltd.
Gloucestershire, UK, 1910/11

Der dänische Schmied und Erfinder Mikael Pedersen (1855–1929) kam 1889 nach England, um beim Zusammenbau der aus Dänemark gelieferten Teile einer von ihm entwickelten Butterzentrifuge behilflich zu sein. Im Gepäck hatte er wohl auch schon die Idee für sein bequemes Fahrrad. Mit seinem ungewöhnlichen, bereits 1893 patentierten Rahmendesign schlug er völlig neue Wege ein: Aus dünnen Rohren entwickelte Pedersen einen nur aus Dreiecken bestehenden Rahmen, der eine hohe Stabilität bei minimalem Gewicht ermöglichte. Allerdings bedingten die vielen Lötstellen mehr Aufwand und damit höhere Kosten als der Bau konventioneller Fahrräder.

Eine besondere Neuentwicklung stellte sein geflochtener, seitlich schwingender Sattel dar, der wie eine Hängematte eingehängt wurde. Produziert wurde das Fahrrad sowohl von seinem eigenen 1896 gegründeten Unternehmen Pedersen Cycle Frame Co. als auch von mehreren anderen Firmen von 1897 bis 1914 und von 1920 bis 1922 in England, ferner seit den 1970er-Jahren von verschiedenen anderen europäischen Herstellern. Pedersens 1903 vorgestellte, jedoch noch unausgereifte 3-Gang-Nabenschaltung, die auf dem Prinzip der Vorlegewelle basierte, führte 1905 zur Liquidation der Pedersen Cycle Frame Co.

Danish blacksmith and inventor Mikael Pedersen (1855–1929) arrived in England in 1889 in order to assist with the assembly of parts supplied from Denmark for a butter centrifuge he had developed. He evidently also brought with him the idea for his comfortable bicycle. With his unusual frame design, and he obtained a patent for it as early as 1893, he took a completely new direction: Pedersen used thin tubes to develop a frame consisting only of triangles that combined great stability with minimal weight. However, the many welding points required more work and thus higher costs than were involved in the assembly of conventional bicycles.

One special new development was his plaited saddle that swung sideways and was suspended like a hammock between the handlebars and the saddle pin. The bicycle was manufactured by his own company Pedersen Cycle Frame Co., founded in 1896, and from 1897 to 1914 and from 1920 to 1922 by other firms in the UK, and as of the 1970s by various other European corporations. In 1903 Pedersen presented a three-speed hub that relied on the principle of a drive shaft. However, it was not yet perfected and led to the Pedersen Cycle Frame Co. going into liquidation in 1905.

08

„Der Teil der Maschine im allgemeinen Gebrauch, den ich am unvollkommensten fand, war der Sitz."[5]

"The part of the machine in general use which I found most imperfect was the seat."

Mikael Pedersen

Tonk Manufacturing Co.
Chicago, USA

Gelöst wurde bei diesem Fahrrad das Problem der Verbindungen zwischen den einzelnen Holzstreben des Rahmens über aufwendig verzierte und durchbrochene Metallmuffen. Als Rahmenmaterial fand das namensgebende Hickoryholz (nordamerikanischer Walnussbaum) Verwendung. Jede Strebe besteht aus sechzehn Lagen laminiertem Holz, das ohne Fügungen an den Ecken gebogen und verleimt wurde. Selbst die Gabel, Streben, Felgen, Lenker und Lenkergriffe und das Tretlagergehäuse sind aus Holz gefertigt.

This bicycle design solved the problem of joints between the individual wooden struts of the frame by relying on elaborately decorated open metal muffs. The frame was built from North American hickory wood, from which it took its name. Each strut was made of 16 layers of laminated wood, bent and glued without seams at the edges. Even the forks, the struts, the rims, the handlebars and the bottom bracket were made from wood.

„Eine vollkommen sichere Verbindung zwischen Holz- und Metallanschlüssen ist eine der schwierigsten Aufgaben, die man sich ausdenken kann, und dies war der einzige gewichtige Einwand gegen Fahrradrahmen aus Holz, die ansonsten einen gewissen Reiz für kleinere Hersteller haben."

"A perfectly safe joint between wood and metal connections has been one of the most difficult things to devise, and this has been the one great objection to wood bicycle frames, which otherwise have a certain charm for makers on a small scale." [6]

Cycling Life 1897

Franz Grundner

Bambusfahrrad
Bamboo bicycle

c. 1898

Grundner & Lemisch
Klagenfurt, AT

Angeregt von einer Pressemitteilung aus London – auf der Stanley Cycle Show hatte im November 1894 die Bamboo Cycle Co. Ltd. das erste Bambusfahrrad vorgestellt –, entwickelte Franz Grundner (1861–1945) ein eigenes Bambusfahrrad. Den Prototyp präsentierte er Weihnachten 1895. Im April 1896 wurde ihm zusammen mit Karl Bräuer ein Privilegium (Patent) dafür erteilt. Über die jeweiligen Anteile an der Erfindung kam es zum Streit zwischen den beiden. Aus der öffentlichen Auseinandersetzung lässt sich jedoch schließen, dass das Bambusfahrrad im Wesentlichen auf Grundner zurückgeht. Bräuer verkaufte kurz danach seine Rechte an Otto Lemisch, sodass der Gründung des Unternehmens Grundner & Lemisch nichts mehr im Wege stand. Wenige Jahre später entstand daraus einer der weltgrößten Hersteller von industriell gefertigten Bambusfahrrädern.

Das Bambus-Rohmaterial kam aus Shanghai, die Metallteile, Kettenschutz, Ausfallenden, Versteifungsrohre sowie die Muffen, mit denen die Bambusrohre geklemmt und verschraubt werden, stellte das Unternehmen selbst her. Durch diese Art der Verbindungen war es möglich, das Fahrrad zu zerlegen und einzelne Teile problemlos auszutauschen.

Inspired by a London press release describing the launch of the very first bamboo bicycle by the Bamboo Cycle Co. Ltd. at the Stanley Cycle Show in November 1894, Franz Grundner (1861–1945) developed his own bamboo cycle. He presented the prototype at Christmas the following year. In April 1896 he was granted a privilege (patent) for it together with Karl Bräuer. A dispute arose between the two over who had contributed what to the invention. However, from the public debate we can deduce that essentially the bamboo bicycle was Grundner's idea. Shortly thereafter Bräuer sold his rights to Otto Lemisch, meaning that there was nothing preventing the foundation of the company Grundner & Lemisch any longer. It took only a few years for the firm to evolve into one of the world's largest manufacturers of industrially made bamboo bicycles.

The raw bamboo was imported from Shanghai, whereas the company itself made the metal parts, chain guard, dropouts, stiffening tubes and the muffs used to slot and screw the bamboo tubing into place. These connections meant it was possible to take the bicycle apart and replace individual parts whenever needed.

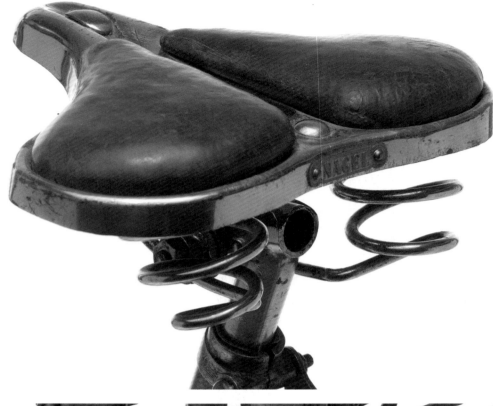

„Die neue Rahmen-Construktion jedoch ist von mir erdacht und ausgearbeitet und hat Herr Bräuer nicht das Mindeste dazu beigetragen …"[7]

"The new frame construction is something I invented and finalized, and Mr. Bräuer contributed not even in the slightest to it …"

Franz Grundner 1896

Adler Fahrradwerke   Kettenlos No. 7   c. 1903

Adler Fahrradwerke, vormals Heinrich Kleyer
Frankfurt a. M., DE

Als Alternativen zum Kettenantrieb kamen bereits Ende des 19. Jahrhunderts Stirnrad-, Kegelrad- oder Rollenantriebe zum Einsatz. Dabei diente eine Welle zur Kraftübertragung von den Pedalen auf das Hinterrad. Der technisch nicht ganz korrekte Begriff Kardanantrieb entstand erst Anfang der 1930er-Jahre. In Deutschland gab es um 1900 eine große Nachfrage nach kettenlosen Fahrrädern, die von mindestens 37 Herstellern bzw. unter 37 Marken angeboten wurden.

Dazu gehörte auch das Frankfurter Unternehmen Adler. Um 1899/1900 wurde das erste Modell eingeführt, dessen Rollenantrieb auf dem Patent von James Henry Sager basierte. Wenige Jahre später (ca. 1902/03) ging Adler dazu über, einen Antrieb mit Kegelrädern zu verwenden, wie ihn das Modell Kettenlos No. 7 aufweist, ein Herrenrad mit Diamantrahmen, das in seiner Rahmengeometrie gegenüber dem Vorgängermodell nicht verändert wurde.

At the end of the 19th century there were alternatives to the chain drive, such as spur gears, bevel gears, or roll drives. In these systems, a shaft functioned to transfer the power from the pedals onto the back wheel. The technically not quite accurate term "shaft drive" did not arise until the early 1930s. In Germany, there was great demand for chainless bicycles around 1900 – and they were on offer from at least 37 manufacturers/brands.

Among them was the Frankfurt-based Adler corporation. Around 1899–1900 the first model was introduced featuring a roll drive based on the patent held by James Henry Sager. A few years later (c. 1902-3) Adler switched over to bevel-gear drives such as that in the Kettenlos No. 7 model, a men's bicycle with a diamond-shaped frame that was not altered in terms of its geometry from that in the predecessor model.

Hesperus-Werke GmbH
Stuttgart, DE, 1921/22

Paul Jaray (1889–1974), Luftfahrtingenieur und Schöpfer der Stromlinienform, optimierte auch das Fahrraddesign: Die niedrige Sitzposition ergab einen günstigen Schwerpunkt und verringerte den Luftwiderstand, die Trethebelkonstruktion mit den drei Positionen, die dadurch den Effekt von drei Antriebsübersetzungen hatte, sollte den Kraftaufwand für den Fahrer reduzieren.

Nach einem tödlichen Unfall aufgrund eines Materialfehlers und dem darauffolgenden Gerichtsverfahren wurde die Produktion 1923 eingestellt.

Paul Jaray (1889–1974), aerospace engineer and creator of the streamlined form, also optimized bicycle design. Indeed, the low seating position resulted in a favorable point of gravity and reduced drag, and the cylinder construction with the three positions, which thus worked like three drive gearings, was intended to decrease the effort the cyclist needed to make.

After a fatal accident owing to faulty materials and the resulting law suit, production of the bicycle was discontinued in 1923.

„Das J-Rad ist das ideale Tourenrad. Von technischen und ärztlichen
Autoritäten praktisch erprobt und
begutachtet."

"The J-Rad is the ideal randonneur.
Technical and medical authorities
have put it to practical tests and
inspected it."

Werbeanzeige / Advertisement c. 1921

Anker-Werke A.G.
Bielefeld, DE

Bereits 1933 meldete Gustav Lind (1885–1979) von den 1886 gegründeten Anker-Werken seine Erfindung zum Patent an, das ihm allerdings erst 1939 unter der Nr. 671164 erteilt worden ist. Die sichelförmig gebogene Vorderradgabel sollte eine bessere Federwirkung haben als die bisher übliche Bauform und somit das Radfahren bequemer machen sowie das Lenken erleichtern. Um das zu belegen, wurden für die Patenterteilung Federungsdiagramme angefertigt. Durch die gesteigerte Federwirkung konnte vorne auf Ballonreifen verzichtet werden, wodurch das Fahrrad auch ein eleganteres Aussehen erhielt. Neben dem Herren- und Damenmodell gab es auch eine Ausführung als Rennrad mit Kettenschaltung, Holzfelgen, Hochdruckreifen und Rennlenker – und für ein Rennrad, dessen „Spezial-Sichelgabel" eine etwas steilere Form hatte, kamen natürlich keine Ballonreifen in Betracht.

1936 vermeldeten die Anker-Werke voller Stolz die Rekordfahrt des Dortmunders Ewald Kaufhold, der mit seinem Sichelrad in 31 Tagen 7363 km gefahren war.

As early as 1933 Gustav Lind (1885–1979) of Anker-Werke, founded in 1886, filed for a patent that was not granted until 1939 as no. 671164.

The sickle-shaped curved front forks were intended to provide better shock absorption than the hitherto customary shape and thus make cycling more comfortable and steering easier. To prove this, diagrams of the springs were attached to the patent application. The improved shock absorption meant there was no need for balloon tires, meaning the bicycle looked more elegant. Alongside the men's and women's models there was also a version as a road racer, with chain gears, wooden wheel rims, high-pressure tires, and racing handlebars. Indeed for a racing bike, where the "special sickle forks" were of a slightly more acute angle, balloon tires were simply out of the question.

In 1936 Anker-Werke proudly reported the record set by Dortmund's Ewald Kaufhold, who had covered 7,363 km in a mere 31 days.

„Zum Gelingen der Weltrekordfahrt hat selbstverständlich die ANKER-Sichelgabel sehr viel beigetragen, denn federnd über Schlaglöcher, elastisch alle Bodenunebenheiten und Stöße auffangend erleichterte sie dem Fahrer die ungeheuren Strapazen."[8] "The world record attempt was of course strongly aided by relying on an ANKER sickle fork, because it absorbs potholes, ensures elastic handling over all uneven surfaces and bumps, and thus makes it easier for the cyclist to endure the terrible exertions."

RadMarkt, Sept. 1936

Jacques Schulz
La Garenne-Colombes, FR

Jacques Schulz hatte einen flexiblen Rahmen, ein „federndes Tragwerk", konstruiert, der angeblich komfortabler war als die herkömmlichen Modelle. Es ist jedoch nicht nur der dünnwandige, ofenrohrförmige Hauptrahmen, der dieses Fahrrad auszeichnet, sondern es besticht durch die von Schulz völlig neu entwickelten Komponenten und Ausstattungsdetails, angefangen bei den extrem leistungsstarken Cantilever-Bremsen mit langen Bremsschuhen, den innen im Rahmen verlaufenden Bremskabeln, den aus Aluminiumblechen genieteten Felgen, über die Naben und Pedale aus Aluminium bis hin zur indexierten Schaltung mit großer Übersetzungsbreite (Ritzel bis zu 40 Zähnen), die es erlaubte, mit nur einem vorderen Zahnkranz (Kettenblatt) problemlos Steigungen zu bewältigen. In dieser Hinsicht könnte das Funiculo als früher Vorläufer der Mountainbikes bezeichnet werden. Zudem konstruierte Schulz leicht abnehmbare Gepäckträger und Lampengehäuse, die vorne und hinten den Wechsel der Glühbirnen erleichtern. Das untere Sattelrohr dient als Werkzeug- und Luftpumpenfach.

Die extrem aufwendige Herstellungsweise – bis auf die Standardreifen ist fast jedes Bauteil handgefertigt – schlug sich natürlich auf die Kosten und die von Schulz gefertigte Stückzahl nieder. Angeblich existiert in Europa heute nur eine Handvoll dieser ungewöhnlichen Räder.

Jacques Schulz developed a flexible frame, a "suspension system" that was ostensibly more comfortable than conventional models. The bicycle does not just stand out for the thin, oven-pipe-like tubes, but also for the components and fine details all specially developed by Schulz, starting with the extremely powerful cantilever brakes with the long brake pads, brake cables located inside the tubes, rims made of riveted sheet aluminum, hubs and pedals likewise made of aluminum through to the indexed gear shifts with a large range (cogs of up to 40 sprockets) that enabled cyclists to surmount inclines smoothly with only one main chain ring. In this regard, the Funiculo can be considered an early precursor of mountain bikes. Moreover, Schulz constructed pannier racks that could be easily removed, as could the lamp casings to facilitate bulb changes at the front or back. The lower saddle pin served as a compartment for the tools and pump.

The extremely elaborate manufacturing process (other than the standard tires almost everything was handmade) was of course reflected in the costs, and the number of units Schulz made. Possibly only a handful of these extraordinary bicycles have survived in Europe.

„Das federnde Tragwerk Jacques Schulz (patentiertes S.G.D.G.-System) ist das ultimative Fahrrad für den Tourenfahrer."

"Jacques Schulz's supple suspension system (patented S.G.D.G. system) is the ultimate bicycle for those wanting a great touring experience."

Werbeanzeige / Advertisement
c. 1937

Etablissements Caminade
Bois-Colombes, FR

Der französische Rahmenbauer Pierre Caminade (*1879) brachte ab 1936 unter dem Markennamen Caminargent seine ersten Aluminiumräder auf den Markt. Die Idee, mit diesem leichten Material Fahrräder herzustellen, war zwar nicht neu, aber Caminade gelang es, ein spezielles Design und eine eigene Technik dafür zu entwickeln. Er arbeitete mit Klemm- und Schraubverbindungen, da zu seiner Zeit das Schweißen von Aluminiumlegierungen, die damals hauptsächlich im Flugzeugbau Verwendung fanden, noch nicht allgemein üblich war. Seine in verschiedenen Modellen erhältlichen Rahmen bestanden aus achteckigen, innen doppelt konifizierten Duraluminiumrohren mit korkgefüllten Dämpfungsenden. Als Verbindungselemente dienten gegossene Aluminiumlaschen mit gegenüberliegenden Gewindestiften, die es ermöglichten, die Hauptrohre zusammenzudrücken und auszurichten. Die Schrauben waren mit dem Caminade-Schildlogo versehen. Aus Aluminiumgussteilen bestehen das Steuerrohr mit den Steuerköpfen und den imitierten Muffen sowie die Gabelkrone. Von Caminade eigens gestaltet waren Lenker, Vorbau, Felgen und Naben. Anscheinend wurde nur eine relativ kleine Anzahl von Fahrrädern hergestellt (wahrscheinlich insgesamt einige Hundert), die als Rolls-Royce unter den Fahrrädern für den gehobenen Markt, für professionelle Fahrer und ambitionierte Amateure bestimmt waren.

French frame-builder Pierre Caminade (*1879) launched his first aluminum bicycles on the market from 1936 under the Caminargent brand. The idea of building bicycles from this light material was not new, but Caminade succeeded in developing a special design and his very own technology. He relied on clamp and bolt connections, as back then it was not customary to weld aluminum alloys such as were mainly used in aircraft construction at that time.

His frames were available in different models and consisted of octagonal, double-butted Duralumin tubes with cork-filled absorption ends. The connecting elements were cast aluminum lugs with threaded pins opposite that enabled the main tubes to be clamped together and thus aligned. The bolts bore the Caminade shield logo. The top tube with the top head were made of cast aluminum, as were the imitation muffs and the crown of the forks. Caminade designed his own handlebars, handlebar stem, rims, and hubs.

Evidently a relatively small number of bicycles were manufactured (probably a total of several hundred), the Rolls Royce of bycicle destined for the high-end market for professional riders and ambitious amateurs.

Adolf Bareuther

Blattfeder-Fahrrad c. 1937

Bicycle with leaf-spring suspension

Adolf Bareuther u. Co Fahrradfabrik Eger
Cheb/Eger, CS

Adolf Bareuther überlegte sich ein besonderes Federungssystem, um das Fahren auf den schlechten Straßen komfortabler zu gestalten. Er ersetzte einfach das Ober- und Unterrohr durch Blattfederbündel. Diese sind recht starr und federn nur bei starken Stößen. Das Fahrrad schwingt nicht auf und schluckt dadurch kaum Energie. Zudem bleibt es relativ verwindungssteif. Der Aufbau des Fahrrads mit den zahlreichen verchromten Teilen spricht dafür, dass es sich hier um ein Rad für eine gehobene Klientel handelte.

Adolf Bareuther devised a special spring system in order to make riding on poor roads more comfortable. He simply replaced the upper and lower tubes with bundles of leaf springs. These are very rigid and only absorb strong shocks. The bicycle does not therefore bounce and hardly loses forward momentum as a consequence. Moreover, it remains relatively torsion resistant. The structure of the bicycle, with its countless chrome-plated parts, would suggest that it was intended for higher-end clients.

Camille Piquerez   Stella-Landi-Velo   c. 1939

Camille Piquerez S. A.
Bassecourt, CH

Aufgrund von wirtschaftlichen Schwierigkeiten musste Georges Rebetez 1934 seine zehn Jahre zuvor gegründete Fabrik für Fahrradrahmen an seinen ebenfalls in Bassecourt ansässigen Konkurrenten Camille Piquerez (1901–1963) verkaufen, der dadurch den Markennamen „Stella" erwarb. Neben Fahrrädern produzierte Piquerez auch Möbel aus Stahlrohr.

Auf der Schweizer Landesausstellung „Landi" in Zürich 1939 präsentierte Piquerez als Sondermodell das Stella-Landi-Velo, das bis in die Nachkriegszeit als Aero-Stella in verschiedenen Ausführungen angeboten wurde.

Die Rahmenform mit dem doppelten Oberrohr, das in einem Bogen über das Sattelrohr zu den Ausfallenden des Hinterrads führt und um das Steuerrohr mit einem aerodynamischen Gehäuse für Schalthebel und Instrumente ausgestattet ist, erinnert an amerikanische Cruiser der Stromlinienzeit. Das Fahrrad besitzt eine Dreigang-Nabenschaltung. Kilometerzähler, Tachometer, Uhr, Schalthebel und Abblendschalter für die Beleuchtung befinden sich in einem Gehäuse, das mit der an einen Autoscheinwerfer erinnernden Frontleuchte abschließt. Hinzu kommt ein Verriegelungsschloss am Steuerrohr. Damit fällt das Stella-Landi-Velo sicherlich in die Luxuskategorie der damaligen Fahrräder.

Owing to economic difficulties, in 1934 Georges Rebetez had to sell his frame-building factory, opened ten years earlier, to his rival Camille Piquerez (1901–1963) who was likewise based in Bassecourt and thus acquired the Stella brand. Alongside bicycles, Piquerez also made tubular-steel furniture.

At the 1939 Swiss National Exhibition Landi in Zurich, Piquerez presented a special-edition model, the Stella-Landi-Velo, which was on offer in various versions through to the post-War period as the Aero-Stella.

The frame shape features a double upper tube that leads in a curve via the saddle tube to the dropouts for the back wheel and at the head tube features an aerodynamic casing for the gear shifts and instruments. It is somehow reminiscent of a US limousine from the Streamline age. The cycle had a three-speed hub as well as an odometer, a speedometer, a clock, gear shift levers, and a dimming switch for the lights, all located in a casing that culminates in the headlamp which resembles a car headlight in shape. There was also a lock attached to the head tube. In other words, the Stella-Landi-Velo can definitely be classified as a luxury bicycle of its time.

„Diese Maschine, die Stil und
Komfort perfekt vereint, stellt den
Inbegriff des Fahrrads dar." [9]
"This machine perfectly
unites style and comfort and is
the true epitome of the bicycle."

Firmenkatalog / Catalog 1946

Cycles Lida
Ixelles, BE

Die Idee, auch die Kraft der Arme für den Antrieb eines Fahrrads einzusetzen, ist nicht neu, auch wenn sie immer wieder als neu verkauft wird. Bereits 1894 beantragte der Franzose Jean Marty ein Patent für die „Durch Auf- und Abbewegen der Lenkstange bethätigte Hilfs-Antriebsvorrichtung für Fahrräder."

Das Modell Guip von Cycles Lida setzte dieses Prinzip funktional überzeugend und elegant um. Durch das Umlegen einer Arretierung am Lenker konnte man in den Wiegetritt gehen und gleichzeitig die Lenkerenden mit den Armen abwechselnd auf und ab bewegen. Mithilfe einer Kette, die verdeckt in den beiden Unterrohren läuft, wird die Kraft auf das Tretlager übertragen.

The idea of also using the power of the arms to propel a bicycle forward is not new, even if it is repeatedly marketed as being new. As long ago as 1894, Frenchman Jean Marty applied for a patent for an "auxiliary drive system for bicycles activated by moving the handlebars up and down".

The Guip model produced by Cycles Lida put the principle into practice in a manner that was as elegant as it was functionally convincing. By flipping over a locking mechanism on the handlebars, the cyclist got out of the saddle and at the same time started moving the handlebars back and forth for additional propulsion. A chain concealed and running inside the two lower tubes transfers the power from the handlebars onto the bottom bracket.

Albert Edward Wood
William Henry Taylor

Airborne

c. 1940

Birmingham Small Arms (BSA)
Birmingham, UK

Entwickelt, um die Truppen hinter der Frontlinie mobiler zu machen, kam dieses Fahrrad im Zweiten Weltkrieg zum Einsatz. Zusammengeklappt und aufgehängt an den Laufrädern konnte es mit dem Fallschirm abgeworfen werden. Sattel und Gabel dämpften dabei den Aufprall auf dem Boden, da sie so weit wie möglich ausgezogen und die Schrauben nur leicht fixiert waren, sodass sich die Rohre ineinanderschieben konnten. Häufiger als bei den Fallschirmjägern kam das Fahrrad jedoch bei den Landungstruppen zum Einsatz.

Der einfache Klappmechanismus des fischähnlich gestalteten Doppelrohrrahmens sowie die Bolzenpedale zum Durchschieben ermöglichten eine kompakte Größe und erleichterten dadurch den Transport.

Nach dem Zweiten Weltkrieg wurden nicht nur die Restbestände preiswert verkauft, sondern das Fahrrad noch weiterhin produziert.

Developed to increase the mobility of troops behind the front line, this bicycle was deployed during World War II. Folded up and suspended from the wheels it could be attached to a parachute and dropped from a plane. The saddle and forks absorbed the shock of the impact on the ground as they were pulled as far apart as possible, and the screws were only slightly tightened so that the tubes could be pushed into each other. The bicycle was used less by paratroopers and more by landing parties.

The simple folding mechanism of the fish-like double-tube frame plus the retracting pedals meant that the bike was very compact and thus easier to transport.

After World War II, not only were the cycles left in stock sold off, but the bicycle continued to be manufactured.

„Eine Drehung zweier Flügelschrauben, und der Rahmen faltet sich zusammen ... Es sieht einfach aus – aber es waren jahrelange Experimente nötig, um diese Maschine zu perfektionieren und die unverzichtbare Leichtigkeit, Steifigkeit und Haltbarkeit zu erreichen."

"A turn of two butterfly screws and the frame folds up ... It looks simple – but years of experiment have been necessary to perfect this machine and to achieve the indispensable lightness, rigidity and durability."

The CTC Gazette, 1944

Trussardi
Mailand / Milan, IT

Das Klappfahrrad von BSA (Nr. 19) diente der Modefirma Trussardi als Vorbild für ein eigenes Fahrrad. 1983 brachte Trussardi 3000 Exemplare davon als luxuriöses Tourenrad mit Nabenschaltung, Packtaschen und Leder-Applikationen auf den Markt.

Italian fashion company Trussardi produced a bicycle of its own modeled after the BSA (No 19) folding bicycle. In 1983, Trussardi marketed 3,000 of the luxury touring bikes, which boasted a three-speed hub, two rear panniers and leather detailing.

Fratelli Vianzone
Turin, IT

Materialknappheit und hohe Kosten führten auch in der Fahrradgeschichte zur Verwendung von Ersatzmaterialien, um den Bedarf an bestimmten Produkten zu decken. In Italien kam es durch die nach dem 1935 erfolgten Einmarsch in Abessinien (heute Äthiopien) vom Völkerbund verhängten Sanktionen zur Verknappung von Stahl. Das Unternehmen Fratelli Vianzone, das neben Fahrrädern aus Aluminium Radfelgen, Skier und andere Produkte aus Bugholz produzierte, übertrug diese Herstellungstechnik auf den kompletten Fahrradbau und entwickelte Rahmen aus gebogenem Schichtholz mit Muffen und Ausfallenden aus Aluminium. Formbestimmend sind hier das Material und die Produktionstechnik, die nur gerundete und keine abgewinkelten Übergänge gestattete. Gabel, Sattelstütze, Lenker, „Schutzblech", Felgen und Griffe bestehen bei diesem Fahrrad ebenfalls aus Holz. Zwischen 1938 und 1956 konnten zwischen 250 und 300 Stück, darunter auch Damenmodelle, gefertigt werden.

A scarcity of materials and high costs led not only generally, but also in the history of bicycles to the use of substitute materials in order to cover requirements for certain products. In the wake of Italy's invasion of Abyssinia (present-day Ethiopia) in 1935, the League of Nations imposed sanctions on the country, which resulted in a shortage of steel. A company such as Fratelli Vianzone, which made bicycles from aluminum and bike wheel rims, skis, and other products from bentwood, then started using the latter material for all structural parts of its bicycles, developing frames made of bent laminated wood with muffs and dropouts made of aluminum. The materials and the production technology define the shape of the bicycle, as only rounded transitions were possible, meaning no angular sections. The forks, saddle pin, handlebars, "mudguards," wheel rims and handles were all made of wood, too. Between 250 and 300 of the bicycles, including women's models, were made from 1938 to 1956.

Reyé Bardet
Bordeaux, FR

Von den Folgen des Zweiten Weltkriegs blieben auch die Fahrradhersteller in ganz Europa nicht verschont. Die Produktion war vielerorts unterbrochen und musste erst wieder aufgebaut werden. Wie man sich dennoch behelfen konnte, zeigte der Franzose Reyé Bardet, der seinen Fahrradrahmen aus nicht mehr gebrauchten Flugzeugbauteilen konstruierte. Die Aluminiumprofile mit ihren aus Gewichtsgründen durchbrochenen Strukturen lieferten ein leichtes, aber dennoch stabiles Rahmenmaterial und verleihen diesem Fahrrad eine ganz eigene Ästhetik. Komplettiert wurde das Rad schließlich mit Fahrrad-Standardkomponenten.

Bicycle manufacturers throughout Europe were not spared the impact of World War II. In many places, production had been discontinued and processes thus re-established. It was possible to muddle through, however, as Frenchman Reyé Bardet showed: He built his bicycle frame out of airplane parts that were no longer required. The aluminum profiles were perforated in order to reduce the aircraft's weight and now they enabled him to construct a light yet sturdy frame while giving the bicycle a quite unique aesthetic. The cycle was rounded out with standard bike components.

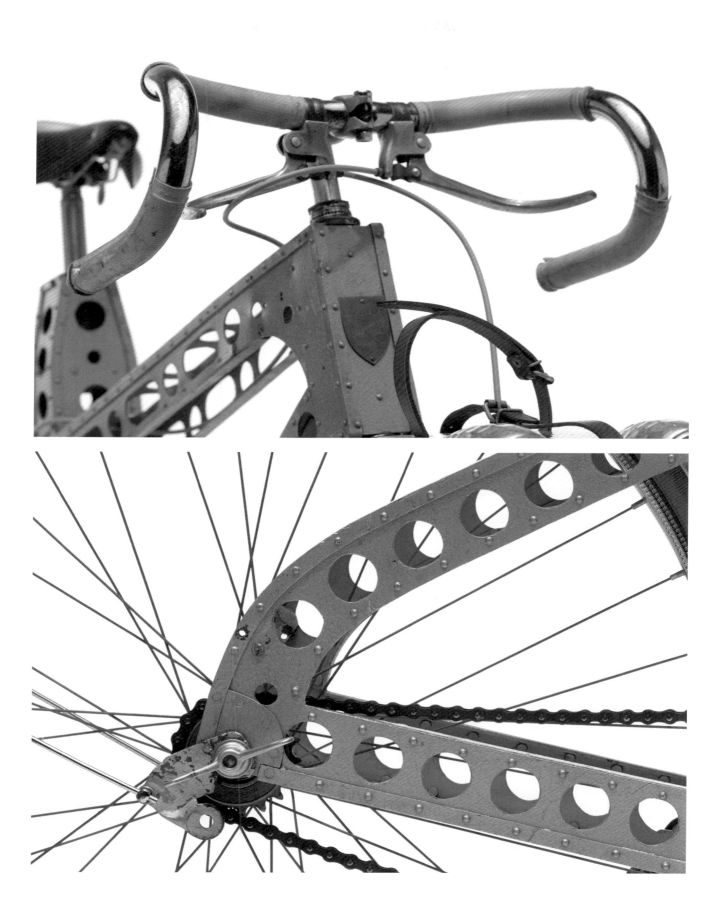

Mitsubishi Heavy-Industries, Ltd.
Tokio / Tokyo, JP

Die Flugzeugkonstrukteure des ehemaligen Werks Tsu von Mitsubishi Heavy Industries, ein Unternehmen, das Schiffe, schwere Maschinen, Flugzeuge und Eisenbahnwaggons herstellte, gestalteten nach dem Ende des Zweiten Weltkriegs ein Fahrrad aus Duraluminium. Material und Technik übernahmen sie dabei vom Flugzeugbau, der Japan nach dem Krieg durch das GHQ (General Headquarters) der Alliierten untersagt worden war.

Sie entwickelten einen Kreuzrahmen mit einem kantigen Längsträger, der jedoch nicht geschweißt, sondern genietet war. Die ersten Modelle hatten zudem eine in gleicher Technik gefertigte Gabel. Insgesamt gab es drei Grundmodelle, die sich unter anderem durch die Gabelform und weitere Details unterscheiden. Für das zweite Modell ist die Rohrgabel charakteristisch. Der auffällig gerundete Gepäckträger brachte dem Fahrrad auch den Spitznamen „Tennisschläger" ein. Überraschenderweise war dieses Fahrrad für die damalige Zeit relativ erfolgreich. Rund 31.000 Stück wurden produziert und ein Teil davon auch unter dem Namen Dujee exportiert.

After World War II, the aircraft engineers at the former Tsu factory run by Mitsubishi Heavy Industries, which otherwise built ships, heavy machinery, airplanes, and railway wagons, designed a bicycle made of Duralumin. They relied here on materials and technology from airplane construction, which by order of the Allies' GHQ (General Headquarters) was forbidden in Japan after the War.

The engineers developed a cross-shaped frame with a rectangular main strut that was not welded but riveted. Moreover, the first models featured forks made using the same technique. In total there were three basic models that differed by the shape of the forks and other details. The second model came with tubular forks. The strikingly rounded rear pannier earned the bicycle its nickname, the "tennis racket." Surprisingly given the period when it was made, the bicycle was relatively successful. Some 31,000 units were produced, and some of them exported, to which end they were given a new name: the Dujee.

H. & W. Sudbrack GmbH,
Schötmar in Lippe,
für / for Artur Wegmann & Co
Recklinghausen i. W., DE

Das Rennrad wurde für den deutschen Radfahrer Karl-Heinz Kramer angefertigt, der damit 1950 bei einem Steherrennen, einem Bahnrennen im Windschatten eines motorisierten Schrittmachers, über eine Distanz von einem Kilometer einen neuen Weltrekord mit 154,5 km/h aufstellte. Dieser Rekord hielt 71 Jahre und wurde erst 2021 gebrochen.

Die funktionalen und gestalterischen Besonderheiten bestehen in der umgekehrten Gabelkrümmung, von der man sich Vorteile im Fall der Berührung der Walze des Schrittmachermotorrads durch das Vorderrad versprach. Das riesige Spezialkettenblatt mit dem Namen des Herstellers wurde extra für hohe Geschwindigkeiten entwickelt.

This bicycle was specially made for German racing cyclist Karl-Heinz Kramer, who rode it in 1950 in a motor-paced race, an indoor track race in the slipstream of a motorized pacemaker run over a distance of one kilometer. Kramer set a new world record of 154.5 km/h, which held for 71 years and was first broken in 2021.

The bicycle's special features included an inverted fork curve, which was hoped to offer advantages should the front wheel touch the roller of the pace-making motorcycle. The huge special chain ring displaying the manufacturer's name was purpose-developed for high speeds.

Klaue-Bremse GmbH
Überlingen, DE

Auf den promovierten Ingenieur Hermann Klaue (1912–2001) gehen nicht nur zahlreiche Entwicklungen im Fahrzeugbau, wie etwa die Scheibenbremse, zurück, sondern auch ein ganz besonderer Fahrradrahmen. Seine vom Flugzeugbau inspirierte Idee eines Fahrrads in Leichtbauweise wollte er durch die Verwendung eines in einem Stück gegossenen Rahmens aus Silumin (Aluminium-Silizium-Magnesium-Legierung) umsetzen. Dafür entwickelte er einen markanten Kreuzrahmen mit einem Zentralrohr im Rechteckprofil. Bereits 1949 ließ er sich diese Idee patentieren. Der Öffentlichkeit stellte er sein Fahrrad 1950 vor, das er bis 1954 in geringer Stückzahl in seinem eigenen Werk in Überlingen fertigen ließ.

Hermann Klaue (1912–2001), who held a doctorate in Engineering, came up with countless new ideas for building bicycles, among them the disk brake. Indeed, he invented a very special bicycle frame. Taking his cue from aircraft construction, he set out to build a lightweight bicycle based on a frame cast from a single piece of silumin (an aluminum-silicon-magnesium alloy). To this end, he developed a striking cross-shaped frame using rectangular profiles. He had the idea patented as early as 1949. The bicycle was launched officially in 1950 and he continued to make it in small unit numbers in his own workshop in Überlingen until 1954.

Hermann Klaue
Hercules-Werke

Hercules 2000   1949/57

Hercules-Werke
Nürnberg / Nuremberg, DE

Hermann Klaue vergab zahlreiche Lizenzen für sein Fahrrad. 1957 begannen auch die Hercules-Werke in Nürnberg mit der Produktion seines zukunftsweisenden Entwurfs, der unter dem Namen Hercules 2000 auf den Markt kam, jedoch nicht mit der von Klaue entwickelten Technik, Nabenbremse etc., ausgestattet war.

Hermann Klaue issued numerous licenses to build his bicycle. In 1957, the Hercules-Werke in Nuremberg started manufacturing his trailblazing design, which was marketed under the name Hercules 2000. However it was not equipped with the technology invented by Klaue, such as a hub brake.

Alex Moulton Limited
Bradford-on-Avon, UK, 1964

Die von der Suez-Krise 1957 ausgelöste Benzinrationierung brachte den britischen Ingenieur Alex Moulton (1920–2012) auf den Gedanken, ein kompaktes Fahrrad ganz nach seinen Vorstellungen zu entwickeln. Durch seine Erfahrungen in der Luftfahrt- und Automobilindustrie – er hatte unter anderem an der Entwicklung des MINI mitgearbeitet – boten sich ihm die besten Voraussetzungen dafür. So setzte er auf kleine Laufräder mit Hochdruckreifen, die sich positiv auf den Rollwiderstand, das Trägheitsmoment und damit auch auf die Beschleunigung auswirkten. Die durch die geringe Radgröße bedingten Komforteinbußen glich er mit seinen neuentwickelten Federungssystemen für die Vorder- und Hinterräder aus. Völlig neuartig war auch der sogenannte F-Rahmen, der mit allen Konventionen des traditionellen Fahrraddesigns brach. Für Moulton stand die Kompaktheit des Fahrrads und nicht die prinzipielle Zerlegbarkeit im Vordergrund. Deshalb ist auch die häufig verwendete Bezeichnung Faltrad nicht korrekt, da seine Fahrräder erst ab 1964 geteilt bzw. gesteckt werden konnten.

Petrol rationing caused by the Suez Crisis of 1957 prompted British engineer Alex Moulton (1920–2012) to set about developing a compact bicycle fully in line with his own ideas. The experience he had garnered in the aerospace and automobile industries (he had, among other things, been involved in developing the MINI) meant he was well equipped for the task. He thus opted for small wheels with high-pressure tires, a choice that impacted favorably on roll resistance, the moment of inertia, and thus also on acceleration. He offset the loss of comfort caused by the small wheel size by inventing new suspension systems for the front and back wheels. The so-called F frame was also completely new, breaking with all the conventions of traditional bicycle design. For Moulton, the emphasis was on compactness and not on the element of disassembly. Which is why the term folding bicycle often used to describe the Stowaway is not correct, as it was not until 1964 that he designed bikes that could be separated and slotted back together.

„Meine Absicht bei der Gestaltung des Moulton-Fahrrads war es, die Entwicklung dieses bemerkenswerten Geräts eine Stufe über seine klassische Form hinaus zu führen. Mit anderen Worten, ein Fahrrad zu schaffen, das mehr Spaß macht und angenehmer zu benutzen ist."

"My intention in the creation of the Moulton bicycle was to take the evolution of that most remarkable device a stage beyond its classical form. In other words, to produce a bicycle which was more pleasing to have and to use." [10]

Alex Moulton, 1980

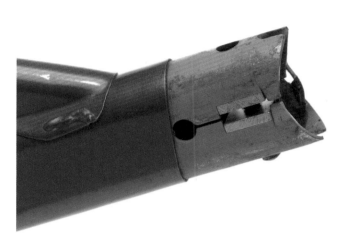

Alex Moulton Limited
Bradford-on-Avon, UK

Alex Moulton beschäftigte sich fortwährend mit der Verbesserung seiner Fahrräder. Wie kompliziert ein Faltsystem sein kann, zeigt die Entwicklung des Gitterrahmens für das spätere AM 7, die allein sechs Jahre beanspruchte.

Alex Moulton was forever trying to improve his bicycles. The development of the lattice frame for the later AM 7, which took a full six years, shows just how complicated it can be to get a folding system right.

Bernard Marcel
Marius Johan Overing

Strano   1962

Union Rijwielfabriek
Den Hulst, NL

Der Fachzeitschrift Fietsenwereld zufolge (1963) war dieses Rad eine Erfindung von Bernard Overing aus Deventer, der eineinhalb Jahre daran gearbeitet hatte und 1962 ein Patent dafür beantragte (NL-Patent von 1965). Allerdings meldete bereits um 1933 Ernesto Pettazzoni aus Bologna ein Patent für sein Velocino an (US-Patent von 1935), das enorme Ähnlichkeit mit dem Strano aufweist: sehr kleines Vorderrad, Sitz über dem normal großen Hinterrad, umkehrbarer Lenker, mit dem man unter dem Sitz lenken und die Beine darüber platzieren konnte. Außerdem gab es bereits 1896 mit dem Humber-Open-Front-Damenmodell ein Fahrrad mit Untersitzlenkung.

Der Hersteller nannte das Fahrrad Meeneemfiets, Mitnehm-fahrrad, da es aufgrund seiner geringen Größe und des per Hebelgriff abnehmbaren Lenkers bequem im Kofferraum transportiert werden konnte. Obwohl die Idee für ein kompaktes und leicht zu verstauendes Fahrrad auch Anfang der 1960er-Jahre Anklang fand, brachte es für Union keinen Erfolg. Bis zur Einstellung der Produktion 1965 wurden lediglich 1000 Stück hergestellt.

Trade journal Fietsenwereld (1963) reported that this bicycle was invented by Bernard Overing from Deventer, who had spent 18 months working on it and filed for a patent on the design in 1962 (Dutch patent of 1965). However, much earlier, namely in 1933, Bologna's Ernesto Pettazzoni had registered a patent for his Velocino (US patent of 1935) which strongly resembles the Strano: a very small front wheel, the seat over the back wheel, which is of a normal size, and reversed handlebars positioned for use below the level of the saddle with your legs placed on top of it. Moreover, back in 1896 the Humber-Open-Front women's bicycle had the handlebars below the seat.

The manufacturer named the new bicycle Meeneemfiets, a bicycle you could take with you. Indeed, given its small size and the fact that the handlebars could be removed simply by unlocking a lever, it easily fitted into a car trunk. Although the idea for a compact and easily stored bicycle was also well received in the early 1960s, Union was not successful with the design. By the time production was discontinued in 1965, only 1,000 units had been made.

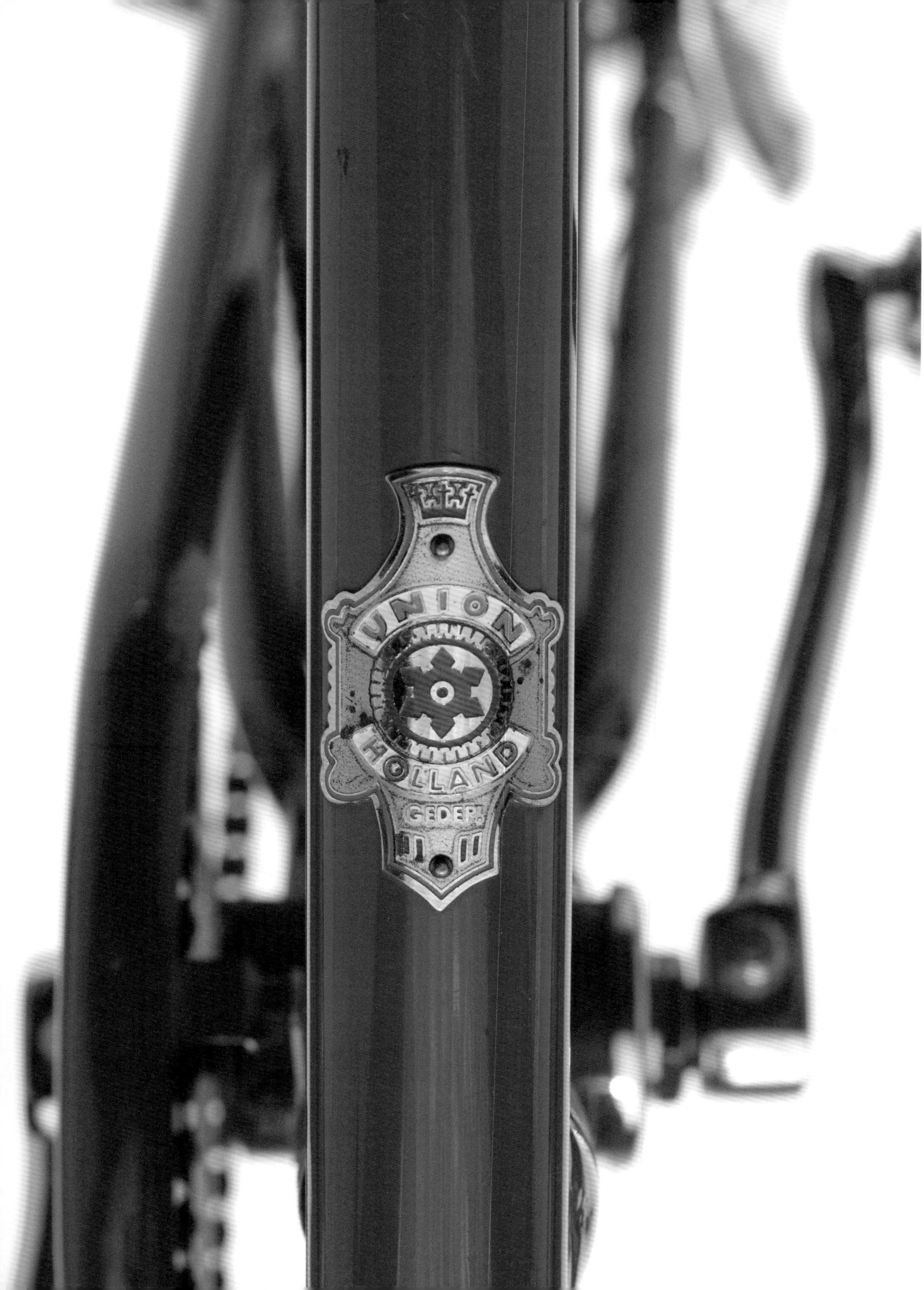
UNION
HOLLAND
GEDEP.

C. Rizzato & Co.
Padua, IT

Die Anzeige (S. 166) bezieht sich auf die verstellbaren Lenker bzw. klappbare Sattelstütze des 1965 auf der internationalen Klappradmesse in Mailand vorgestellten Fahrrads. Für Aufsehen sorgten dabei nicht nur die trapezartige, nahezu extravagante Rahmenform, sondern auch die zahlreichen ungewöhnlichen gestalterischen Details: Angefangen bei der sichelartigen Gabelkonfiguration, die einen Frontgepäckträger mit integriertem Licht ermöglicht, über das vordere Schutzblech, das parallel zum abfallenden Rahmenrohr geführt ist, bis zum Klappmechanismus des Sattelrohrs mit dem großen Sattel. Hinzu kommen hinten ein zweiter Gepäckträger und vor allem die kontrastreiche Farbgestaltung, bei der zwischen tragenden Strukturen und aufgesetzten Elementen, wie Schutzblechen, Lenkerrohrummantelung oder Leuchtengehäusen differenziert wird. Zusammengeklappt misst das Duemila 78 × 66 cm und kostete damals 38.000 Lire. Zudem war auch eine kleinere Version als Kinderfahrrad erhältlich.

The advertisement (p. 166) refers to the adjustable handlebars and/or folding saddle pin of the Duemila, which was presented in 1965 at the international folding bicycle trade fair in Milan. Not only did its trapezoidal, almost outlandish frame shape cause a real stir, but so did the countless unusual design details, such as the sickle-like configuration of the forks, a choice that made space for a front pannier with an integrated light, the front mudguard which runs parallel to the downward line of the frame tube, and the folding mechanism of the saddle tube with the large saddle. Then there is the second pannier, not to mention the contrasting color concept that distinguishes the load-bearing parts from the added elements, such as the mudguards, the faring round the top tubes, and the lamp casings. When folded closed, the Duemila was 78 × 66 cm in size and at the time cost 38,000 lire. A smaller version was also available as a children's bike.

„Ein DUEMILA ist nicht nur faltbar,
sondern auch wandelbar."
"Besides being foldable, a
DUEMILA is transformable."
Anzeige / Advertisement c.1968

Albert John Fritz

Schwinn Fastback Sting-Ray

1967

Schwinn Bicycle Company
Chicago, USA

Wie sehr das Fahrraddesign von der Jugendkultur der späten 1950er- und frühen 1960er-Jahre in den USA beeinflusst wurde, zeigt das sogenannte Bonanzarad. In Kalifornien waren es die Chopper, die stark modifizierten Motorräder, die vielen Jugendlichen als Vorbilder für den Umbau ihrer eigenen Fahrräder dienten. Diese Anregungen griff Al Fritz (1924–2013), ein Ingenieur von Schwinn, auf, und entwickelte mit dem Sting-Ray einen der ersten High Riser. 1967 kam das Ram's Horn Fastback auf den Markt.

Charakteristisch sind der Bananensattel mit der großen Lehne, der hochgezogene Hirschgeweih-Lenker, die kleinen 20-Zoll-Räder und der an die Gangschaltung eines Automobils erinnernde Schalthebel der 5-Gang-Nabenschaltung, der mittig auf dem Oberrohr sitzt.

Bicycle design in the late 1950s and early 1960s in the United States was strongly influenced by youth culture, as can be seen from the so-called Bonanza bicycle. In California, many youths took their cue from choppers (strongly modified motorcycles) when converting their own bicycles. Al Fritz (1924–2013), an engineer at Schwinn, took up the idea and in the form of the Sting-Ray developed one of the first "high risers" in 1963. Schwinn's Ram's Horn Fastback was brought to market in 1967.

Characteristic features were the banana saddle with the high backrest, the high antler-like handlebars, the small 20-inch wheels, and the gear shift for the five-speed hub – the stick shift resembles that in a car and was positioned in the middle of the upper tube.

Otto Kynast
GmbH & Co. KG

Super de Luxe   c. 1972

Otto Kynast GmbH & Co. KG
Quakenbrück, für / for Neckermann, DE

Im Unterschied zum Schwinn High Riser weisen die in Deutschland produzierten Bonanzaräder meist zwei gerade, parallele Oberrohre auf. Die doppelten Gabelrohre sind mit funktionslosen Schraubenfedern versehen. Das ursprünglich vom Versandhändler Neckermann vertriebene Bonanzarad fand viele Nachahmer, die diesen Typus in zahlreichen Varianten herstellten.

Unlike the Bonanza bikes manufactured in Germany, the Schwinn High Riser had a curved upper tube that morphed into the saddle pin section, and no double upper tube. It also lacked the spiral spring on the forks that actually had no function, and the dual socket for the fork tubes. Originally marketed by mail-order company Neckermann, the Bonanza bike was copied many times over and there were countless variations on the high riser type.

Fritz Fleck
Mannheim, DE

Titan ist rund 50 Prozent leichter als Stahl und weist eine ähnliche Zugfestigkeit auf, war damals wie heute erheblich teurer und nur begrenzt verfügbar. Titanrahmen kamen Anfang der 1970er-Jahre auf. Zu den frühesten Beispielen zählen die Renn- und Bahnräder des Mannheimer Konstrukteurs und Rahmenbauers Fritz Fleck (1928–2013), die unter der Marke FLEMA (FLEck, MAnnheim) vertrieben wurden. Fleck fertigte aus den Titanrohren der Firma Steinzeug in Friedrichsfeld ungefähr 25 Räder sowie mehrere Prototypen.

Nachdem ein erster Prototyp bei einem Rennen durch Flattern bei extrem hoher Geschwindigkeit zu Bruch ging – das Elastizitätsmodul von Titan ist kleiner als bei Stahl –, setzte Fleck entsprechende Verstärkungen an den gefährdeten Stellen ein. Mit dem hier gezeigten, derartig modifizierten Rad errang Günter Haritz 1972 die Goldmedaille im Bahnvierer bei den Olympischen Spielen in München.

Titanium is about 50 percent lighter than steel while possessing similar tensile strength, but then as now was considerably more expensive and availability was and is limited. Titanium frames first appeared in the early 1970s. Among the earliest examples were the racing bikes and track bikes made by Mannheim-based engineer and frame-builder Fritz Fleck (1928–2013) and marketed under the FLEMA (FLEck, MAnnheim) brand. Fleck used titanium tubes from the company Steinzeug in Friedrichsfeld to produce about 25 different bicycles and several prototypes.

During a race, an initial prototype cracked at an extremely high speed owing to wheel shimmy – titanium's elasticity is less than that of steel – and Fleck introduced corresponding strengthening at the frame points at risk. The model on show here is one of those modified accordingly, and Günter Haritz rode it in 1972 to claim a Gold medal in the track team pursuit at the Munich Olympic Games.

„Zunächst habe ich mir die Konstruktion von Standard-Stahlrahmen angesehen. Mit jedem neuen Rahmen gewann ich an Erfahrung und modifizierte die Konstruktion. Den Flatter-Effekt bekam ich mit Verstärkungs-platten am Steuerrohr und um das Tretlagergehäuse in den Griff. Außerdem fertigte ich spezielle Verstrebungen an Gabelschaft und Gabelkopf an."

"I started by looking at the design of standard steel frames. With each new frame I gained experience and modified the construction. I got a grip on the shimmy with reinforcing plates on the head tube and around the bottom bracket shell. I also made special braces on the front fork tube and crown." [11]

Fritz Fleck 2005

Five Rams (chin. Wu Yang)
Guangdong, CN

Five Rams (Wu Yang) gehört zu den größten Fahrradherstellern in China. Der Firmensitz befindet sich in Guangdong, die Fabrik in Guangzhou. Mit dem XQ51 gelang dem Unternehmen ein ungewöhnlicher Entwurf, der eigentlich im Globalen Norden den Bereich der Kinderfahrräder hätte revolutionieren können. Statt den heranwachsenden Kindern alle paar Jahre ein größeres Fahrrad zu kaufen, hätten sich die Eltern für ein „mitwachsendes" Gefährt entscheiden können, denn das XQ51 lässt sich in der Größe anpassen und somit über einen längeren Zeitraum benutzen. Ermöglicht wird dies durch eine verstellbare Rahmenkonstruktion. Das horizontale, im Querschnitt rechteckige Hauptrohr ist vorne fest mit der Gabel verbunden, kann hinten jedoch stufenlos durch das speziell konstruierte doppelte Sattelrohr durchgeführt und fixiert werden. So lässt sich der Abstand zwischen der Antriebseinheit mit dem Sattel und dem vorderen Fahrradteil verlängern oder auch verkürzen. Lenker und Sattel sind höhenverstellbar, sodass das Fahrrad individuell anpassbar ist, ohne dass Teile davon ausgetauscht werden müssen.

Five Rams (Wu Yang) is one of China's largest bicycle makers. The company's headquarters is in Guangdong, the factory in Guangzhou. With its XQ51 the corporation came up with an unusual design that could actually have revolutionized the children's bicycle segment in the Global North. Instead of having to buy children a new, larger bicycle every few years as they grew, parents could have chosen a bicycle that grew with the kids, for the size of the XQ51 can be adjusted and therefore it can be used over a longer period of time. This was made possible by an adjustable frame structure. The horizontal main tube, with a rectangular cross section, is firmly connected to the front forks, but at the back can be slotted through the specially constructed double saddle tube and fixed at any point. As a result, the distance between the drive unit with the saddle and the front section of the bicycle can be lengthened or shortened as required. The height of both the handlebars and saddle can be adjusted, so that the bicycle as a whole can be individually adapted without any parts needing to be replaced.

Heinz Kettler Metallwarenfabrik
Ense-Parsit, DE

Die Erfahrungen im Bereich der Metallverarbeitung erwarb sich das 1949 von Heinz Kettler gegründete Unternehmen durch die Produktion von Sportgeräten, Gartenmöbeln, Spielgeräten und Spielfahrzeugen. Vor allem die Gartenmöbel lieferten die Erfahrungswerte für das direkte Verschweißen von Alurohren für die Fahrradrahmen. Die Gestaltung berücksichtigte in besonderer Weise die geringere Steifigkeit des Materials, indem Sitz- und Unterrohr entsprechend große Durchmesser erhielten und das dünnere, in die Sattelstrebe übergehende Oberrohr verdoppelt wurde. Das Alu-Rad 2600 gilt als das vermutlich weltweit erste geschweißte Großserien-Aluminium-Fahrrad. Kettler gehörte zu den wenigen Fahrradherstellern im Westen, die in der Lage waren, Aluminiumrahmen so günstig herzustellen wie ihre Konkurrenten im Fernen Osten.

Trotz der immer noch vorhandenen Schwächen des Materials wurde das Modell in großer Stückzahl verkauft. 20 Jahre Garantie auf Rahmen und Gabel suggerierten hohe Qualität. Die Großserienproduktion ermöglichte günstige Preise und der Verkauf durch die Warenhäuser erschloss ein breiteres Publikum als der Fahrradfachhandel.

Founded in 1949 by Heinz Kettler, the company had gained know-how in metalworking by producing sports equipment, garden furniture, toys, and toy vehicles. Above all the garden furniture provided the knowledge of how to directly weld aluminum tubes for bicycle frames. The design particularly took into account the fact that aluminum had little rigidity by giving the saddle tube and the lower tube larger diameters and doubling up the thin top tube, which culminates in the saddle pin. The 2600 aluminum bicycle was probably the world's first welded aluminum bicycle to be mass produced. Kettler was one of the few bicycle manufacturers in the West capable of manufacturing aluminum frames as cheaply as their competitors in the Far East.

Despite the weaknesses of the material that had not been overcome at the time, the model sold in large numbers. The 20-year guarantee on the frame and forks intimates high quality. Mass production translated into favorable prices, and sales through department stores locked into a larger swath of potential buyers than would have sales through specialist cycle dealerships.

„Superleicht, rostfrei und komplett
ausgestattet."

"Super-light, rustproof and with all
the trimmings."

Anzeige / Advertisement 1977

Hercules-Werke
Nürnberg / Nuremberg, DE

Der Maschinen- und Flugzeugbauingenieur Hans Günter Bals (*1930) beschäftigt sich seit Jahrzehnten mit der Idee einer den ganzen Körper einbindenden Fortbewegung: 1956 entstand zunächst ein Kinderfahrrad, in den 1970er-Jahren ein erster Prototyp für Erwachsene, der zu dem 1978 vorgestellten Modell weiterentwickelt wurde, für dessen Herstellung die Hercules-Werke die Lizenz erwarben. Das Fahrrad wurde ab 1979 mit gravierenden Abweichungen vom ursprünglichen Entwurf produziert. Obwohl das neuartige Antriebskonzept der in den 1970er-Jahren aufkommenden Trimm-dich-Bewegung sehr entgegenkam, blieb der wirtschaftliche Erfolg aus. Bals entwickelte seine Idee weiter und brachte später in Eigenregie eine verbesserte Version unter dem Namen Swingbike auf den Markt.

Das Cavallo wird nicht mit den Beinen über Pedale angetrieben, sondern über Bewegungen des ganzen Körpers: Arme, Beine, Bauch, Brust und Rücken kommen dabei zum Einsatz. Bals konstruierte hierfür einen Rahmen mit vier Gelenken, die mit dem Sattel verbunden sind. Zwei Rahmenrohre wirken als Pleuel auf die Kurbelarme des Antriebszahnrades. In einer schwingenden, entfernt an das Reiten eines Pferdes erinnernden Bewegung erfolgt der Antrieb.

Mechanical and aerospace engineer Hans Günter Bals (*1930) dedicated decades to the idea of locomotion that used the entire body: In 1956 he came up with a children's bicycle and in the 1970s a first prototype for adults, which he then refined to arrive at the model launched in 1978 – Hercules-Werke acquired the license to manufacture it. The bicycle went into production from 1979 onwards but departed significantly from the original design. Although the novel drive concept very much appealed to the keep-fit movement that arose in the 1970s, the bicycle was not a commercial success. Bals continued to tweak the idea and later himself brought out an improved version which he called the Swingbike.

The Cavallo is not powered by the feet via the pedals, but by movements of the entire body: The arms, legs, stomach, chest and back are all involved. To this end, Bals constructed a frame with four joints that are linked to the saddle. Two frame tubes function like piston rods to the cranks of the driving chain ring. The bicycle is thus driven forwards by a swinging movement remotely reminiscent of riding a horse.

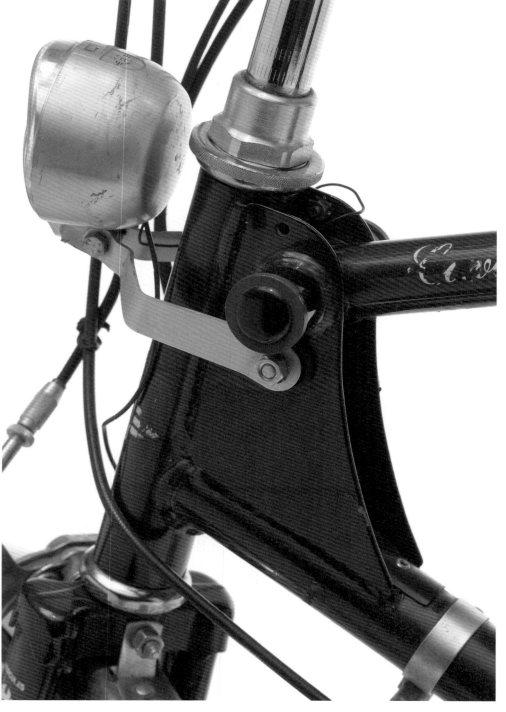

„Fahrer und Fahrzeug zu einer Einheit werden zu lassen, den ganzen Körper, alle Muskeln und den gesamten Organismus in die körperliche Leistung einzubeziehen …"[12]

"Making a unity of cyclist and cycle, including the whole body, all the muscles, and the entire organism in the physical performance …"

Hans Günter Bals 2010

Luigi Colani Designfactory
Schloss Harkotten, DE

Luigi Colanis Designstudie konzentriert sich auf die aerodynamisch-biomorphe Form des Oberrohrs, das am Ende mit dem Sattel verschmilzt. Die anderen Rahmenteile bestehen aus dünnen Doppelrohren und verleihen dem Fahrrad eine optische Leichtigkeit, zugleich zeigt sich in der Kombination mit dem massiven Oberrohr die Heterogenität des Entwurfs. Aus diesem von Colani als Vorstudie für ein Karbonfahrrad bezeichneten Prototyp – eine zweite, nahezu identische Version war mit der japanischen Aufschrift „Gekkeikan" versehen – entwickelte er zehn Jahre später einen kompletten Karbonrahmen, der wie seine anderen Fahrradstudien, unter anderem für Schauff, nicht in Produktion ging.

Luigi Colani's design study concentrates on the aerodynamic-biomorphic shape of the upper tube, which melds at the end with the saddle. The other frame sections consist of thin dual tubes and give the bicycle a sense of visual lightness, while when combined with the massive upper tube the design is clearly heterogeneous. Colani designated this to be a preliminary study for a prototype he classified as a carbon bicycle (a second, almost identical version was marked with the Japanese label "Gekkeikan") and ten years later he developed from it a complete carbon frame which, like his other bicycle studies (among others for Schauff), did not go into production.

„Mein großes Interesse
war immer schon die
Nahtstelle zwischen Mensch
und Maschine."[13]
"My greatest interest has
always been in the interface
between humans and machines."

Luigi Colani

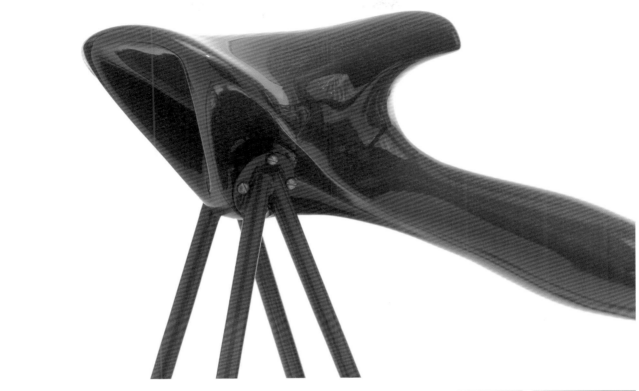

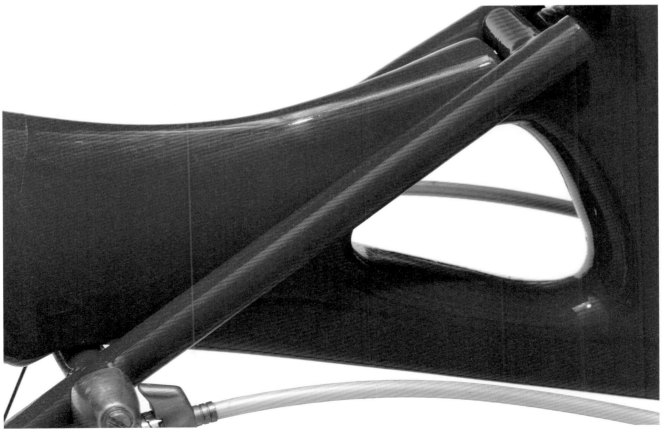

Peter Fendt
Klaus Hofgärtner

FEHO STS 1–26   1979/80

Fendt & Hofgärtner GmbH
Marktoberdorf, DE

Als Studenten entwickelten Peter Fendt und Klaus Hofgärtner 1979 die Idee, ein Fahrrad mit Kardanantrieb auf den Markt zu bringen. In der Annahme, damit den Fahrradantrieb zu revolutionieren, mussten sie jedoch bei der Patentanmeldung feststellen, dass bereits Ende des 19. Jahrhunderts Räder mit Wellenantrieb entstanden waren. Im Herbst 1981 stellten sie ihr erstes Fahrradmodell mit der Bezeichnung FEHO STS 1–26 der Presse vor und begannen mit der Serienfertigung. Der Rahmen wurde damals vom Traditionsunternehmen Falter in Bielefeld gefertigt, die Montage erfolgte am Firmenstandort in Marktoberdorf. Die technischen, vertrieblichen aber auch internen Anlaufschwierigkeiten führten dazu, dass der erhoffte kommerzielle Erfolg ausblieb und von diesem ersten Modell mit Druckgussfelgen nur 400 Stück produziert wurden. Das 1982 vorgestellte, technisch verbesserte Nachfolgemodell Fendt Cardano Comfort erreichte eine höhere Stückzahl.

In 1979, while still students, Peter Fendt and Klaus Hofgärtner had the idea of marketing a bicycle with a shaft drive. Assuming they were thus revolutionizing cycle drive systems, when registering the idea for a patent they discovered that bicycles with shaft drives had existed as long ago as the late 19th century. In fall 1981 they then presented their first bicycle model, named the FEHO STS 1–26, to the press and it went into series production. At the time, the frame was made by the long-standing Falter corporation in Bielefeld, and the bikes were assembled at the company base in Marktoberdorf. Technical, distribution and internal difficulties in the initial phase led to the idea not being a commercial success and only 400 of this first model with its cast metal rims were made. In 1982, a successor model with technical improvements, the Fendt Cardano Comfort, was launched and manufactured in larger numbers.

„… Während wir glaubten,
die Fahrradinnovation des
Jahrzehnts entdeckt zu haben,
haben wir in Wirklichkeit nur eine
uralte Klamotte reaktiviert."[14]
"… Whereas we thought we had
discovered the bicycle innovation
of the decade, in fact we had only
reactivated an ancient item."

Peter Fendt 1985

Itera Development Center AB
Vilhelma, SE

Mit den Argumenten Gewichtsersparnis, preiswertere Herstellung, größere Haltbarkeit (kein Rost) und völlig neuem Erscheinungsbild konnte der schwedische Staat als Förderer für dieses von Ingenieuren des Autoherstellers Volvo konzipierte Tourenrad mit Dreigang-Nabenschaltung gewonnen werden. Die Planungen für das erste komplett aus Kunststoff (Glasfaser-verstärktes Polyamid) bestehende Fahrrad mit seinen in einem Stück spritzgegossenen Nabenaufnahmen, Speichen und Felgen – nur Klingel, Schloss und Kette waren aus Metall – begannen bereits 1973 mit Beteiligung von Bayer, SKF (Svenska Kullagerfabriken) und der KTH (Kungliga Tekniska Högskolan) in Stockholm. 1980 konnte der erste Prototyp vorgestellt werden, 1982 begann der Verkauf. Die Teile wurden geliefert und mussten nach dem Ikea-Prinzip vom Kunden selbst zusammengebaut werden. Das Fahrrad hatte trotz aller Versprechungen bald einen schlechten Ruf, da häufig Teile fehlten, Ersatz nicht ohne Weiteres zu bekommen war und es bei extremen Temperaturen im Sommer und im Winter zu Problemen mit dem Material kam, die teilweise, etwa bei den Kurbeln, zu Brüchen führten. Das Rad wurde mit einigen Modifikationen, wie etwa einem Metalllenker, noch bis 1985 produziert, sodass insgesamt 30.000 Stück auf den Markt kamen.

The Swedish government was won over to support production of this randonneur with a three-speed hub designed by engineers at carmakers Volvo by the arguments that it saved weight, was cheaper to make, was more durable (no rust) and had a completely new appearance. Planning for the first bicycle completely made of plastic (fiberglass-reinforced polyamide) with its dropouts, spokes and rims all injection molded at once (only the bell, lock, and chain were made of metal) started as early as 1973 – with the involvement of Bayer, SKF (Svenska Kullagerfabriken) and the KTH Royal Institute of Technology in Stockholm. In 1980, the first prototype was presented and sales commenced in 1982. The parts were supplied to customers, who had to assemble the bikes themselves according to the IKEA principle.

For all the promises made, the bicycle soon had a bad reputation. Indeed, frequently parts were missing, replacements were not easy to get, and in the case of extreme summer and winter temperatures there were problems with the material, which in part cracked or snapped, for example the crank arms. The bicycle remained in production (with some modifications, such as metal handlebars) until 1985, meaning a total of 30,000 units sold.

„Freude am Radfahren
ohne harte Arbeit."

"Joys of cycling
without hard work."

Volvo-Werbespruch / Volvo ad slogan

Cinelli
Caleppio di Settala (MI), IT

Antonio Colombo übernahm 1978 die Fahrradmarke Cinelli von deren Gründer Cino Cinelli. Hintergrund des jungen Industriellen war die Fabrikation für Stahlrohre, Columbus, die er im Vorjahr von seinem Vater übernommen hatte. Voller Tatendrang und fasziniert von den Designströmungen der damaligen Zeit – kein Geringerer als der Grafikdesigner Italo Lupi schuf 1979 das neue Cinelli Logo –, sorgte er für bahnbrechende Innovationen in der Fahrradwelt. Inspiriert von den ersten aerodynamischen Fahrrädern aus Frankreich, skizzierte Antonio Colombo 1981 das Cinelli Laser. Zusammen mit dem Columbus-Ingenieur Paolo Erzegovesi und dem Rahmenbauer Andrea Pesenti realisierte man eines der schönsten und auch erfolgreichsten aerodynamischen Rennräder. Die Rahmen basierten auf einer muffenlosen Konstruktion, deren Knotenpunkte durch dünnwandige Stahlbleche abgedeckt wurden. Der Effekt: Eine aerodynamische Wirkung, die konstruktive Verstärkung der Knotenpunkte und eine beeindruckende, fließend organische Form.

In 1978, Antonio Colombo acquired the Cinelli bicycle brand from its founder Cino Cinelli. The young industrialist had a background in the production of Columbus steel tubes, having taken the latter business over from his father the prior year. Full of energy and fascinated by the design trends of the day (no less a graphic designer than Italo Lupi created the new Cinelli Logo in 1979), he drove trailblazing innovations in the world of bicycles. Inspired by the first aerodynamic bikes from France, in 1981 Antonio Colombo drew a sketch of what was to become the Cinelli Laser. Together with Columbus engineer Paolo Erzegovesi and frame-builder Andrea Pesenti he thus created what is one of the most beautiful and successful aerodynamic racing bikes of all time. The frames were based on a construction that required no lugs, with the nodal points covered by thin steel sheet. The result was an aerodynamic effect, structural strengthening of the nodal points, and an impressive flowing organic shape.

„Für mich ist ein Fahrrad
nicht nur Geschwindigkeit.
Es ist nicht nur Technik.
Und es ist nicht nur Kunst.
Man muss immer
die Balance halten."
"For me, a bicycle is not
only speed. It is not only
technology. And it is
not only art. You must
always balance them." [15]

Antonio Colombo 2020

Sprick Fahrräder GmbH
Oelde, DE

Im September 1982 bezeichnete die Presse das Comfortable auf der Internationalen Fahrrad-Ausstellung in Köln als „zukunftsweisendste Neuentwicklung der letzten Jahrzehnte." Zu den technischen Besonderheiten dieses 1983 patentierten Entwurfs von Odo Klose (1932–2020) gehören Laufräder aus glasfaserverstärktem Kunststoff mit schlauchlosen Reifen, abschließbarer Gepäckkasten, Flugzeuglenker und ein moderner Unisex-Rahmen aus zwei parallel verlaufenden, gebogenen Rundrohren, die über Kunststoffelemente verbunden waren; hinzu kommen geschlossener Kettenkasten, Abstandshalter, Halogenscheinwerfer und Rücklicht mit Standlichtautomatik, Reflektor am Gepäckträger, integriertes Rahmenschloss. Verkauft wurde dieses bemerkenswerte, häufig als „Colani-Rad" bezeichnete Fahrrad nicht über den einschlägigen Handel, sondern über eine Kaufhauskette.

In September 1982, the press referred to the Comfortable when it launched at the International Bicycle Show in Cologne as the "most pioneering new development of recent decades." The technical features of the design by Odo Klose (1932–2020), which was patented in 1983, included fiberglass-reinforced plastic wheels with tubeless tires, a lockable luggage box, airplane handlebars, and a modern unisex frame consisting of two parallel curved round tubes that were connected by plastic elements; added to which there was a closed chain box, a safety distancer, halogen lamps and a rear taillight that kept shining when stationary, a reflector on the luggage box, and a lock integrated into the frame. This remarkable bicycle, often referred to as the "Colani bike," was not sold through the usual retailers but only through a department store chain.

„Beim Sprick Comfortable gab es ja einige Neuheiten. Zum Beispiel die speichenlosen Räder, den kleinen Kofferraum, einen Sicherheitsabstandhalter und den sogenannten Spannrahmen ... Er federt und macht das Fahren komfortabler. Deshalb heißt das Rad ja auch „Comfortable"... [zum Lenker] Ich wollte eine Form schaffen, in der alle Funktionen integriert sind, also Bremse, Schaltung, Klingel und Tacho. Die Bedienhebel sind ja normalerweise alle einzeln aufgesetzt auf ein Rohr."[16]

"The Sprick Comfortable featured a few novelties, such as the spokeless wheels, the small trunk, a safety distancer, and a single-piece frame ... It absorbs shocks and makes cycling more comfortable. Hence the reason for the bicycle's name... [On the handlebars:] I wanted to create a shape into which all the functions were integrated, meaning the brakes, the gear shifts, the bell and the speedo. The control levels are, after all, normally positioned individually along a tube."

Odo Klose 2018

Wolfgang Taubmann
Paul Rinkowski

Textima

c. 1985

VEB Kombinat Textilmaschinenbau
Karl-Marx-Stadt, DDR/GDR

Hervorgegangen aus dem VEB Fahrradwerke Elite Diamant bestand zwischen Anfang 1970 und 1990 eine eigens eingerichtete Forschungsabteilung im VEB Kombinat Textilmaschinenbau Karl-Marx-Stadt, um mit Spezialanfertigungen den Radsport in der DDR, vor allem für das Olympia- und Nationalteam, konkurrenzfähig zu machen. Mit muffenlosen Rahmen sollte zunächst das Gewicht reduziert, später auch die Aerodynamik verbessert werden. Weitere Modifikationen am Rahmen und an den Anbauteilen dienten dazu, den Luftwiderstand weiter zu verringern, um so bei gleichem Kraftaufwand höhere Geschwindigkeiten zu erzielen. Im Windkanal wurden neben den Verbesserungen am Fahrrad auch die Haltung und Kleidung der Fahrer und Fahrerinnen getestet. Optimierungen erfuhren die Räder durch die Verwendung von Hörnerlenkern, ein an das hintere Laufrad angepasstes Sitzrohr sowie ein deutlich nach vorne abfallendes Oberrohr, das eine entsprechende Verkürzung des Steuerrohrs ermöglichte, sodass der Fahrer seine Sitzposition verbessern und damit der Windwiderstand insgesamt gesenkt werden konnte. Mit diesem bis ca. 1986 gebauten Zeitfahrrad erreichte die Rennrad-Entwicklung dieser Forschungsabteilung ihren Höhepunkt.

The successor to VEB Fahrradwerke Elite Diamant, between early 1970 and 1990 there was a dedicated research department at VEB Kombinat Textilmaschinenbau Karl-Marx-Stadt focusing on creating competitive custom-built bikes for East German cycling, above all for the Olympics squad and the national team. The idea was to create frames that required no muffs in order to reduce weight, with later efforts destined to improve aerodynamics. Additional modifications to the frame and the components served to lower drag in order to achieve higher speeds for the same power output. Wind tunnel tests were used to improve not only the bicycles, but also the position and clothing of the cyclists.

Optimizations included the introduction of horn handlebars, a seat tube adjusted to the back wheel, and an upper tube that clearly angled downward to the front, enabling a correspondingly shorter top tube to improve the cyclist's position on the saddle and thus reduce wind drag. Built until about 1986, this time trialing bike marked the culmination of the research department's efforts.

AC 4 prototype

CON-RAD-DESIGN
Leinfelden-Oberaichen, DE

Auf der Suche nach einer Alternative zum Millionen Mal produzierten Diamantrahmen aus Metallrohr begann Michael Conrad (*1940), mit Verbundwerkstoffen zu experimentieren. So entstand einer der ersten in Westdeutschland realisierten Karbon-Monocoque-Rahmen, der sowohl durch das Material als auch durch die Form neue Wege wies. Auffallendes Designmerkmal ist die eigenwillige Interpretation des Kreuzrahmens mit dem versetzten, an eine liegende 4 erinnernden Sattelrohr.

Dem an der HfG Ulm ausgebildeten Designer ging es weniger darum, ein reines Profirennrad zu entwickeln, sondern vielmehr um ein leichtes, sportliches Tourenrad, das ästhetische Qualität mit günstigen Produktionskosten verbinden sollte – ein Ziel, das zum damaligen Zeitpunkt noch nicht erreicht werden konnte, aber immerhin die ersten Ansätze dafür bot.

Hunting for an alternative to the metal-tube diamond-shaped frames that had been produced millions of times, Michael Conrad (*1940) started experimenting with composites. The result was one of the first carbon-monocoque frames made in WestGermany – it blazed the trail in terms of both material and shape. The striking design feature is the idiosyncratic interpretation of the cross-frame with the staggered saddle tube, reminiscent of a 4 on its side.

Having trained at Ulm School of Design, the designer was interested less in developing a thoroughbred racing bike and more in creating a light sports randonneur that combined aesthetic quality with favorable production costs – it was an objective that was not yet possible at that point in time, but at least showed the way forward.

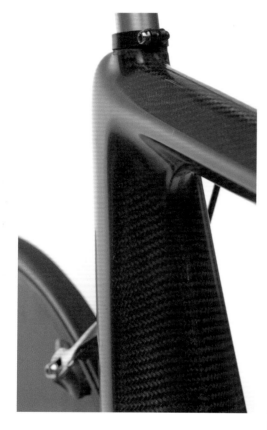

„1984 entstand das erste Rendering mit der charakteristischen ‚4' … Es folgten ‚VELO' 3 und 4. Sie unterschieden sich durch unterschiedliche Querschnitte: V 3 zu breit, V 4 schmaler = eleganter … V 4 war mir immer noch zu klobig, deshalb realisierte ich 1989 AC 4 (advanced composite) mit noch geringerem Querschnitt. Ich hatte damals noch nicht die Möglichkeit die Rahmenstruktur zu berechnen, ich musste mich herantasten." [17]

"In 1984 we made the first rendering with the characteristic '4' … Followed by 'VELO' 3 and 4. They differ in terms of cross sections: V 3 was too wide, V 4 narrower = more elegant … V4 I still found too bulky, which is why in 1989 I came up with the AC 4 (advanced composite) with an even slimmer cross section. Back then I was not yet able to calculate the frame structure; I simply had to feel my way there."

Michael Conrad 2022

Cycles A. Sablière
Saint-Étienne, F

Der Radrennfahrer und Konstrukteur André Sablière stellte in seinem Unternehmen zunächst Stahlrahmen her, bevor er den Werkstoff Aluminium für sich entdeckte. Er entwickelte hierzu eine eigene Legierung, die sich besonders für den Bau seiner extrem leichten, muffenlosen Fahrradrahmen eignete. Die unlackierten, komplett aus Aluminium gefertigten Fahrräder – selbst der Gabelschaft und die Ausfallenden sind aus Aluminium – mit ihren perfekt verschliffenen und polierten Schweißnähten beeindrucken nicht nur durch die geschmeidig fließenden Rohrformen, sondern auch durch das geringe Gewicht. In diesem Punkt war Sablière den Rahmenbauern seiner Zeit deutlich voraus.

Racing cyclist and engineer André Sablière initially built steel frames in his company before discovering aluminum as a material. In this context, he developed his own alloy that was most suitable to build his extremely light frames that had no muffs. His unpainted bicycles, with the perfectly sanded and polished welding seams made entirely of aluminum (even the forks and the dropouts are made of aluminum), are impressive, thanks to not only the sleekly fluid tube shapes, but also their low weight. In this regard, Sablière was far ahead of the other frame-builders of his day.

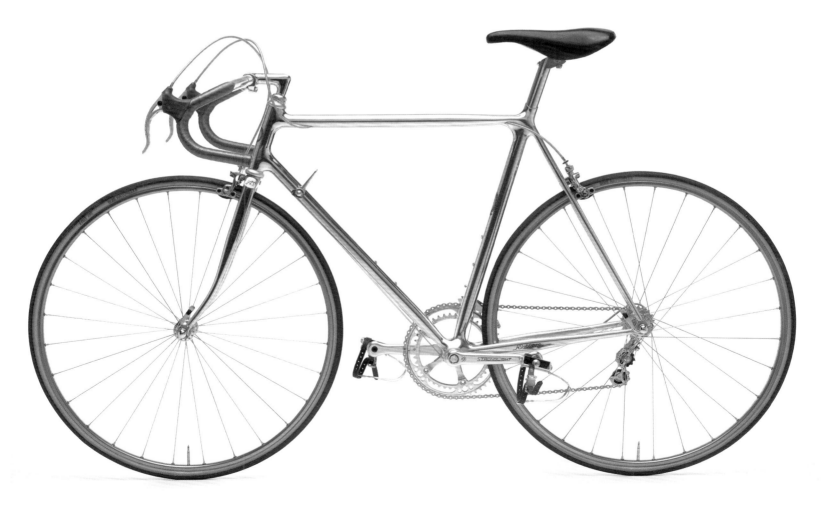

„Ich suche den besten
Kompromiss zwischen
Leichtigkeit und Steifigkeit.
Zweitens: Ich opfere
nie die Leichtigkeit der
Steifigkeit."
"I search for the best
compromise between
lightness and rigidity.
And, secondly,
I never sacrifice
lightness to rigidity." [18]

André Sablière

Bridgestone Cycle Co., Ltd.
Tokio / Tokyo, JP

Bridgestone Cycle, ein Tochterunternehmen des gleichnamigen Reifenherstellers, begann 1946 mit der Produktion von Fahrrädern und entwickelte sich in den Folgejahren zu einem der größten Fahrradhersteller Japans. 1985 stellte das Unternehmen das Modell Blouson vor. Der aus dem Französischen kommende Name für legere Herrenjacken sollte für die schlichte, dennoch elegante Bauweise des Fahrrads stehen, dessen Gestaltung der italienische Automobil- und Industriedesigner Giorgetto Giugiaro (*1938) übernommen hatte. Sein Designansatz für dieses Unisex-Fahrrad ging jedoch weit über die angestrebte Vereinfachung der Konstruktion hinaus, indem er den klassischen Kreuzrahmen über den Lenker nach vorne verlängerte. Das Steuerrohr setzt sich nicht wie üblicherweise über die Gabelkrone und die eigentliche Gabel nach unten fort, sondern nach vorne und knickt etwa auf Höhe der Nabe nach hinten um. Dadurch bietet der Lenker eine angenehmere Griffposition und zugleich eine größere Beinfreiheit.

Bridgestone Cycle, a subsidiary of the eponymous tire manufacturer, started making bicycles in 1946 and in subsequent years emerged as one of Japan's largest bicycle manufacturers. In 1985, the company rolled out its Blouson model. The name came from the French for light men's jackets and was supposed to evoke the simple yet elegant build of the bicycle, which was the brainchild of Italian automobile and industrial designer Giorgetto Giugiaro (born 1938). His design for this unisex bicycle went far beyond the brief of simplifying the construction, as he extended the classical cross frame forwards beyond the handlebars. The top tube is not positioned conventionally downwards above the crown of the forks and the actual forks, but forwards and bends backwards approximately above the hub. The handlebars are therefore more comfortable to grip and there is more freedom of movement for the legs.

Strida Ltd.
Glasgow, UK

Der britische Designstudent Mark Sanders gestaltete das Strida 1985 als Abschlussarbeit für den gemeinsamen Masterstudiengang Industrial Design Engineering (IDE) des Imperial College und des Royal College of Art in London.

Inspiriert von der Technik eines Kinderbuggys, entwickelte Sanders einen Faltmechanismus, der das Fahrrad nach dem Einklappen von Lenkrad und Pedalen innerhalb von wenigen Sekunden in ein handliches Paket verwandelt. Durch die einseitig gelagerten Laufräder, die sich im geklappten Zustand nebeneinander befinden und durch Magnete aneinanderhaften, lässt sich das Fahrrad bequem mit einer Hand schieben. Außerdem werden dadurch Reifentausch bzw. Reparatur erleichtert. Der Riemenantrieb bewahrt den Benutzer bzw. die Benutzerin vor der Verschmutzung der Kleidung durch die beim traditionellen Kettenantrieb verwendete Kettenschmiere.

Durch das minimalistische Design mit dem A-förmigen Rahmen, der dem Fahrrad die Gestalt eines großen Dreiecks gibt, unterscheidet sich das Strida deutlich von den üblichen Falträdern. Interessanterweise ließ sich der Berliner Otto Spiess bereits 1897 ein formal ähnliches Fahrrad patentieren.[19]

British design student Mark Sanders created the Strida in 1985 as his graduation project for the joint Master's program in Industrial Design Engineering (IDE) at Imperial College and the Royal College of Art in London.

Inspired by the technology of children's pushchairs, Sanders developed a folding mechanism that transformed the bicycle after folding up the handlebars and pedals into a handy package in mere seconds. The single-side wheel mountings mean that the wheels are next to each other once folded and held there by magnets such that the bicycle can easily be pushed with one hand. This also makes changing tires or making repairs easier. Thanks to its belt drive, the user doesn't sully any clothing, such as can happen with the grease from a customary chain.

The minimalist design with the A-shaped frame that gives the bicycle the look of a large triangle means Strida stands out clearly from the customary folding bicycles. Interestingly, Berlin-based Otto Spiess was awarded a patent in 1897 for a formally similar bicycle.

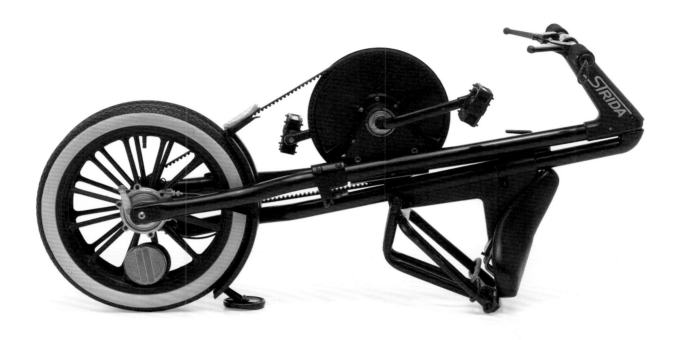

„Das Strida ist aufgrund seiner Form, seiner Einfachheit und der Tatsache, dass es zusammengeklappt auf den Rädern gerollt werden kann, ziemlich einzigartig in der Welt der Klappräder. Dadurch ist es viel einfacher zu handhaben, wenn man zu Fuß unterwegs ist (also nicht fährt), als herkömmliche Klappräder, die sehr schwer zu tragen sind, zum Beispiel in Zügen, in Gängen, auf Bahnsteigen usw."

"Strida is pretty unique in the folding bike world due to its shape, simplicity and the fact that it can be wheeled along when folded. This makes it much easier to handle in the walking (i.e., non-riding) parts of a journey than conventional folding bikes, which get awfully heavy to carry, for example inside trains, down corridors and along platforms etc." [20]

Mark Sanders 2008

Strida Ltd.
Ming, Taipeh, TW

Im Unterschied zum Strida 1 wird das Strida 5 von Ming Cycle in Taiwan produziert. Außerdem ist es mit Scheibenbremsen, einem exzentrischen Riemenspanner, Metallspeichenrädern und Hochdruckreifen ausgestattet.

Unlike Strida 1, Strida 5 is made by Ming Cycle in Taiwan. Moreover, it comes with disk brakes, an eccentric belt tightener, metal spoke wheels, and high-pressure tires.

Kirk Precision Ltd.
Basildon, UK

Frank Kirks Idee, ein Fahrrad aus Magnesium im Druckguss-verfahren zu produzieren, brachte völlig andere Erfordernisse für die Konstruktion und damit das Rahmendesign mit sich, als dies bei der Verwendung von Stahl- oder Aluminiumrohren der Fall ist. Gegossene Rahmen bieten große Vorteile für eine preiswerte Massenproduktion.

Magnesium gehört zu den leichtesten Metallen. Auch wenn die Steifigkeit geringer als bei Aluminium oder Stahl ist, eignet es sich gut für den Rahmenbau. Allerdings ist der Rahmen nicht hohl gegossen, sodass dadurch die Gewichtsersparnis aufgehoben wird. Magnesium kann zwar entflammbar und korrosionsanfällig sein, wenn es nicht richtig lackiert wird, doch insgesamt gesehen ist das Material kostengünstig und die Gewinnung umweltfreundlich.

Mithilfe neuester CAD-Programme entwickelte Kirk, ein damals im Automobilbau als Konstrukteur tätiger Luft- und Raumfahrt-ingenieur, seine ungewöhnliche, auf das Material und den Produktionsprozess genau abgestimmte Rahmenform. Dennoch gab es Probleme mit der Verwindungssteifigkeit, aber auch mit abgebrochenen Schalthebelaufnahmen oder dem Bremssteg, sodass diesem Magnesium-Fahrrad letztendlich der kom-merzielle Erfolg versagt blieb.

Frank Kirk's idea of making a bicycle with pressure die-cast magnesium spelled completely new requirements as regards structure and frame design than was the case with steel or aluminum tubes. Die-cast frames offered major advantages when it came to cheap mass production.

Magnesium is one of the lightest metals. Even if it is less rigid than steel or aluminum, it is very suitable for building frames. However, the frame is not cast as a hollow body, meaning the weight savings are forfeited. Magnesium can be inflammable and prone to corrosion if it is not duly lacquered, but on balance the material is cost effective and its extraction eco-friendly.

Using the latest CAD programs, Kirk, an aerospace engineer active as a construction engineer in automobile manufacture at the time, developed his unusual frame shape that was perfectly aligned to the material and the production process. There were nevertheless problems with torsional rigidity as well as with gear-shift mounts snapping and the brake mount, and this magnesium bicycle was in the final instance not a commercial success.

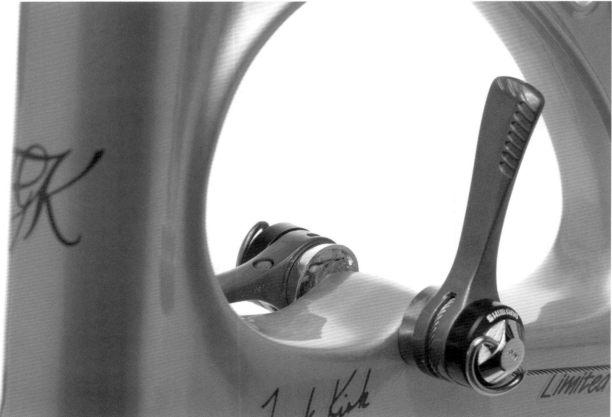

„Ich dachte, wenn wir die Materialien und die Mittel haben, um ein viel größeres Gussteil als bisher zu machen, erscheint es logisch, die Produktion zu vereinfachen. Mit anderen Worten, die Herstellung sollte billiger, gleich-bleibend genau und obendrein besser werden ... Wir konnten CAD für kleine Feinabstimmungen und zur Verfeinerung der Ästhetik nutzen.“ "I thought that if we had the materials and the means to make a much larger casting than before, it seemed logical to simplify the production. In other words, make it cheaper to make, consistently accurate and better into the bargain ... We were able to use CAD for small finetuning adjustments and for refining the aesthetics." [21]

Frank Kirk 2009

Cycle Composites, Inc. (CCI)
Santa Cruz, USA

Das von Bevil Hogg und Tom French, ehemaligen Mitarbeitern von Trek Bicycles, gegründete Unternehmen setzte sich das Ziel, die ersten Fahrradrahmen aus Vollkarbon zu entwickeln, zu bauen und kommerziell zu vermarkten. Zusammen mit Brent J. Trimble, der zuvor schon Karbonräder entworfen hatte, gelang es dem Unternehmen, mit dem Kestrel 4000 das erste in größerer Serie produzierte Fahrrad auf den Markt zu bringen, dessen aerodynamisch geformter Rahmen komplett aus Kohlefaserrohren bestand.

Brent J. Trimble ließ sich Design und Verfahren durch mehrere Patente schützen (US5158733A, US4902458A). Zudem entstand der Entwurf mithilfe der Finite-Elemente-Analyse (FEA), einer computergestützten Methode, die berechnet, wie der Rahmen auf physikalische Kräfte wie Vibrationen, Hitze, Luftströmung usw. reagieren wird und so dem Designer eine Perfektionierung seines Rahmens ermöglicht. Mit dem Kestrel 4000 wurde der Standard für die spätere Serienfertigung von Karbonfahrrädern geschaffen.

Founded by Bevil Hogg and Tom French, former staff members at Trek Bicycles, the company set out to develop, build and market the first fully carbon bicycle frames. Together with Brent J. Trimble, who had already designed carbon bicycles, the company succeeded in launching the first carbon frame on the market made in larger numbers – the Kestrel 4000. Its aerodynamic frame was made completely of carbon-fiber tubes.

Trimble had the design and process protected by several patents (US5158733A, US4902458A). Moreover, the design relied on finite element analysis (FEA), a computer-assisted method for calculating how the frame would respond to physical forces such as vibrations, heat, air current, etc., thus enabling the designer to perfect the frame. The Kestrel 4000 set the standard for the later mass production of carbon bicycles.

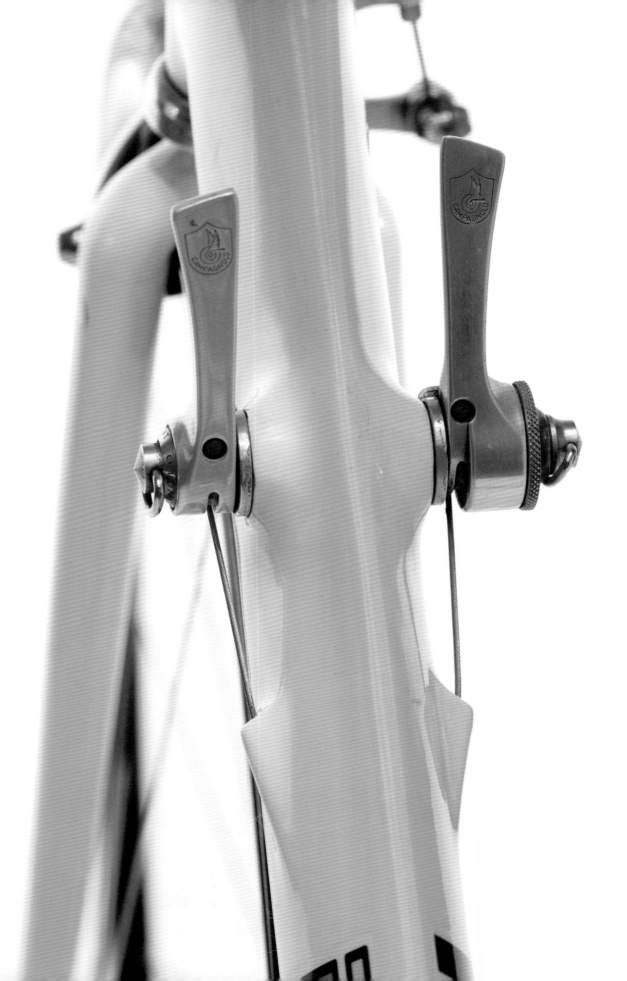

Cycle Composites, Inc. (CCI)
Santa Cruz, USA

Das Kestrel 500SCi geht in der Gestaltung weit über Brent J. Trimbles Kestrel 4000 hinaus. Auch wenn es sich dabei nicht um das erste Fahrrad mit dieser durch den Verzicht auf das Sitzrohr entstandenen trapezförmigen Rahmenform handelt, ließ sich daran die strukturelle Flexibilität der Verbundwerkstoffbauweise überzeugend demonstrieren.

The Kestrel 500SCi went one step further. By eliminating the seating tube, a trapezoidal frame shape arose that convincingly demonstrated the structural flexibility of composite constructions.

Bottecchia Cicli S.r.l.
Vittorio Veneto, IT

Ottavio Bottecchia (1894–1927) gewann 1924 als erster Italiener die Tour de France und gründete zwei Jahre danach zusammen mit Teodoro Carnielli in Vittorio Veneto die Fahrradfabrik Bottecchia, die heute zu den größten italienischen Herstellern von Renn- und Tourenrädern gehört. Das Unternehmen hat sich auch im Profisport einen Namen gemacht, etwa durch die Erfolge von Gianni Motta beim Giro d'Italia 1966 oder von Greg LeMond bei der Tour de France 1989.

Die hier ausgestellte Zeitfahrmaschine von Bottecchia stellt einen Höhepunkt des aerodynamischen Rennraddesigns aus Stahlrohr dar, unmittelbar bevor das damals neue Material Karbon seinen Siegeszug antrat. Die schmalen, annähernd tropfenförmig gestalteten Rohrprofile und die Aero-Profil-Zwickel an den Hauptdreiecksverbindungen sowie auf der Rückseite des Sitzrohrs sollten den Luftwiderstand minimieren und so die Fahrräder noch schneller und damit auch die Fahrer und Fahrerinnen erfolgreicher machen.

In 1924, Ottavio Bottecchia (1894–1927) became the first Italian to win the Tour de France and two years afterwards joined forces with Teodoro Carnielli to found the Bottecchia bicycle factory in Vittorio Veneto, which today is one of Italy's largest manufacturers of racing bikes and randonneurs. The company has a strong reputation in professional cycle racing, for example with Gianni Motta's successes at the 1966 Giro d'Italia or Greg LeMond's win at the 1989 Tour de France. The Bottecchia time-trialing bicycle on show here marks a high point in aerodynamic designs for racing bikes made of tubular steel, directly before the then new material of carbon started to gain sway. The slender, almost tear-drop profiles of the tubes and the aero-profile spandrels at the main connections of the triangular frame as well as behind the saddle tube were intended to minimize drag and thus make the bike faster to give the rider a greater chance of success.

Togashi Engineering Ltd.
Tokio / Tokyo, JP

In der Werkstatt eines japanischen Motorradherstellers entstand dieser futuristische Karbonrahmen. Die diagonale Hauptstrebe verschmilzt mit zwei durchbrochenen Dreiecksformen. An der Spitze des oberen, nach hinten gerichteten Dreiecks befinden sich die Metallstreben der Sattelhalterung, das untere nimmt das Kurbelgehäuse auf, dient als Kettenstrebe und endet in der Nabenaufnahme des Hinterrads (Ausfallende). Von diesem aufwendig in Handarbeit laminierten Rahmen existieren nur sehr wenige Exemplare mit verschiedenen Ausstattungen, unter anderem mit einseitig aufgehängtem Vorderrad. Den Stolz des Herstellers auf sein ungewöhnliches Produkt veranschaulicht die Aufschrift: „Made with quality and Pride".

This futuristic carbon frame was built in the workshop of a Japanese motorbike manufacturer. The diagonal main strut melds with the two triangular shapes it perforates. The metal saddle pin is located at the tip of the upper, backward-oriented triangle, while the lower triangle houses the bottom bracket, serves as the chain stay, and ends in the dropouts for the rear wheel. Only very few examples of this handmade wet-laminated frame have survived, among others with the single fork. The manufacturer's pride in this extraordinary product is manifested in the slogan "Made with quality and Pride".

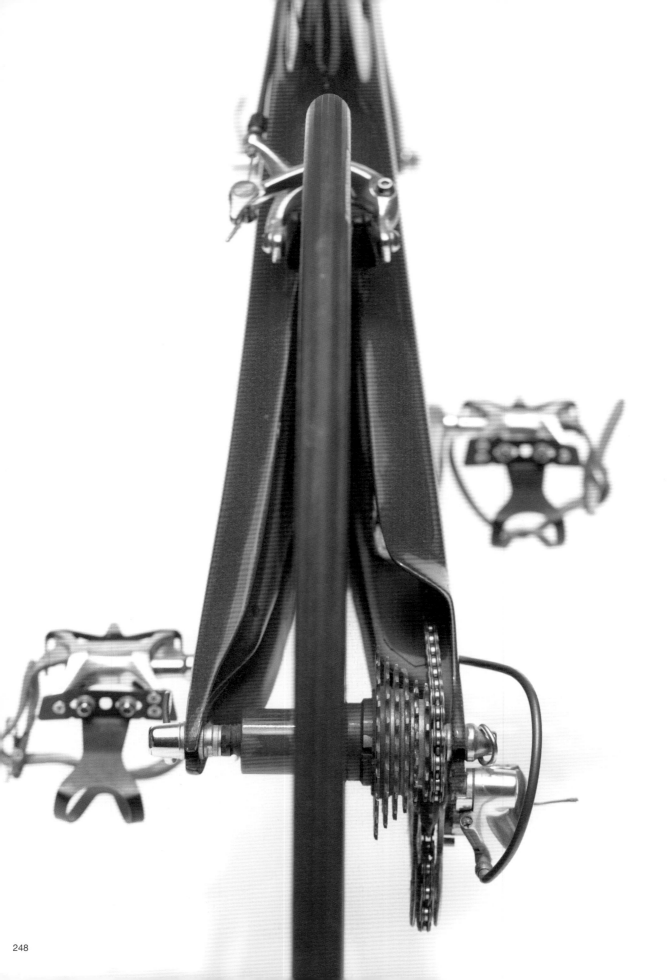

Institut für Forschung und
Entwicklung von Sportgeräten (FES) e. V.
Berlin, DDR/GDR

Seit 1970 widmete sich das 1963 als Entwicklungsabteilung für Sportgeräte der Forschungsstelle der DHfK (Deutsche Hochschule für Körperkultur und Sport) gegründete Institut für Forschung und Entwicklung von Sportgeräten (FES) dem Fahrradbau in der DDR. Ab 1984 entstand das erste selbsttragende Scheibenlaufrad aus Karbon und ab 1987 der erste karbonfaserverstärkte Fahrradrahmen. 1988 wurde die bahnbrechende Entwicklung des Instituts FES durch die olympische Goldmedaille im 100-km-Mannschaftszeitfahren in Seoul gekrönt. 1992 folgte die nächste Auszeichnung mit der Goldmedaille bei den Olympischen Spielen in Barcelona.

From 1970 onwards, what had been founded in 1963 as the Department for the Development of Sports Equipment attached to the Research Division of the DHfK (Deutsche Hochschule für Körperkultur und Sport) became the FES and focused on bicycle design and construction. As of 1984, the first self-supporting disc wheel made of carbon was built there, followed in 1987 by the first carbon-fiber-reinforced bike frame. In 1988, Institut FES's trailblazing invention was crowned by the East German team winning gold in the 100 km team time trial at the Seoul Olympic Games. In 1992, an Institut FES bicycle also won gold at the Barcelona Games.

„Wir sind es nicht, die Gold
produzieren; das sind die Sportler
und Trainer. Wir verstehen uns
als technologischen Baustein."
"We're not the ones who produce
the gold medals. That's down to
the athletes and coaches. We see
ourselves as the technological
element." [22]
Harald Schaale 2018

Aerodyne Space Technology, SA,
für / for Lotus Cars Limited
Norfolk, UK

Auf Grundlage des von Mike Burrows entwickelten und von Lotus leicht modifizierten Bahnrads Lotus 108, auf dem Chris Boardman 1992 in Barcelona eine olympische Goldmedaille gewann, sollte eine Straßenrennradversion entstehen. Ohne Mike Burrows an dieser Weiterentwicklung zu beteiligen – immerhin hatte er die Grundlagen dafür geschaffen –, gestalteten die Lotus-Ingenieure das Modell 110. Sie änderten die Rahmenform und damit die Aerodynamik sowie die Verwindungssteifigkeit. Außerdem sahen sie von der einseitigen Aufhängung der Lauräder ab, führten eine verstellbare Sattelstütze ein und ermöglichten die Verwendung von Standardgruppen. Das Straßenrad war nun nicht mehr nur auf Chris Boardman zugeschnitten, sondern konnte auch von anderen Fahrern eingesetzt werden. Erfolge gab es weiterhin zu feiern: Zunächst wurden bei DPS Composites in Norfolk sechs Entwicklungsmodelle hergestellt, dann folgte eine Serie von 50 Stück, bevor die Produktion nach Südafrika zu Aerodyne verlagert wurde.

The idea was to create a road racing version of the Lotus 108 track racing bike that Mike Burrows had developed and was slightly modified by Lotus (Chris Boardman won a gold medal at the 1992 Barcelona Olympics riding one). Without involving Mike Burrows in this new version (although he had laid the foundations for it), the Lotus engineers designed the Lotus Sport 110. They changed the frame shape and thus the aerodynamics and the torsional stiffness. Moreover, they dispensed with the single-side dropouts, introduced an adjustable saddle pin, and enabled the use of standard group-sets for the chain rings, gears, and brakes. The road-racing version was no longer tailored to Chris Boardman but could also be used by other cyclists. And other successes were not long in coming. Initially, DPS Composites in Norfolk made six development models, then series production of 50 units followed before manufacturing was shifted to Aerodyne in South Africa.

„Es wurde so konzipiert, dass
es weniger verwindungssteif
ist als das 108er, vertikal mehr
Nachgiebigkeit bietet, eine
Standardgruppe aufnehmen
kann und eine verstellbare
Sattelstütze hat. Es war
ein Fahrrad, das von jedem
benutzt werden konnte …"
"It was designed to be less
torsionally stiff than the 108,
to have more compliance
vertically and to take a
standard groupset and to have
an adjustable seatpost. It was
a bike that was designed
to be used by anybody ..."[23]

Richard Hill 2017

C4 sas di Marco Bonfanti & C.
Airuno, IT

Marco Bonfanti gehörte zu den Pionieren der Karbon-Mono-coquerahmen. Bereits 1986 entwarf er seinen Aero-Rahmen, der 1987 beim Giro d'Italia durch das Bianchi Racing Team zum Einsatz kam. Bei dem 1993 entstandenen Modell Joker gestaltete Bonfanti einen trapezförmigen Schleifenrahmen mit angesetzter Kurzschwinge für den Sattel. Diese offene, schlanke Rahmenform ermöglichte über das Material Karbon eine leichte Federung des Fahrrads, ohne die Steifigkeit zu beeinträchtigen. Hier gehen Design und Funktion Hand in Hand. Bei hoher Ferti-gungsqualität blieb der Preis jedoch relativ günstig, sodass sich ein breiterer Kreis an Rennradfahrern und Rennradfahrerinnen diesen Fahrkomfort leisten konnte.

Marco Bonfanti was one of the pioneers of carbon monocoque frames. As early as 1986 he designed his aero-frame, used by the Bianchi Racing Team in the 1987 Giro d'Italia. The Joker model, brought to market in 1993, saw Bonfanti relying on a trapezoidal loop-shaped frame with a short saddle cantilever. Thanks to the use of carbon, this open, slender frame shape offered a degree of suspension without impairing rigidity. In this case, form and function blended superbly. Despite the exceptional manufacturing quality, the price was relatively cost-effective and thus a broader circle of racing cyclists was able to afford the comfort.

„Das Unternehmen wurde mit dem Ziel gegründet, Rahmen herzustellen, die aus einem einzigen Stück bestehen."

"The company was founded with the objective of manufacturing single-piece frames."[24]

Marco Bonfanti 2005

Ivan Lypa
Serhii Nytka

Antonov Enei

c. 1994

Antonov Aeronautical
Scientific-Technical Complex
Kiew / Kyiv, UA

Die Ingenieure des Flugzeugherstellers Antonov waren nicht nur in der Lage, eines der schwersten Flugzeuge der Geschichte, die An-225 Mriya, zu bauen, sondern entwickelten auch ultraleichte Fahrräder aus Aramid. Nach einem ersten kreuzförmigen Rahmen (Bi 2) stellten Ivan Lypa und Serhii Nytka 1994 das Modell Enei vor, dessen z-förmige Rahmengeometrie entfernt an das Lotus 110 erinnert, sich jedoch durch den Aufbau des Sattelrohrs mit der hochgezogenen Spitze deutlich davon unterscheidet. Das Enei schwang sich rasch zum Erfolgsmodell des ukrainischen Nationalteams auf, war jedoch aufgrund seiner Qualität und des geringen Preises auch für Radrennfahrer und Radrennfahrerinnen anderer Nationen von Interesse.

The engineers at aircraft manufacturer Antonov were not only able to build one of the heaviest airplanes in history, the An-225 Mriya, but also developed one of the lightest bicycles, using Aramid. Initially opting for a cross-frame (Bi 2), Ivan Lypa and Serhii Nytka presented their Enei model, with a z-shaped frame geometry vaguely reminiscent of the Lotus 110, but with a significant difference as regards the saddle tube with its acute angle and tapering shape. The Enei swiftly emerged as the successful model of the Ukrainian national team, but given its quality and low price was also of interest to racing cyclists from other countries.

Ivan Lypa
Serhii Nytka

Antonov Aeronautical
Scientific-Technical Complex
Kiew / Kyiv, UA

Als die Union Cycliste Internationale (UIC) 1997 Rahmen verbot, die nicht auf zwei Dreiecken basierten, sahen sich Ivan Lypa und Serhii Nytka gezwungen, eine neue Rahmenform zu gestalten, um den Sportlern und Sportlerinnen wieder die Teilnahme an den Radrennen zu ermöglichen.

Zunächst entstand ein Übergangsmodell, das ein kleines Dreieck zwischen Sattelrohr und Kettenstrebe aufwies, sodass damit die Forderungen der UCI erfüllt wurden. Doch die Produktion dieser ungewöhnlichen aerodynamischen Rahmenform wurde schnell wieder eingestellt, weshalb nur sehr wenige Exemplare hergestellt wurden. Bereits ein Jahr später erschien das Elin in seiner bekannten Form. Das Übergangsmodell erhielt die Bezeichnung Elin 2, obwohl es eigentlich vor dem späteren, eher traditionell aussehenden, aber bei den Wettbewerben sehr erfolgreichen Elin entstanden ist.

When the Union Cycliste Internationale (UIC) outlawed the frame in 1997 because it was not based on two diamonds, Ivan Lypa and Serhiy Nytka found themselves forced to develop a new frame shape in order to enable athletes to continue to take part in cycle races.

Initially, they built a transitional model with a small triangle between the saddle pin and the rear tube in order to conform with the UCI requirements. However, production of this unusual, aerodynamic frame shape was soon discontinued and only a few units were made. Only one year later, the Elin came out with its well-known shape. The transitional model was named Elin 2, although it actually came before the somewhat traditionally shaped Elin, which was highly successful in races.

Giant Manufacturing Co. Ltd.
Dajia (Taichung), TW

1994 begann Mike Burrows (1943–2022) als Design Consultant für die taiwanesische Firma Giant zu arbeiten, einen der Pioniere in der Herstellung von Fahrradrahmen aus Kohlenstofffasern. Für einen Designer wie ihn, der sowohl erfinderisch als auch praktisch veranlagt war, bot Giant mit seiner effektiven Produktionstechnik die idealen Voraussetzungen. Das Unternehmen verfügt über die Größe und die Ressourcen, um mit Materialien zu arbeiten, die in der Massenproduktion preiswert sind, aber teuer in der Herstellung von Werkzeugformen.

Das erste Produkt dieser Zusammenarbeit war das MCR-Rennrad mit seinem aerodynamischen Rahmen in Karbon-Monocoque-Bauweise, bei dem mehrere von Burrows' Innovationen zum Einsatz kommen, etwa die Einstellvorrichtung für die interne Kabelführung oder die Laufräder mit flachen Aero-Speichen aus spritzgegossenem, karbonverstärktem Nylon. Hinzu kam die Entwicklung eines neuen, besser verstellbaren Vorbaus. Das MCR war zu seiner Zeit eines der aerodynamischsten Rennräder auf dem Markt.

Noch im gleichen Jahr entwarf Burrows das TCR-Rennrad, das mit seinem nach hinten abfallenden Oberrohr die Rahmengeometrie revolutionierte.

In 1994, Mike Burrows (1943–2022) started working as a design consultant for Taiwan's Giant corporation, one of the pioneers in manufacturing bicycle frames from carbon fibers. For a designer like him, who was as inventive as he was practical, Giant with its effective production technologies offered ideal conditions. The company had the size and the resources to work with materials that were cost-effective in mass production, but expensive when it came to making the machine tools.

The first outcome of the collaboration between the two was the MCR road racing bike with its aerodynamic carbon-monocoque frame, which featured several of Burrows' innovations, such as the adjuster for the internal cable guides or the wheels with their flat aero spokes made of injection-mold, carbon-reinforced nylon. Moreover, it incorporated a new handlebar stem that was easier to adjust. In its day, the MCR was one of the most aerodynamic racing bikes on the market.

That same year, Burrows designed the TCR racing bike which featured a top tube that sloped downwards toward the saddle, revolutionizing the geometry of the bicycle frame.

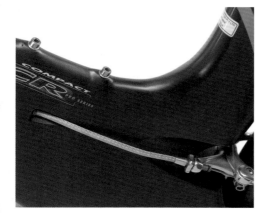

„Wenn Designer und Konstrukteure jemals bessere Fahrräder herstellen wollen, müssen sie auf jegliche Art von Rohren verzichten. Stattdessen müssen sie darüber nachdenken, den Rahmen direkt zu formen, und zwar aus einer Art Verbundwerkstoff oder sogar aus Kunststoff."

"If designers and engineers are ever to produce better bicycles, they have to forget about tubing of any sort. Instead they need to think about forming the frame directly, using some form of composite or even plastic material." [26]

Mike Burrows 2000

Biria GmbH
Neukirch, DE

Das Fahrrad sollte zu einem Vorzeigeprojekt eines der drei größten europäischen Fahrradherstellers werden. Bereits 1992 angekündigt, wurde das Unplugged 1996 vorgestellt, konnte jedoch erst ab 1998 ausgeliefert werden. Von den geplanten 143 Stück wurden nur 17 aufgebaut und verkauft; 10 ungelabelte Rahmensets kamen nach dem Konkurs Birias auf den Markt. Die Details des Aufbaus konnten von den Kunden frei gewählt werden, von einfachen Komponenten bis zu sehr hochwertigen, die in einer goldenen Kette bei der teuersten Variante gipfelte.[25]

Die ungewöhnliche Form verweist auf den ursprünglichen Zweck des Entwurfs. Man wollte demonstrieren, wie vielseitig das Material Karbon im Fahrradbau einsetzbar ist, etwa durch das winkelförmig an den diagonalen Hauptträger angesetzte Tretlager, das extremen Belastungen ausgesetzt ist. Die Laufräder sind einseitig, jeweils gegenüber aufgehängt (Einarmschwinge), jedoch wirken alle Kräfte perfekt mittig. Der Verzicht auf eine Federung ist der minimalistischen Gestaltung geschuldet.

This bicycle was to become a showcase project of one of the three largest European bicycle makers. Announced in 1992, the Unplugged was presented to the public in 1996 but deliveries were not possible until 1998. Of the 143 units planned, only 17 were built and sold; 10 unlabelled frame sets hit the market after Biria had gone bankrupt. Clients were free to choose the details of the bike as built, from simple components through to very high-end versions, culminating in a golden chain for the most expensive one.

The unusual shape alludes to the designers' original intention. They wanted to show how multifaceted carbon was as a material for cycle building, for example with the bottom bracket attached at an angle to the diagonal main struts and thus exposed to extreme strain. The wheels rest on one-side dropouts, the one on the right, the other on the left (single-arm cantilevers), yet all force exerted is concentrated perfectly in the middle. The lack of suspension results from the minimalist design.

BMW AG
München / Munich, DE

Auch vor dem gegenwärtigen E-Bike-Boom hatten viele Automobil- und Motorradhersteller Fahrräder im Programm, allerdings liefen diese häufig unter Accessoires mit entsprechend nachrangiger Wertschätzung. Ausnahmen gab es immer wieder.

Bei BMW widmete man sich seit den 1950er-Jahren dem Thema Fahrrad, aber erst der Mountainbike-Boom der 1990er-Jahre führte zu entsprechenden Neuentwicklungen, da man hier die bereits vorhandene Motorrad-Technologie sinnvoll einsetzen konnte. Für das Super-Tech-Mountainbike verwendete man das Telelever-System, um beim Bremsen das nach vorne Eintauchen des gefederten Vorderrads zu vermindern und so ein Überschlagen zu verhindern. Das System hatte man zwar von HS-Products übernommen, aber durch die Verbindung dieses Systems mit einem eigens entwickelten Klappmechanismus entstand ein vollgefedertes und zugleich klappbares Mountainbike, das modernste Technologie, Sicherheit und Design vereinigt.

Even before the current surge in e-bikes, many automobile and motorbike manufacturers also built bicycles, although these were often simply marketed as accessories and were thus only accorded secondary importance – Peugeot is one of the few exceptions here.

BMW was involved in bicycle making from the 1950s onwards, but it was the mountain bike boom of the 1990s that prompted corresponding new development efforts as now existing motorbike technology could be meaningfully deployed. For the Super-Tech mountain bike, the company relied on its Telelever system to reduce the front wheel, with its suspension, from dropping sharply if the rider braked hard, and thus potentially sending the person head over heels. The system was bought in from HS-Products, but by connecting the system to the folding mechanism developed inhouse at BMW a full-suspension and also folding mountain bike arose, combining ultra-modern technology, safety, and design.

Richard Sapper
Francis Ferrain

Zoombike

1998/2000

Elettromontaggi S.r.l.
Massa Martana, IT

Nach langer Entwicklungsarbeit wurde das Zoombike 1998 auf der Internationalen Automobil-Ausstellung (IAA) in Frankfurt der Öffentlichkeit vorgestellt und ab 2000 in 60 Exemplaren produziert. Es lässt sich im Handumdrehen zu einem länglichen Paket zusammenfalten und mit einem einzigen Knopfdruck in zwei Teile zerlegen, sodass es bequem transportiert werden kann, sei es in öffentlichen Verkehrsmitteln oder in privaten Fahrzeugen. Alle mechanischen Teile, einschließlich der Antriebskette und der Dreigang-Kettenschaltung, sitzen ebenso im Zentralrohr wie das Vorderlicht samt Akku. Um seinen Entwurf umzusetzen, griff Richard Sapper (1932–2015) auf Techniken der Luft- und Raumfahrtindustrie zurück: Die Rahmenstruktur besteht aus stranggepressten, hochfesten Aluminiumprofilen mit sehr dünnen Wandungen; in die Enden dieser Profile sind Aluminium-Druckguss-Verbindungen geklebt, die eine extrem steife Struktur mit minimalen Toleranzen bilden. Die sehr kleinen Raddurchmesser werden durch eine spezielle, aus dem Automobilbau stammende Technik der Radaufhängung möglich.

After a long development lead-time, the Zoombike went on public display for the first time in 1998 at the International Automobile Fair (IAA) in Frankfurt, and 60 units were rolled out from 2000 onwards. At the flick of a wrist, it can be folded to form a lengthwise package and at the press of a button broken down into two parts for ease of transportation, be it on public transport or in private vehicles.

All the mechanical parts, including the drive chain and the three-speed derailleur, are located in the central tube, as is the front light and battery. To realize his design, Richard Sapper (1932–2015) relied on aerospace technology: The frame was made of extruded, high-tensile aluminum profiles with very thin walls; into the ends of these profiles, diecast aluminum connections are glued that ensure an extremely rigid structure with minimal tolerances. The very small wheel diameters are possible thanks to a special wheel suspension method adopted from automobile making.

„Das Zoombike ist eine große technische Errungenschaft und das Ergebnis jahrelanger Arbeit, die bis zu meinem ersten Klapprad aus dem Jahr 1979 zurückreicht. Seitdem hatte ich darüber nachgedacht, wie ein Faltrad, das in Verbindung mit Bussen und Bahnen genutzt wird, eine Alternative zum Auto darstellen und die verstopften europäischen Städte wie Mailand entlasten könnte."
"The Zoombike is a great technical achievement, and the result of many years of work, going back to the first folding bike I designed in 1979. Since then I had been considering how a folding bike, used in conjunction with buses and trains, could offer a transportation alternative to the automobile, and some relief to congested European cities like Milan." [27]

Richard Sapper, 2014

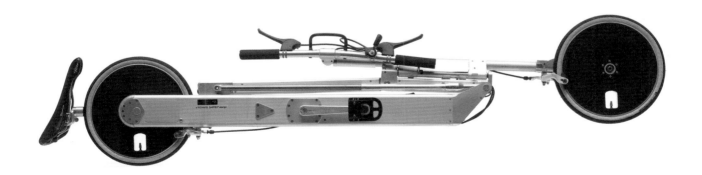

B. J. O'Hare RocketWing 1998
M. G. Allsop / J. Allsop

Softride Inc.
Bellingham, USA

Basierend auf dem Modell Classic TT von 1996, dem ersten Rennrad von Softride mit Aluminiumrahmen, entstand das Modell RocketWing. Dafür wurde das vor allem bei Ultramarathon- und Triathlonfahrern beliebte Sitz-Federungs-System, das die Brüder James (Jim) und Michael G. Allsop 1989 zusammen mit David Calopp entwickelt hatten, nicht nur angepasst, sondern völlig neu gedacht. Sie setzten ein nicht schwingendes Aluminiumrohr als Sattelschwinge ein und montierten den neuen Federungsmechanismus am Übergang zum Rahmen. Michael G. Allsop ließ sich die zusammen mit Brady J. O'Hare ausgearbeitete Idee 1998 patentieren. Durch das Fehlen der Sitzstreben und die lange Sattelschwinge verändert sich die Rahmenform deutlich. Damit erfolgte nicht nur eine Reduzierung des Luftwiderstands, sondern zugleich auch eine Verbesserung des Fahrkomforts.

The RocketWing was based on the 1996 Classic TT model – the first Softride racing bike with an aluminum frame. To this end, the seat suspension system developed by brothers James (Jim) and Michael G. Allsop and David Calopp in 1989, which was very popular with ultramarathon and triathlon competitors, was not only adapted but completely reengineered. The brothers now opted for a non-oscillating aluminum tube for the saddle cantilever and mounted the new suspension mechanism at the transition to the frame. In 1998, Michael G. Allsop applied for a patent for the system, which he had elaborated together with Brady J. O'Hare. The new frame's shape was very different owing to the absence of the seat pin and the long saddle cantilever, which not only reduced drag but also improved riding comfort.

Trek Bicycle Corporation
Waterloo (Wisconsin), USA

Als ein früher Anwender der Kohlefasertechnologie entwickelte Trek ab 1991 das sogenannte OCLV-Verfahren (Optimum Compaction, Low Void). 1992 kamen die ersten in dieser Technologie produzierten Vollkarbon-Rahmen auf den Markt, die das Gewicht reduzierten und außerdem für ein hohes Maß an Festigkeit und Steifigkeit sorgten. Bei der computergestützten Gestaltung setzte man auf die Finite-Element-Analyse, um zu berechnen, wie unterschiedliche Rohr- und Rahmenformen auf unterschiedliche Belastungen reagieren. Die aerodynamischen Eigenschaften des Entwurfs wurden mit Strömungssimulationen getestet.

Die typischen Y-förmigen Rahmen fanden 1995 erstmals bei Mountainbikes Verwendung. In Abwandlung davon entstand kurz danach der Y-Foil-Rahmen, bei dem die ursprüngliche Grundform subtil weiterentwickelt wurde. Charakteristisch sind dabei die fehlende Sattelstrebe und das freitragende Oberrohr, das eine gewisse Federung des Sattels ermöglicht.

As an early user of carbon fiber technology, from 1991 onwards Trek advanced its so-called OCLV tubes (Optimum Compaction, Low Void). In 1992, the first fully carbon frame produced using this technology hit the market – the process lowered frame weight while nevertheless guaranteeing great rigidity and stiffness. The computer-aided design relied on finite-element analysis in order to calculate how the different tube and frame shapes responded to different types of strain, and the design's aerodynamic properties were tested in the wind-tunnel simulations.

The typical Y-shaped frames were first utilized in 1995 for mountain bikes. In a modification of them, a little later Trek brought out its Y-Foil frame that is a subtle advance on the original shape. It is characterized by not needing a saddle stay and an upper tube secured at only end that offers a degree of spring for the saddle.

Biomega ApS
Hellerup, DK

Das 1998 gegründete dänische Start-up-Unternehmen Biomega hatte sich das Ziel gesetzt, das Fahrrad als Lifestyle-Objekt zu etablieren, und beauftragte dazu den australischen Designer Marc Newson (*1963). Sein Entwurf basiert auf dem Einsatz einer aus dem Flugzeugbau bekannten Herstellungstechnologie für Aluminium, dem Superforming-Verfahren. Der in zwei Hälften gefertigte Rahmen sollte verklebt und nicht geschweißt werden, da dies einfacher und schneller ging und so auch Schweißnähte vermieden werden konnten.

Das Fahrrad zeichnet sich durch eine reduzierte, pure Form aus, charakterisiert durch den markanten Aluminiumrahmen in Z-Form, der die Körperspannung eines Sprinters im Startblock assoziiert. Zudem nimmt der Rahmen nicht nur im Innern alle Kabel für Bremsen und Schaltung auf, sondern verbindet sämtliche Fahrradbestandteile. Da der Rahmen mit einer Leuchtfarbe lackiert ist, erscheint er bei Tageslicht weiß, leuchtet im Dunkeln jedoch neongrün.

Founded in 1998, Danish start-up Biomega's objective was to establish bicycles as a lifestyle object, and to this end it commissioned Australian designer Marc Newson (born 1963). His idea is based on the use of a manufacturing technology for aluminum developed by the aerospace industry, known as super-forming. Made in two parts, the frame was to be glued rather than welded together, as that was simpler and faster and avoided creating any weld seams.

The bicycle stands out for its reduced, pure shape, characterized by the striking z-shaped aluminum frame that conjures up associations of a sprinter tensed up in the blocks waiting for the starting gun. Moreover, all the brake and gear cables were housed inside the frame, which also connects all the elements of the bike. Since the frame was coated with a luminous paint, it looks white during the day, but glows neon-green in the dark.

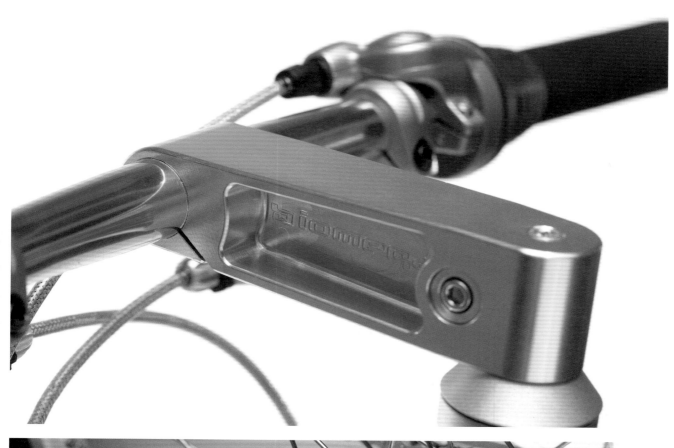

„Biomega wollte ein urbanes Fahrrad, also habe ich mich umgesehen, wie ich etwas Besonderes machen könnte. Zu dieser Zeit arbeitete ich an einem Flugzeug und dachte viel über die Luftfahrtindustrie nach. Ich hatte über dieses unglaubliche neue englische Verfahren zur Herstellung von Aluminium gelesen, das Superforming. Es ist eine erstaunliche Technologie, die es mir ermöglichte, ein Fahrrad ohne Schweißnähte zu bauen und all den überflüssigen Mist, der normalerweise den Rahmen verunstaltet, darin zu verstauen."

"Biomega wanted an urban bike, so I set about looking around to see how I could do something distinctive. I was working on the jet at the time, and was thinking a lot about the aviation industry. I'd read about this incredible new English process of fabricating aluminum, called Super-forming. It's an amazing technology and enabled me to build a bike with no welds and all the extraneous shit that usually clutters up the frame tucked inside it." [28]

Marc Newson 2002

Biomega ApS
Hellerup, DK

Die ungewöhnliche Rahmenform entspricht den biomorphen Designprinzipien Ross Lovegroves. Ursprünglich in Aluminium in der gleichen Superforming-Technologie wie Marc Newsons MN02-Rahmen konzipiert, entwickelte Lovegrove wenig später daraus einen leichten Karbon-Monocoquerahmen.

Das längsovale Loch im vorderen Drittel ist nicht nur Lovegroves ästhetischen Vorstellungen geschuldet, sondern hat auch rein funktionale Gründe: Gewichtsersparnis und die Möglichkeit für eine Aufhängung des Fahrrads als flache Wandskulptur. Zudem können Pedale und Lenker eingeklappt werden, sodass das Rad leicht über enge Treppenhäuser in die eigene Wohnung transportiert werden kann. Mit dem in einem hermetisch abgedichteten, ölgefüllten Gehäuse untergebrachten Kardanantrieb lassen sich schmutzige Ketten und fettverschmierte Beine vermeiden.

The unusual frame shape accords with Ross Lovegrove's biomorphic design principles. Originally intended to be made in aluminum using the same super-forming technology as Marc Newson's MN02 frame, a little later Lovegrove advanced the idea to create a light carbon monocoque frame.

The longitudinal oval cut-out in the forward third derives not only from Lovegrove's aesthetic notions, but also has purely functional purposes. It saves weight and enables you to hang the bike on the wall as a flat sculpture. Moreover, the pedals and handlebars can be folded so that the bicycle can be easily carried up tight stairwells to the owner's apartment. The shaft drive tucked away in the hermetically sealed, oil-filled casing makes dirty chains and grease-tattooed legs a thing of the past.

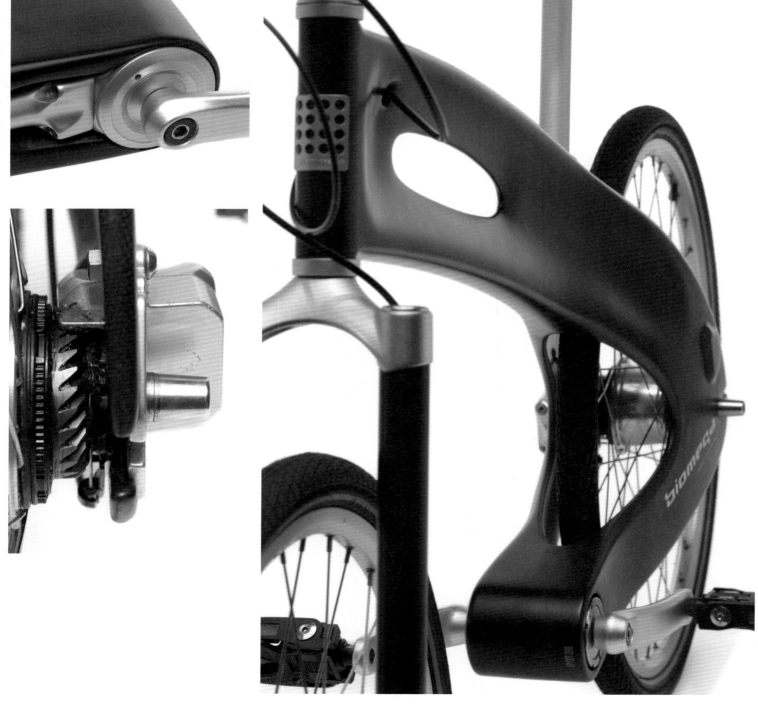

„Das LDN- oder BIOLOVE-Fahrrad steht für eine ganz neue Geometrie, was das durch die Karbonfasern optimierte Verhältnis von Steifigkeit und Gewicht angeht. Die gegenläufige Bewegung, die vom Lenker zurück zur hinteren Nabe und dann freitragend nach vorne zu den Pedalen führt, erzeugt eine geschlechtslose Architektur mit einem Volumen, das die zukünftige Aufnahme von wiederaufladbaren Batterien in den Rahmen vorwegnimmt. Das Loch dient dazu, überflüssiges Material zu vermeiden, das Design leichter zu machen und die Aufhängung an der Wand zu erleichtern, um seine Präsenz über ein rein funktionales Objekt hinaus zu zelebrieren, was eine Grundbedingung für alle meine Arbeiten ist."

"The LDN or BIOLOVE bicycle represents a very new geometry in the way that the stiffness to weight ratio of carbon fibre can provide. The reverse logic of running from the handlebar back to the rear hub then cantilevering forward to the pedals generates a genderless architecture of a volume that anticipated the frames future inclusion of rechargeable batteries. The hole is there to remove extraneous material, lighten the design and facilitate its hanging on a wall, celebrating its presence beyond a purely functional object which is a condition of all my work." [29]

Ross Lovegrove 2022

UBC GmbH
Murr, DE

Der Produktdesigner Christian Zanzotti (*1985) konnte und sollte ohne Rücksicht auf technische Machbarkeit und Marketing ein Fahrrad entwickeln, das die Kompetenz des Auftraggebers in Hinblick auf Design, Forschung und Entwicklung sowie Fertigung eindrucksvoll zur Schau stellt.

Der Rahmen besteht nicht wie bei den meisten Karbonfahrrädern aus Standard-Karbonfasern, sondern aus der für die Herstellung von Monocoque-Chassis in der Formel 1 verwendeten hochfesten T1000-Kohlefaser.

Charakteristisch für den Entwurf sind die in der Seitenansicht sehr dünn wirkenden Ober- und Unterrohre, die dem Fahrrad eine optische Leichtigkeit verleihen und mit den wuchtigen Laufrädern kontrastieren. Riemenantrieb und CNC-gefräste Ausfallenden mit integrierten Riemenspannern vervollständigen die detaillierte Ausarbeitung dieses Fahrrads, das mit dem für die Fertigung herausfordernden Knick im Oberrohr zu den Vorreitern der heute üblichen Rahmengeometrie gehört.

Das für verschiedene Ausführungen (Singlespeed, Pedelec und Fixie) konzipierte Fahrrad sollte 25.000 Euro kosten, ging jedoch nicht in Serie.

The brief given to product designer Christian Zanzotti (*1985) was to develop a bicycle that impressively visualized the manufacturer's expertise in design, R&D, and manufacturing – and he did not need to concern himself with the technical feasibility and marketing of the final result.

Unlike customary carbon bicycles, the frame was not made of standard carbon fibers but of high-tensile T1000 carbon fiber as is used to make the monocoque chassis of Grand Prix racing cars.

The design stands out for what look like very thin upper and lower tubes when seen side-on and which lend the bicycle a sense of visual lightness and contrast with the hefty wheel. A belt drive and CNC-milled dropout with an integrated belt tensioner round out the detailed concept underlying the bike which, with the bend in the upper tube (a real challenge for the makers) was one of the pioneers of the frame geometry customary today.

The bicycle was designed for different versions (single-speed, pedelec, and fixed gear) and was expected to cost 25,000 Euros, but never went into series production.

„Außergewöhnlich filigrane Fügestellen, ungewöhnlich dünne Rohrquerschnitte und eine markante Oberrohrsilhouette prägen den unverkennbaren Charakter dieses in limitierter Serie hergestellten Stadtfahrrades".[30]

"Extraordinarily refined tube connections, unusually thin tube cross sections, and a striking upper tube silhouette combine to create the unmistakable appearance of this urban fixed-gear bicycle, brought out as a limited series."

Christian Zanzotti 2022

Keim Cycles
Savonnière (Indre-et-Loire), FR

Um das Potenzial des Naturmaterials Holz optimal zu nutzen, entwickelten die französische Designerin Paule Guérin und ihr Partner, der deutsche Tischler Till Breitfuss, diesen ungewöhnlichen Rahmen in Form eines asymmetrischen Fünfecks. Gebaut wird der Rahmen aus 24 Lagen Eschenholz, die speziell ausgerichtet und vakuumgeschichtet mit einem biobasierten Hochleistungsharz verleimt werden – ein Verfahren, wie es ganz ähnlich bei der Fertigung von Hockeyschlägern oder Skiern eingesetzt wird.

Steuerrohr, Vorbau, Lenker und Gabel bestehen dagegen aus Karbon. Die Rahmenform, die Kombination des Naturmaterials Holz mit dem modernen Hightech-Material Karbon, der nahtlose Übergang des hölzernen Rahmens in das Steuerrohr bzw. in den Vorbau aus Karbon verleihen dem Fahrrad sein ungewöhnliches Aussehen, das durch den Verzicht auf ein Sattelrohr – der Sattel sitzt direkt auf dem Oberrohr auf – noch gesteigert wird. Eine Höhenverstellung ist nicht notwendig, da die auf 20 Stück begrenzte Edition in Handarbeit und auf Maß erfolgte.

In order to make optimal use of the potential of wood as a natural material, French designer Paule Guérin and her partner, German cabinetmaker Till Breitfuss, created this unusual frame in the shape of an asymmetrical pentagon. The frame is made of 24 layers of ash that are specially aligned and vacuum bonded using a biobased high-performance resin – a method very similar to that used to make hockey sticks and skis.

By contrast, the front tube, stem, handlebars, and forks are made of carbon. The frame shape, the combination of wood as a natural material with modern high-tech carbon, and the seamless transition from the wooden frame to the front tube and the stem, both of which are carbon, lend the bicycle an unusual appearance, one emphasized by the absence of a saddle pin – the saddle is mounted direct on the top tube. No height adjustment of the saddle is necessary as the Arvak was produced in an edition limited to 20 units, each handmade and customized to the owner.

Nick Foley/Jacob Bouchard/Michael Liu

Jump, Mod. 5.6

2018

Progear China Co. Ltd. für Jump
San Francisco, USA

Mit der Entwicklung von E-Bikes, die stationsunabhängig über eine App mietbar sind, schlug Jump ein neues Kapitel im Bereich des Sharing-Systems auf. Durch die Verlegung der Technologien – GPS, Zahlungssystem, Kundenschnittstelle – auf das Fahrrad selbst fallen die kostspieligen Stationen weg.

Für das Design entstehen dadurch ganz spezifische Herausforderungen: Die große Beanspruchung infolge der gemeinsamen Nutzung durch unterschiedliche Menschen und von Wettereinflüssen erfordert nicht nur eine gesteigerte Robustheit, sondern auch ein hohes Maß an Anpassungsfähigkeit. So entstand ein Rahmen mit höherem Lenker, der sich nur leicht zum Benutzer hin wölbt und so eine etwas aufrechtere Haltung ermöglicht, wodurch er für die meisten Körpergrößen einigermaßen bequem ist. Außerdem wurde der niedrige Rahmen so gebaut, dass er eine lange, verstellbare Sattelstütze aufnehmen kann. Der tiefe Einstieg, aber auch die Farbigkeit sind genderneutral.

When Jump developed its station-free e-bike for app-based hiring, it started a new chapter in the history of the bike-sharing system. Locating the technologies – GPS, payment system, customer interface – inside the bicycle meant there was no need for expensive bike stations.

This spelled very specific challenges for the design: Hefty wear-and-tear owing to the bike's shared use by different people and its exposure to the elements called not only for exceptional robustness, but also for a high degree of adaptability. The result was a frame with higher handlebars that curve slightly toward the user to allow for a more upright cycling posture, making it more or less comfortable for most body sizes. Moreover, the low frame was built such that it could house a long, adjustable saddle pin. The low frame and the color are both destined to be gender-neutral.

„Als wir mit dem Designprozess für das JUMP-Fahrrad begannen, wusste jeder in der Fahrradindustrie, dass E-Bikes das Potenzial haben, die Fahrradbewegung zu revolutionieren, aber ein großartiges E-Bike allein löst nicht die allgemeinen Hindernisse für das Fahrradfahren: Kosten, Lagerung, Bequemlichkeit, körperliche Fähigkeiten und persönliche Sicherheit. Diese Faktoren leiteten unseren Designprozess und die Möglichkeit, Technologie und Design so zu kombinieren, dass das Radfahren für mehr Menschen einfacher und angenehmer wird."

"When we started the JUMP bike design process, everyone in the bicycle manufacturing industry knew that e-bikes had the potential to revolutionize the bike movement, but a great e-bike alone doesn't holistically address the common barriers to biking: cost, storage, convenience, physical ability, and personal safety. These factors guided our design process and this powerful opportunity to bring together technology and design in a way that makes biking fundamentally easier and more enjoyable for more people." [31]

Nick Foley 2018

Vässla AB
Stockholm, SE

Mit einem ungewöhnlichen Ansatz versucht das junge Stockholmer Unternehmen Vässla, die Verkehrsprobleme unserer Städte anzugehen. Seit 2021 bietet das Unternehmen seine umweltfreundlichen E-Scooter und E-Bikes im Abo-Modell an. Man kann die hochwertigen Fahrzeuge für eine bestimmte Zeit mieten, später aber auch kaufen. Außerdem lassen sie sich über IoT-Technologie vernetzen. Das Abonnement beinhaltet die Lieferung des fahrbereiten Fahrzeugs sowie Helm, Schließfach, Versicherung, Wartung und Service.

Bei der Gestaltung eines auf diese Weise genutzten E-Bikes spielten verschiedene Aspekte eine wichtige Rolle: zum einen eine gewisse Vielseitigkeit und Robustheit bei gleichzeitiger funktionaler und ästhetischer Akzeptanz. Der Kreuzrahmen ermöglicht den niedrigen Einstieg und damit die Nutzung für alle Geschlechter und Größen, zugleich sind darin alle technischen Komponenten integriert. Das geringe Gewicht (Karbongabel) und die besondere Ergonomie des klar und zurückhaltend gestalteten E-Bikes sorgen für den entsprechenden Fahrkomfort.

The young Stockholm-based company Vässla has taken an extraordinary approach to tackling the transportation problems in our cities. Since 2021, the company has been offering its eco-friendly e-scooters and e-bikes on subscription. The high-grade vehicles can be rented for a specific period and purchased later on. Moreover, they can be networked using IoT technology. The subscription includes delivery of the ready-to-go vehicle as well as a helmet, locker, insurance, maintenance, and servicing.

Various aspects play a key role in the design of an e-bike to be used in this way: first, a degree of versatility and robustness, and at the same time functional and aesthetic acceptance. The cross frame has a low entry point, making the bike suitable for use by riders of any gender and size, and also integrates all the technical components. The low weight (carbon forks) and special ergonomics of the e-bike with its clear and restrained design come good in terms of real cycling comfort.

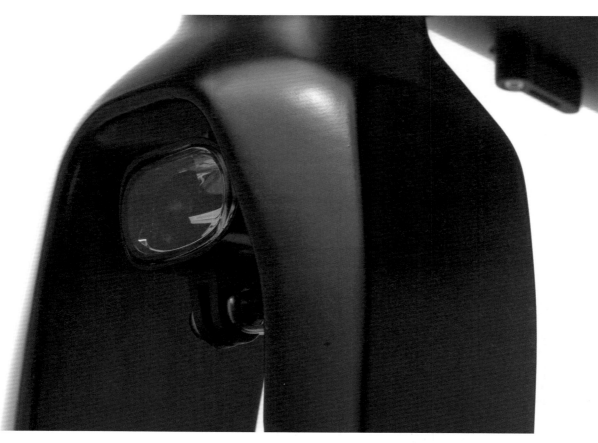

„Die Auslegung auf eine rein urbane
Anwendung und volle Konnektivität
resultieren beim Vässla Pedal zu einem
neuen Archetyp, getrieben von radikaler
Simplifizierung des Rahmens und Kom-
ponentenverzicht"
"Vässla Pedal is designed for purely
urban use and full connectivity, which
has resulted in a new archetype inspired by a radical simplification of the
frame and a corresponding reduction
in components." [32]

Christian Zanzotti 2022

Pierpaolo Ruttico, Francisco Martins
Carabetta, Federico Bordoni, Salvatore Urso

eXgineering
Manno, CH

Die 3D-Drucktechnik hat schon seit Längerem Einzug in die Fahrradherstellung gehalten, jedoch mehr im experimentellen Bereich als in der Serienproduktion. 2022 entstand für Geschwindigkeitsrekordversuche das angeblich erste komplett 3D-gedruckte Rennrad, das Pinarello Bolide F HR 3D. Hinter dem New01bike verbirgt sich dagegen ein ganz anderer Ansatz, nicht nur produktionstechnisch, sondern auch im Hinblick auf Ästhetik, Nutzerfreundlichkeit und Nachhaltigkeit: Der Rahmen ist transparent, besteht aus recyceltem Polykarbonat und kann selbst wieder recycelt werden. Mithilfe von digitalen Technologien, computergestütztem Design und dem Einsatz entsprechender Materialien lässt sich ein individuell anpassbares Fahrrad schnell, preiswert und in Serie produzieren, ohne den Nachhaltigkeitsaspekt zu vernachlässigen. Dieser erste zu 100 Prozent aus recyceltem Polykarbonat mit einem 3D-Drucker hergestellte Fahrradrahmen unterstützt einerseits den Prozess der Individualisierung und steht andererseits für die Kreislaufwirtschaft, beides ist unabdingbar für eine bessere Zukunft.

For some time now, 3D printing technology has made an entry into bicycle manufacture, albeit more in the experimental field than in mass production. In 2022, the purportedly first completely 3D-printed racing or time trial bike was made for the hour-world-record attempt, the Pinarello Bolide F HR 3D. Behind the New01bike is a quite different approach, however, not only in terms of production technology but also as regards aesthetics, user friendliness, and sustainability: The frame is translucent, made of recycled polycarbonate, and can itself be recycled. Thanks to digital technologies, computer-aided design, and the use of corresponding materials, an individually adjustable bicycle can thus be made swiftly, cheaply, and in series without neglect of the aspect of sustainability. It is the very first bicycle frame to be made completely of recycled polycarbonate using a 3D printer and promotes not only the process of individual customization but also the circular economy – both of which are imperative for a better future.

„Maßgeschneiderte ergonomische Fahrräder sind nicht nur kostspielig und langsam in der Herstellung, sondern auch sehr schwierig in der Massenproduktion, da sie auf bestimmte Bedürfnisse und Verwendungszwecke zugeschnitten sind. Auf der anderen Seite sind seriengefertigte Fahrräder selten so vielseitig, dass sie sich an unterschiedliche Körperproportionen und -maße der Benutzer anpassen, denn sie sind für Standardbenutzer entstanden. New01bike wurde entwickelt, um diese Lücke zu schließen und ein maßgeschneidertes Fahrrad erschwinglich, schnell und einfach in Massenproduktion und Recycling zu machen.“

"Custom ergonomic bikes are not only costly and slow to manufacture but also very difficult to mass-produce, since they are tailored for particular needs and usages. On the other hand, mass-serialized bikes are seldom so versatile that they accommodate different user body proportions and measures, as they are made for the 'standard user'. New01bike was created to fill this gap, make a custom bike affordable, fast, and easy to mass-produce and recycle." [33]

Indexlab 2022

1 Zitiert nach Hans-Erhard Lessing u. Tony Hadland, Evolution des Fahrrads. Berlin/Heidelberg 2021 (Übersetzung der engl. Edition: Tony Hadland and Hans-Erhard Lessing, Bicycle Design. An Illustrated History. Cambridge, Massachusetts 2014), 14.
2 Zitiert nach Jacques Seray, Deux roues. La véritable histoire du vélo. Rodez 1988, 101. Vgl. auch Lessing/Hadland 2021 (wie Anm. 1), 93.
3 Verbesserungen der Gestelle und Räder für Vélocipède und andere Wägen, Österreichisches Privilegium No 696, Cl. XX/254, 16.6.1878, zitiert nach Walter Ulreich, Bicycles of Josef Erlach and Valentin Wiegele, in: Cycle History, 10. Proceedings, 10th International Cycling History Conference, Nijmwegen 1999, San Francisco 2000, 48, 55 Anm. 6 (dt. Text nach Zita Breu, Konservierung, Restaurierung und Hist[orische] Dokumentation einer Muskelkraftmaschine von 1878. Diplomarbeit, Hochschule für angewandte Kunst. Wien 1987, 90).
4 Kat. Eagle Bicycles. The Eagle Bicycle Mfg. Co. Stamford 1891, 7.
5 Zitiert nach Lessing/Hadland 2021 (wie Anm. 1), 198.
6 Zitiert nach Robert Cobcroft, American Wood Bicycle Components 1896–1897, 15 June 2012, Bikes, Cycling History, https://veloaficionado.com/blog/american-wood-bicycle-components-1896-1897 (13.9.2022).
7 Zitiert nach Oswald Wieser, Grundner & Lemisch. Bambusfahrräder in die Zukunft geholt. Purkersdorf 2019, 22.
8 RadMarkt Nr. 2364, 2.
9 Vorwort im Katalog von 1946; einsehbar unter: https://k-i-n-g.ch/de/velokataloge-schweiz (13.9.2022).
10 Zitiert nach Tony Hadland, The F-Frame Moultons. Zürich 2016, VII (Reprint Tony Hadland, The Moulton bicycle, 1980).
11 www.speedbicycles.ch/interview/fritz_fleck/index.html (27.8.2022).
12 http://swingbiker.de/bilder/20100622swingbike-artikel-gelnhauser-neue-zeitung.jpg (27.8.2022).
13 Albrecht Bangert, Colani. Das Gesamtwerk. Schopfheim 2004, 262.
14 www.fendt.de/die_fahrradbauer.htm (27.8.2022).
15 Interview mit Odo Klose, BIKE BILD, Sept. 17, 2018 (12.6.2022).
16 www.velonews.com/culture/viva-italia-antonio-colombo-industry-leader-and-art-collector/ (13.9.2022).
17 E-mail vom 19.8.2022.
18 https://encycloduvelo.fr/sabliere-andre/ (12.9.2022).
19 Lessing/Hadland 2021 (wie Anm. 1), 435.
20 Rose Etherington, Interview: Strida bike designer Mark Sanders www.dezeen.com/2008/02/03/interview-strida-bike-designer-mark-sanders/(3.8.2022).
21 Ron George, The 8 Second Bicycle, January 17, 2009, http://cozybeehive.blogspot.com/2009/01/8-second-bicycle.html (14.09.2022).
22 Harald Schaale in einem Artikel von Günter Klein, Das Staatsgeheimnis des deutschen Sports, Merkur, 3.2.2018, https://www.merkur.de/sport/mehr-sport/fes-staatsgeheimnis-deutschen-sports-9581301.html (13.9.2022).
23 Zitiert nach Simon Smythe, For the love of Lotus: The story behind the iconic Lotus type 110 bike. Cycling weekly, 25.10.2017, www.cyclingweekly.com/news/product-news/for-the-love-of-lotus-the-story-behind-the-iconic-lotus-type-110-bike-356243 (13.9.2022).
24 Ciclismo 30.11.2005, https://www.ciclismo.it/c4-italiano-al-100-1-c4 (10.9.2022).
25 https://de.wikipedia.org/wiki/Biria_unplugged (13.9.2022).
26 Mike Burrows, Bicycle Design. London 2000, 91.
27 Jonathan Olivares, Richard Sapper. London & New York 2016, 72.
28 Alice Rawsthorn, Marc Newson. London 2002, 16.
29 E-mail vom 29.6.2022.
30 E-mail vom 29.9.2022.
31 https://designawards.core77.com/Transportation/74357/BIKE-SHARE-ELECTRIFIED (13.9.2022).
32 E-mail vom 29.6.2022
33 https://www.3d-grenzenlos.de/magazin/3d-objekte/indexlab-gimac-polycarbonat-3d-druck-fahrradrahmen-27879423/ (13.9.2022).

1 Quoted from Hans-Erhard Lessing & Tony Hadland, Evolution des Fahrrads, (Berlin & Heidelberg, 2021), 14 (trans.).
2 Quoted from Jacques Seray, Deux roues. La véritable histoire du vélo, (Rodez, 1988), 101 (trans.). See also Lessing & Hadland 2021 (see note 1), 93.
3 Verbesserungen der Gestelle und Räder für Vélocipède und andere Wägen, Österreichisches Privilegium No. 696, Cl. XX/254, June 16, 1878, quoted from Walter Ulreich, "Bicycles of Josef Erlach and Valentin Wiegele," in: Cycle History, 10. Proceedings, 10th International Cycling History Conference, Nijmwegen, 1999, San Francisco, 2000, 48, 55, note 6.
4 Cat. Eagle Bicycles, The Eagle Bicycle Mfg. Co., (Stamford, 1891), 7.
5 Quoted from Lessing & Hadland 2021 (see note 1), 198 (trans.).
6 Quoted from Robert Cobcroft, "American Wood Bicycle Components 1896–1897," June 15, 2012, Bikes, Cycling History, https://veloaficionado.com/blog/american-wood-bicycle-components-1896-1897 (last retrieved Sept. 13, 2022).
7 Quoted from Oswald Wieser, Grundner & Lemisch. Bambusfahrräder in die Zukunft geholt, (Purkersdorf, 2019), 22 (trans.).
8 RadMarkt, no. 2364, 2 (trans.).
9 Preface to the 1946 catalog (trans.); accessible at https://k-i-n-g.ch/de/velokataloge-schweiz (last retrieved Sept. 13, 2022).
10 Quoted from Tony Hadland, The F-Frame Moultons, (Zurich, 2016), p. VII (Reprint of Tony Hadland, The Moulton bicycle, 1980).
11 www.speedbicycles.ch/interview/fritz_fleck/index.html (last retrieved Aug. 27, 2022).
12 http://swingbiker.de/bilder/20100622swingbike-artikel-gelnhauser-neue-zeitung.jpg (trans.) (last retrieved Aug. 27, 2022).
13 Albrecht Bangert, Colani. Das Gesamtwerk. Schopfheim 2004, 262.
14 www.fendt.de/die_fahrradbauer.htm (trans.) (last retrieved Aug. 27, 2022).
15 Interview with Odo Klose, BIKE BILD, Sept. 17, 2018 (trans.) (last retrieved June 12, 2022).
16 www.velonews.com/culture/viva-italia-antonio-colombo-industry-leader-and-art-collector/ (last retrieved Sept. 13, 2022).
17 Email of August 19, 2022 (trans.).
18 https://encycloduvelo.fr/sabliere-andre/ (trans.) (last retrieved Sept. 12, 2022).
19 Lessing & Hadland 2021 (see note 1), 435.
20 Rose Etherington, Interview: Strida bike designer Mark Sanders, www.dezeen.com/2008/02/03/interview-strida-bike-designer-mark-sanders/(last retrieved August 3, 2022).
21 Ron George, The 8 Second Bicycle, January 17, 2009, http://cozybeehive.blogspot.com/2009/01/8-second-bicycle.html (last retrieved Sept. 14, 2022).
22 Harald Schaale in an article by Günter Klein, "Das Staatsgeheimnis des deutschen Sports," in: Merkur, Feb. 3, 2018, https://www.merkur.de/sport/mehr-sport/fes-staatsgeheimnis-deutschen-sports-9581301.html (last retrieved Sept. 13, 2022).
23 Quoted from Simon Smythe, "For the love of Lotus: The story behind the iconic Lotus type 110 bike," in: Cycling Weekly, Oct. 25, 2017, https://www.cyclingweekly.com/news/product-news/for-the-love-of-lotus-the-story-behind-the-iconic-lotus-type-110-bike-356243 (last retrieved Sept. 13, 2022).
24 Ciclismo, Nov. 30, 2005, https://www.ciclismo.it/c4-italiano-al-100-1-c4 (last retrieved Sept. 10, 2022).
25 https://de.wikipedia.org/wiki/Biria_unplugged (last retrieved Sept. 13, 2022).
26 Mike Burrows, Bicycle Design, (London, 2000), 91.
27 Jonathan Olivares, Richard Sapper, (London & New York, 2016), 72.
28 Alice Rawsthorn, Marc Newson, (London, 2002), 16.
29 Email of June 29, 2022.
30 Email of Sept. 29, 2022.
31 https://designawards.core77.com/Transportation/74357/BIKE-SHARE-ELECTRIFIED (last retrieved Sept. 13, 2022).
32 Email of June 29, 2022.
33 https://www.3d-grenzenlos.de/magazin/3d-objekte/indexlab-gimac-polycarbonat-3d-druck-fahrradrahmen-27879423/ (last retrieved Sept. 13, 2022).

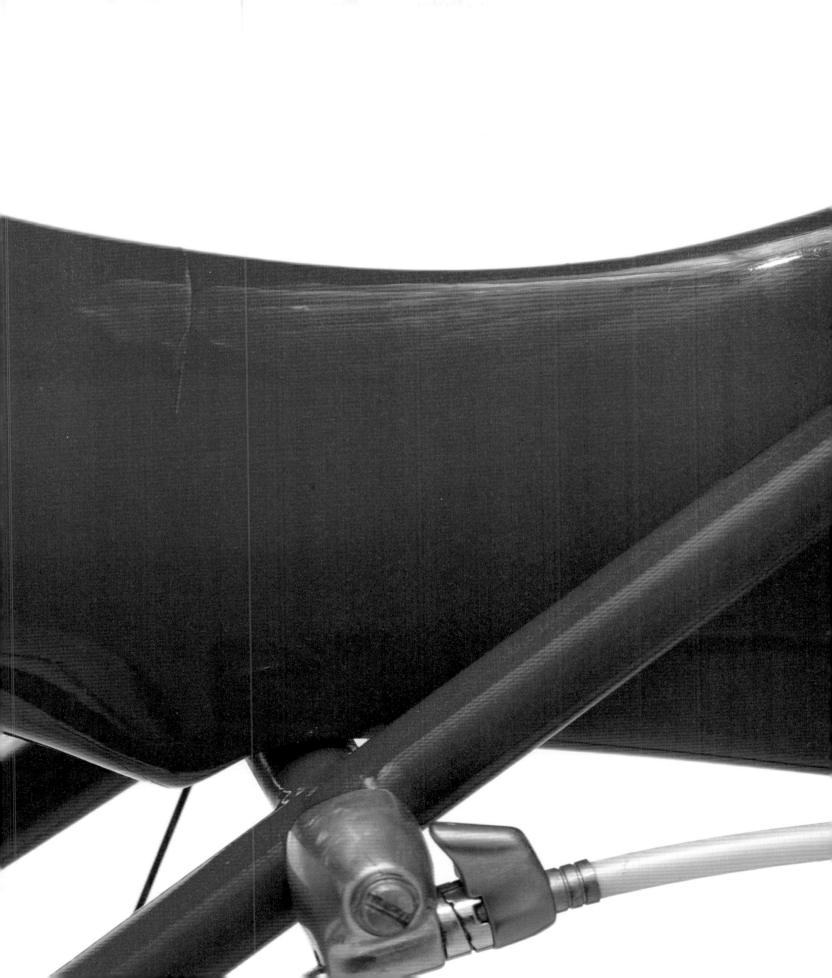

Katalog Catalog

01   054

Karl Friedrich Drais

Laufmaschine
Running Machine

Laufmaschine, 1817 (Nachbau)
Entwurf: Karl Friedrich Drais (1785–1851)
Hersteller: Johann Frey, Stellmacher in
Mannheim (Nachbau Alfred Baltus,
Solingen, c. 2011), Deutschland
Rahmen: Holz (Esche, Nachbau: Buche,
Eiche)
Laufräder: 27 Zoll, eisenbereifte
Wagnerräder
Gewicht: 22,3 kg
Deutsches Fahrradmuseum, Bad Brückenau

1817

Laufmaschine (Running Machine), 1817
(replica)
Design: Karl Friedrich Drais (1785–1851)
Manufacturer: Johann Frey, wheelwright in
Mannheim (replica Alfred Baltus, Solingen,
c. 2011), Germany
Frame: Wood (ash, replica: beech, oak)
Wheels: 27", wooden wheels with iron rims
Weight: 22.3 kg
Deutsches Fahrradmuseum, Bad Brückenau

02   058

Eugène Meyer

Tretkurbelrad
Foot pedal velocipede

Tretkurbelrad, c. 1869/70
Entwurf: Eugène Meyer (1844–1907)
Herst: Eugène Meyer & Cie, Paris,
Frankreich
Rahmen: Eisen, geschmiedet
Laufräder: vorne 38,5 Zoll, hinten 26 Zoll,
vollgummibereift, Drahtspeichen,
Stahlfelgen;
Gewicht: c. 28 kg
Deutsches Fahrradmuseum, Bad Brückenau

c. 1869/70

Foot pedal velocipede (bicycle), c. 1869–70
Design: Eugène Meyer (1844–1907)
Manufacturer: Eugène Meyer & Cie, Paris,
France
Frame: Iron, forged
Wheels: front 38.5", rear 26", solid rubber
tires, wire spokes, steel rims
Weight: c. 28 kg
Deutsches Fahrradmuseum, Bad Brückenau

03   062

Josef Erlach

Sicherheitsniederrad
Low-wheel safety bicycle

Sicherheitsniederrad, c.1880
Entwurf: Josef Erlach (1830–1885)
Hersteller: Valentin Wiegele, Korpitsch
bei Villach, Österreich, c. 1887/88
Rahmen: Winkeleisen, genietet und
verschraubt
Schaltung: Zwei Gänge durch Verstellen
der Schubstange
Laufräder: vorne 26 Zoll, hinten 40 Zoll,
vollgummibereift
Gewicht: 26,3 kg
Deutsches Fahrradmuseum, Bad Brückenau

c.1880

Low-wheel safety bicycle, c. 1880
Design: Josef Erlach (1830–1885)
Manufacturer: Valentin Wiegele,
Korpitsch, nr. Villach, Austria, c. 1887/88
Frame: iron section, riveted and screwed
together
Gears: Two gears by adjusting the push rod
Wheels: front 26", rear 40", solid rubber tires
Weight: 26.3 kg
Deutsches Fahrradmuseum, Bad Brückenau

04 066

Leonard B. Gaylor

Eagle Roadster

1886

Sicherheitshochrad Eagle Roadster, 1886
Entwurf: Leonard B. Gaylor (1857–1931)
Hersteller: Eagle Bicycle Manufacturing
Company, Stamford, USA
Rahmen: Stahl, vernickelt, konische Rohre
Laufräder: vorne 22 Zoll, hinten 52 Zoll,
vollgummibereift
Gewicht: c. 24 kg
Deutsches Fahrradmuseum, Bad Brückenau

Eagle Roadster safety Penny-Farthing, 1886
Design: Leonard B. Gaylor (1857–1931)
Manufacturer: Eagle Bicycle Manufacturing
Company, Stamford, USA
Frame: Steel, nickel-plated, conical tubes
Wheels: front 22", rear 52", solid rubber tires
Weight: c. 24 kg
Deutsches Fahrradmuseum, Bad Brückenau

05 070

Neckarsulmer Strickmaschinen-Fabrik AG

Sicherheitsniederrad
Low-wheel safety bicycle

c. 1888/89

Sicherheitsniederrad, c. 1888/89
Entwurf: Neckarsulmer Strickmaschinen-
Fabrik AG
Hersteller: Neckarsulmer Strickmaschinen-
Fabrik AG, später NSU AG, Neckarsulm,
Deutschland
Rahmen: Stahl, klappbares Tretlager zum
Spannen der Kette
Laufräder: 32 Zoll
Gewicht: 23,7 kg
Deutsches Fahrradmuseum, Bad Brückenau

Low-wheel safety bicycle, c. 1888–9
Design: Neckarsulmer Strickmaschinen-Fabrik
AGManufacturer: Neckarsulmer
Strickmaschinen-Fabrik AG, later NSU AG,
Neckarsulm, Germany
Frame: Steel, hinged bottom bracket for
tensioning the chain
Wheels: 32"
Weight: 23.7 kg
Deutsches Fahrradmuseum, Bad Brückenau

06 074

Manufacture Française d'Armes et Cycles

Hirondelle Superbe

1888/91

Sicherheitsniederrad Hirondelle Modell
Superbe, 1888/91
Entwurf: Manufacture Française d'Armes
et Cycles
Hersteller: Manufacture Française d'Armes
et Cycles de Saint-Étienne, Frankreich,
c. 1891
Rahmen: Stahl
Laufräder: vorne 25,6 Zoll, hinten 29,5 Zoll,
vollgummibereift
Gewicht: 22,8 kg
Deutsches Fahrradmuseum, Bad Brückenau

Hirondelle low-wheel safety bicycle,
model Superbe, 1888/91
Manufacture Française d'Armes et Cycles
Manufacture Française d'Armes et Cycles de
Saint-Étienne, France, c. 1891.
Frame: Steel
Wheels: front 25.6", rear 29.5", solid
rubber tires
Weight: 22.8 kg
Deutsches Fahrradmuseum, Bad Brückenau

07   078

A.G. Spalding & Bros.

Spalding

Sicherheitsniederrad Spalding, c. 1893
Entwurf: A.G. Spalding & Bros.,
Hersteller: A.G. Spalding & Bros., Chicago,
New York, Philadelphia, USA
Rahmen: Stahl; jeweils zu den Muffen hin
konisch sich verjüngende Rohre
Laufräder: 28 Zoll, Holzfelgen
Gewicht: c. 11 kg
Deutsches Fahrradmuseum, Bad Brückenau

c. 1893

Spalding low-wheel safety bicycle, c. 1893
Design: A.G. Spalding & Bros.,
Manufacturer: A.G. Spalding & Bros., Chicago,
New York, Philadelphia, USA
Frame: Steel; tubes tapering towards the
sockets in each case
Wheels: 28", wooden rims
Weight: c. 11 kg
Deutsches Fahrradmuseum, Bad Brückenau

08   082

Mikael Pedersen

Pedersen

Pedersen-Fahrrad, 1893
Entwurf: Mikael Pedersen (1855–1929)
Hersteller: Dursley-Pedersen Cycle Co, Ltd.,
Dursley, England, 1910/11
Rahmen: Stahl, gelötet
Schaltung: Dreigang-Nabenschaltung
Laufräder: 28 Zoll
Gewicht: 14,1 kg
Deutsches Fahrradmuseum, Bad Brückenau

1893

Pedersen Bicycle, 1893
Design: Mikael Pedersen (1855–1929)
Manufacturer: Dursley-Pedersen Cycle Co, Ltd.,
Dursley, England, 1910–11
Frame: Steel, soldered
Gears: Three-speed hub gear
Wheels: 28"
Weight: 14.1 kg
Deutsches Fahrradmuseum, Bad Brückenau

09   086

Tonk Manufacturing Co.

Old Hickory

Niederrad Old Hickory, 1896
Entwurf: Tonk Manufacturing Co.
Hersteller: Tonk Manufacturing Co.,
Chicago, USA
Rahmen: Holz (Walnuss), 16 Lagen laminiert
und gebogen, durchbrochene Muffen
aus Stahl
Laufräder: 28 Zoll, Holzfelgen
Gewicht: 13,8 kg
Deutsches Fahrradmuseum, Bad Brückenau

1896

Old Hickory low-wheel bicycle, 1896
Design: Tonk Manufacturing Co.
Manufacturer: Tonk Manufacturing Co.,
Chicago, USA
Frame: Wood (walnut), 16-ply laminated
and curved, openwork steel muffs
Wheels: 28", wooden rims
Weight: 13.8 kg
Deutsches Fahrradmuseum, Bad Brückenau

10 090

Franz Grundner

Bambusfahrrad
Bamboo bicycle

Bambusfahrrad, c. 1898
Entwurf: Franz Grundner (1861–1945)
Hersteller: Grundner & Lemisch, Klagenfurt,
Österreich
Rahmen: Bambusrohr, Stahl, Stahlmuffen
Laufräder: 26 Zoll, Holzfelgen
Gewicht: 16,2 kg
Deutsches Fahrradmuseum, Bad Brückenau

c. 1898

Bamboo bicycle, c. 1898
Design: Franz Grundner (1861–1945)
Manufacturer: Grundner & Lemisch,
Klagenfurt, Austria
Frame: Bamboo cane, steel, steel lugs
Wheels: 26", wooden rims
Weight: 16.2 kg
Deutsches Fahrradmuseum, Bad Brückenau

11 094

Adler Fahrradwerke

Kettenlos No. 7

Kardanrad Kettenlos No. 7, c. 1903
Entwurf: Adler Fahrradwerke
Hersteller: Adler Fahrradwerke (vormals
Heinrich Kleyer), Frankfurt a. M., Deutschland
Rahmen: Stahl
Laufräder: 28 Zoll
Gewicht: 18,2 kg
Deutsches Fahrradmuseum, Bad Brückenau

c. 1903

Kettenlos No. 7 shaft-driven bicycle, c. 1903
Design: Adler Fahrradwerke
Manufacturer: Adler Fahrradwerke (formerly
Heinrich Kleyer), Frankfurt / M., Germany
Frame: Steel
Wheels: 28"
Weight: 18.2 kg
Deutsches Fahrradmuseum, Bad Brückenau

12 098

Paul Jaray

J-Rad

Liegerad J-Rad, 1919
Entwurf: Paul Jaray (1889–1974)
Hersteller: Hesperus-Werke GmbH,
Stuttgart, Deutschland, 1921/22
Rahmen: Stahl, geschweißt
Schaltung: Dreigang-Trethebelantrieb
mit Drahtzügen
Laufräder: vorne 20 Zoll, hinten 26 Zoll
Gewicht: 21,9 kg
Deutsches Fahrradmuseum, Bad Brückenau

1919

J-Rad recumbent bicycle, 1919
Design: Paul Jaray (1889–1974)
Manufacturer: Hesperus-Werke GmbH,
Stuttgart, Germany, 1921–2
Frame: Steel, welded
Gears: three-speed pedal gear with wire
cables
Wheels: front 20", rear 26"
Weight: 21.9 kg
Deutsches Fahrradmuseum, Bad Brückenau

13   102

Gustav Lind

Anker-Sichelrad

Rennrad Anker-Sichelrad, 1933
Entwurf: Gustav Lind (1885–1979)
Hersteller: Anker-Werke A.G., Bielefeld,
Deutschland
Rahmen: Stahl
Schaltung: Dreigang-Kettenschaltung,
Fichtel & Sachs Torpedo
Laufräder: 28 Zoll, Holzfelgen
Gewicht: 12,1 kg
Deutsches Fahrradmuseum, Bad Brückenau

1933

Anker-Sichelrad racing bike, 1933
Design: Gustav Lind (1885–1979)
Manufacturer: Anker-Werke A.G., Bielefeld,
Germany
Frame: Steel
Gears: Three-speed Fichtel & Sachs Torpedo
derailleur
Wheels: 28", wooden rims
Weight: 12.1 kg
Deutsches Fahrradmuseum, Bad Brückenau

14   106

Jacques Schulz

Funiculo

Randonneur Funiculo, 1935/37
Entwurf: Jacques Schulz
Hersteller: Jacques Schulz,
La Garenne-Colombes, Frankreich
Rahmen: Stahl
Schaltung: Viergang-Kettenschaltung
Laufräder: 26 Zoll
Gewicht: 18 kg
Deutsches Fahrradmuseum, Bad Brückenau

1935/37

Funiculo randonneur, 1935–7
Design: Jacques Schulz
Manufacturer: Jacques Schulz,
La Garenne-Colombes, France
Frame: Steel
Gears: Four-speed derailleur
Wheels: 26"
Weight: 18 kg
Deutsches Fahrradmuseum, Bad Brückenau

15   110

Pierre Caminade

Caminargent

Damenrad Caminargent, 1936
Entwurf: Pierre Caminade (*1879)
Hersteller: Etablissements Caminade,
Bois-Colombes, Frankreich
Rahmen: Duraluminium, achteckige,
konifizierte Rohre, gelötet
Schaltung: Dreigang-Kettenschaltung
Laufräder: 26 Zoll
Gewicht: 12,9 kg
Deutsches Fahrradmuseum, Bad Brückenau

1936

Caminargent women's bicycle, 1936
Design: Pierre Caminade (*1879)
Manufacturer: Etablissements Caminade,
Bois-Colombes, France
Frame: Duralumin, octagonal butted tubes,
soldered
Gears: Three-speed derailleur
Wheels: 26"
Weight: 12.9 kg
Deutsches Fahrradmuseum, Bad Brückenau

16   114

Adolf Bareuther

Blattfeder-Fahrrad
Bicycle with leaf-spring suspension

c. 1937

Blattfeder-Fahrrad, c. 1937
Entwurf: Adolf Bareuther
Hersteller: Adolf Bareuther u. Co Fahrradfabrik
Eger, Cheb/Eger, Tschechoslowakei
Rahmen: Stahl, z. T. Blattfeder, verchromt
Laufräder: 28 Zoll
Gewicht: 20,7 kg
Deutsches Fahrradmuseum, Bad Brückenau

Bicycle with leaf-spring suspension, c. 1937
Design: Adolf Bareuther
Manufacturer: Adolf Bareuther u. Co
Fahrradfabrik Eger, Cheb/Eger,
Czechoslovakia
Frame: Steel, partly leaf spring, chrome-plated
Wheels: 28"
Weight: 20.7 kg
Deutsches Fahrradmuseum, Bad Brückenau

17   118

Camille Piquerez S.A

Stella-Landi-Velo

c. 1939

Fahrrad Stella-Landi-Velo, c. 1939
Entwurf: Camille Piquerez S.A.
Hersteller: Camille Piquerez S.A.,
Bassecourt, Schweiz
Rahmen: Stahl, Doppelrohrrahmen oben
mit Aluminiumverkleidung
Schaltung: Dreigang-Nabenschaltung
Laufräder: 26 Zoll
Gewicht: 17,3 kg
Deutsches Fahrradmuseum, Bad Brückenau

Stella-Landi-Velo bicycle, c. 1939
Design: Camille Piquerez S.A.
Manufacturer: Camille Piquerez S.A.,
Bassecourt, Switzerland
Frame: Steel, double-tube frame on top
with aluminum cladding
Gears: Three-speed hub gear
Wheels: 26"
Weight: 17.3 kg
Deutsches Fahrradmuseum, Bad Brückenau

18   122

Cycles Lida

Guip

c. 1939

Fahrrad mit Fuß- und Handantrieb Mod. Guip
Entwurf: Cycles Lida, c. 1939
Hersteller: Cycles Lida, Ixelles, Belgien
Rahmen: Stahl
Schaltung: Dreigang-Kettenschaltung
Laufräder: 26 Zoll, Holzfelgen
Gewicht: 17,7 kg
Deutsches Fahrradmuseum, Bad Brückenau

Guip bicycle with foot and hand drive
Design: Cycles Lida, c. 1939
Manufacturer: Cycles Lida, Ixelles,
Belgium
Frame: Steel
Gears: Three-speed derailleur
Wheels: 26", wooden rims
Weight: 17.7 kg
Deutsches Fahrradmuseum, Bad Brückenau

19   126

Albert Edward Wood / William Henry Taylor

Airborne

Klapprad Airborne, c. 1940 (1942 patentiert)
Entwurf: BSA (Albert Edward Wood,
William Henry Taylor)
Hersteller: Birmingham Small Arms (BSA),
Birmingham, England
Rahmen: Stahl
Laufräder: 26 Zoll
Gewicht: 14,3 kg
Deutsches Fahrradmuseum, Bad Brückenau

c. 1940

Airborne folding bicycle, c. 1940 (patented
1942)
Design: BSA (Albert Edward Wood,
William Henry Taylor)
Manufacturer: Birmingham Small Arms (BSA),
Birmingham, England
Frame: Steel
Wheels: 26"
Weight: 14.3 kg
Deutsches Fahrradmuseum, Bad Brückenau

20   132

Fratelli Vianzone

Standard

Holzfahrrad Standard, 1946
Entwurf: Fratelli Vianzone
Hersteller: Fratelli Vianzone, Turin, Italien
Rahmen: Schichtholz, gebogen
Laufräder: 28 Zoll, Holzfelgen
Gewicht: 13,6 kg
Deutsches Fahrradmuseum, Bad Brückenau

1946

Standard wooden bicycle, 1946
Design: Fratelli Vianzone
Manufacturer: Fratelli Vianzone, Turin, Italy
Frame: Plywood, curved
Wheels: 26", wooden rims
Weight: 13.6 kg
Deutsches Fahrradmuseum, Bad Brückenau

21   136

Reyé Bardet

Flugzeug-Rad
Airplane bicycle

Flugzeug-Rad, 1946
Entwurf: Reyé Bardet
Hersteller: Reyé Bardet, Bordeaux,
Frankreich
Rahmen: Aluminium, genietet
Laufräder: 26 Zoll
Gewicht: 15,7 kg
Deutsches Fahrradmuseum, Bad Brückenau

1946

Airplane bicycle, 1946
Design: Reyé Bardet
Manufacturer: Reyé Bardet, Bordeaux,
France
Frame: Aluminum, riveted
Wheels: 26"
Weight: 15.7 kg
Deutsches Fahrradmuseum, Bad Brückenau

22   140

Mitsubishi

Dujee

Fahrrad Dujee, 1947
Entwurf: Mitsubishi
Hersteller: Mitsubishi Heavy Industries,
Ltd., Tokio, Japan
Rahmen: Aluminium, genietet
Laufräder: 26 Zoll
Gewicht: 18,1 kg
Heinz Fingerhut – Velo-Classic

1947

Bicycle Dujee, 1947
Design: Mitsubishi
Manufacturer: Mitsubishi Heavy
Industries, Ltd., Tokyo, Japan
Frame: Aluminum, riveted
Wheels: 26"
Weight: 18.1 kg
Heinz Fingerhut – Velo-Classic

23   144

H. & W. Sudbrack GmbH

Vagant

Steherfahrrad Vagant, 1950
Entwurf: H. & W. Sudbrack GmbH
Hersteller: H. & W. Sudbrack GmbH,
Schötmar in Lippe, für Artur Wegmann & Co,
Recklinghausen i. W., Deutschland
Rahmen: Stahl
Laufräder: vorne 24 Zoll, hinten 28 Zoll,
Holzfelgen
Gewicht: 13,5 kg
Deutsches Fahrradmuseum, Bad Brückenau

1950

Vagant bicycle for motor-paced racing, 1950
Design: H. & W. Sudbrack GmbH
Manufacturer: H. & W. Sudbrack GmbH,
Schötmar in Lippe, for Artur Wegmann & Co,
Recklinghausen i. W., Germany
Frame: Steel
Wheels: front 24", rear 28", wooden rims
Weight: 13.5 kg
Deutsches Fahrradmuseum, Bad Brückenau

24   148

Hermann Klaue

HK-Rad
HK bicycle

HK-Rad, 1949/50
Entwurf: Hermann Klaue (1912–2001)
Hersteller: Klaue-Bremse GmbH,
Überlingen, Deutschland
Rahmen: Silumin, gegossen
Laufräder: 26 Zoll
Gewicht: 16,3 kg
Deutsches Fahrradmuseum, Bad Brückenau

1949/50

HK bicycle, 1949–50
Design: Hermann Klaue (1912–2001)
Manufacturer: Klaue-Bremse GmbH,
Überlingen, Germany
Frame: Silumin, cast
Wheels: 26"
Weight: 16.3 kg
Deutsches Fahrradmuseum, Bad Brückenau

25   152

Hermann Klaue / Hercules-Werke

Hercules 2000

1949/57

Kreuzrahmenrad Hercules 2000, 1949/57
Entwurf: Hermann Klaue und Hercules-Werke
Hersteller: Hercules-Werke, Nürnberg,
Deutschland
Rahmen: Aluminium, gegossen
Schaltung: Dreigang Nabenschaltung
Fichtel & Sachs Torpedo
Laufräder: 26 Zoll
Gewicht: 17,2 kg
Die Neue Sammlung – The Design Museum

Hercules 2000 cross-frame bicycle, 1949–57
Design: Hermann Klaue and Hercules-Werke
Manufacturer: Hercules-Werke, Nuremberg,
Germany
Frame: Aluminum, cast
Gears: Three-speed hub gear Fichtel & Sachs
Torpedo
Wheels: 26"
Weight: 17.2 kg
Die Neue Sammlung – The Design Museum

26   154

Alex Moulton

Moulton Stowaway

1962/64

Steckrad Moulton Stowaway, 1962/64
Entwurf: Alex Moulton (1920–2012)
Hersteller: Alex Moulton Limited,
Bradford-on-Avon, England
Rahmen: Stahl
Schaltung: Zweigang Nabenschaltung
Fichtel & Sachs Duomatic
Laufräder: 16 Zoll
Gewicht: 16,9 kg
Die Neue Sammlung – The Design Museum

Moulton Stowaway folding bicycle, 1962–4
Design: Alex Moulton (1920–2012)
Manufacturer: Alex Moulton Limited,
Bradford-on-Avon, England
Frame: Steel
Gears: Two-speed hub gear Fichtel & Sachs
Duomatic
Wheels: 16"
Weight: 16.9 kg
Die Neue Sammlung – The Design Museum

27   160

Bernard Marcel / Marius Johan Overing

Strano

1962

Kompaktrad Strano, 1962
Entwurf: Bernard Marce / Marius Johan
Overing (*8.9.1912)
Hersteller: Union Rijwielfabriek,
Den Hulst, Niederlande
Rahmen: Stahl
Laufräder: vorne 12 Zoll, hinten 24 Zoll
Gewicht: 15,6 kg
Deutsches Fahrradmuseum, Bad Brückenau

Strano compact bicycle, 1962
Design: Bernard Marcel / Marius Johan
Overing (*8.9.1912)
Manufacturer: Union Rijwielfabriek,
Den Hulst, Netherlands
Frame: Steel
Wheels: front 12", rear 24"
Weight: 15.6 kg
Deutsches Fahrradmuseum, Bad Brückenau

28 164

Cesare Rizzato

Duemila

Faltrad Duemila, 1965
Entwurf: Cesare Rizzato
Hersteller: Cesare Rizzato & Co, Padua,
Italien
Rahmen: Stahl
Schaltung: Zweigang Nabenschaltung
Fichtel & Sachs Torpedo Duomatic
Laufräder: 20 Zoll
Gewicht: 19,5 kg
Deutsches Fahrradmuseum, Bad Brückenau

1965

Duemila folding bicycle, 1965
Design: Cesare Rizzato
Manufacturer: Cesare Rizzato & Co,
Padua, Italy
Frame: Steel
Gears: Two-speed hub gear Fichtel & Sachs
Torpedo Duomatic
Wheels: 20"
Weight: 19.5 kg
Deutsches Fahrradmuseum, Bad Brückenau

29 168

Schwinn (Albert John Fritz)

Schwinn Ram's Horn Fastback

Jugendrad Schwinn Ram's Horn
Fastback, 1967
Entwurf: Schwinn Bicycle Company
(Albert John Fritz)
Hersteller: Schwinn Bicycle Company,
Chicago, USA
Rahmen: Stahl
Schaltung: Fünfgang-Nabenschaltung
Laufräder: 20 × 1 3/8 Zoll
Gewicht: 17,4 kg
Deutsches Fahrradmuseum, Bad Brückenau

1967

Schwinn Ram's Horn Fastback youth
bicycle, 1967
Design: Schwinn Bicycle Company
(Albert John Fritz)
Manufacturer: Schwinn Bicycle Company,
Chicago, USA
Frame: Steel
Gears: Five-speed hub gear
Wheels: 20 × 1 3/8"
Weight: 17.4 kg
Deutsches Fahrradmuseum, Bad Brückenau

30 172

Otto Kynast GmbH & Co. KG

Super de Luxe

Bonanzarad Super de Luxe, c. 1972
Entwurf: Otto Kynast GmbH & Co. KG
Hersteller: Otto Kynast GmbH & Co. KG,
Quakenbrück, für Neckermann,
Deutschland
Rahmen: Stahl
Schaltung: Dreigang-Nabenschaltung
Laufräder: 20 Zoll
Gewicht: 20,3 kg
Heinz Fingerhut – Velo-Classic

1972

Bonanza Super de Luxe bicycle, c. 1972
Design: Otto Kynast GmbH & Co. KG
Manufacturer: Otto Kynast GmbH & Co. KG,
Quakenbrück, for Neckermann, Germany
Frame: Steel
Gears: Three-speed hub gear
Wheels: 20"
Weight: 20.3 kg
Heinz Fingerhut – Velo-Classic

31 174

Fritz Fleck

Flema	1972
Rennrad Flema, 1972 Entwurf: Fritz Fleck (1928–2013) Hersteller: Fritz Fleck, Mannheim, Deutschland Rahmen: Titan Laufräder: 28 Zoll Gewicht: 7,5 kg Heinz Fingerhut – Velo-Classic	Flema racing bike, 1972 Design: Fritz Fleck (1928–2013) Manufacturer: Fritz Fleck, Mannheim, Germany Frame: Titanium Wheels: 28" Weight: 7.5 kg Heinz Fingerhut – Velo-Classic

32 178

Five Rams

Five Rams XQ51	1974
Jugendrad Five Rams XQ51, 1974 Entwurf: Five Rams Hersteller: Five Rams (chin. Wu Yang), Guangdong, China Rahmen: Stahl Laufräder: 18 Zoll Gewicht: 16,5 kg Eva Mayer	Five Rams XQ51 bicycle for young people, 1974 Design: Five Rams Manufacturer: Five Rams (chin. Wu Yang), Guangdong, China Frame: Steel Wheels: 18" Weight: 16.5 kg Eva Mayer

33 182

Heinz Kettler Metallwarenfabrik

Kettler Alurad 2600 Kettler 2600 aluminum bicycle	1977
Kettler Alurad 2600, 1977 Entwurf: Heinz Kettler Metallwarenfabrik Hersteller: Heinz Kettler Metallwarenfabrik, Ense-Parsit, Deutschland Rahmen: Aluminium Schaltung: Dreigang Nabenschaltung Fichtel & Sachs Torpedo Laufräder: 26 Zoll Gewicht: 14,4 kg Die Neue Sammlung – The Design Museum	Kettler 2600 aluminum bicycle, 1977 Design: Heinz Kettler metal goods factory Manufacturer: Heinz Kettler metal goods factory, Ense-Parsit, Germany Frame: Aluminum Gears: Three-speed hub gear Fichtel & Sachs Torpedo Wheels: 26" Weight: 14.4 kg Die Neue Sammlung – The Design Museum

34   186

Hans Günter Bals

Hercules Cavallo

Reitrad Hercules Cavallo, 1978
Entwurf: Hans Günter Bals (*1930)
Hersteller: Hercules-Werke, Nürnberg,
Deutschland
Rahmen: Aluminium
Schaltung: 3 Gänge
Laufräder: 26 1 3/8 Zoll
Gewicht: 22 kg
Deutsches Fahrradmuseum, Bad Brückenau

1978

Hercules Cavallo riding bike, 1978
Design: Hans Günter Bals (*1930)
Manufacturer: Hercules-Werke, Nuremberg,
Germany
Frame: Aluminum
Gears: 3 gears
Wheels: 26 x 1 3/8"
Weight: 22 kg
Deutsches Fahrradmuseum, Bad Brückenau

35   190

Luigi Colani

Rennradstudie
Study for a racing bike

Rennradstudie, 1979
Entwurf: Luigi Colani (1928–2019)
Hersteller: Luigi Colani Designfactory, Schloss
Harkotten, Deutschland
Rahmen: Stahl mit Kunststoffverkleidung
Schaltung: 16-Gang-Kettenschaltung Shimano
105
Laufräder: 28 Zoll
Gewicht: 10,4 kg
Die Neue Sammlung – The Design Museum

1979

Study for a racing bike, 1979
Design: Luigi Colani (1928–2019)
Manufacturer: Luigi Colani Designfactory,
Schloss Harkotten, Germany
Frame: Steel with plastic cladding
Gears: 16-speed Shimano 105 derailleur
Wheels: 28"
Weight: 10.4 kg
Die Neue Sammlung – The Design Museum

36   194

Peter Fendt / Klaus Hofgärtner

FEHO STS 1-26

Kardanrad FEHO STS 1-26, 1979/80
Entwurf: Peter Fendt und Klaus Hofgärtner
Hersteller: Fendt & Hofgärtner GmbH,
Marktoberdorf, Deutschland
Rahmen: Stahl
Schaltung: Dreigang-Nabenschaltung
Laufräder: 26 Zoll
Gewicht: 20,5 kg
Heinz Fingerhut – Velo-Classic

1979/80

FEHO STS 1-26 shaft-driven bicycle, 1979/80
Design: Peter Fendt and Klaus Hofgärtner
Manufacturer: Fendt & Hofgärtner GmbH,
Marktoberdorf, Germany
Frame: Steel
Gears: three-speed hub gear
Wheels: 26"
Weight: 20.5 kg
Heinz Fingerhut – Velo-Classic

37   198

Itera Development Center AB

Itera Plastcykel

Kunststoff-Fahrrad Itera, 1980/1982
Entwurf: Itera Development Center AB
Hersteller: Itera Development Center AB,
Vilhelmina, Schweden
Rahmen: Kunststoff Polyamid (PA) 6
Schaltung: Dreigang-Nabenschaltung
Laufräder: 27 Zoll
Gewicht: 18,6 kg
Die Neue Sammlung – The Design Museum

1980/82

Plastic bicycle Itera, 1980–2
Design: Itera Development Center AB
Manufacturer: Itera Development Center AB,
Vilhelmina, Sweden
Frame: Plastic polyamide (PA) 6
Gears: Three-speed hub gear
Wheels: 27"
Weight: 18.6 kg
Die Neue Sammlung – The Design Museum

38   158

Alex Moulton

AM 7

Faltrad AM 7, 1977/83
Entwurf: Alex Moulton (1920–2012)
Hersteller: Alex Moulton Limited,
Bradford-on-Avon, England
Rahmen: Stahl
Schaltung: Siebengang-Kettenschaltung
Laufräder: 16,5 Zoll
Gewicht: 12,6 kg
Deutsches Fahrradmuseum, Bad Brückenau

1977/83

Folding bike AM 7, 1977–83
Design: Alex Moulton (1920–2012)
Manufacturer: Alex Moulton Limited,
Bradford-on-Avon, England
Frame: Steel
Gears: Seven-speed derailleur
Wheels: 16.5"
Weight: 12.6 kg
Deutsches Fahrradmuseum, Bad Brückenau

39   202

Antonio Colombo/Paolo Erzegovesi

Cinelli Laser

Bahnrad Cinelli Laser, 1981/84
Entwurf: Antonio Colombo / Paolo Erzegovesi
Hersteller: Cinelli, Caleppio di Settala (MI),
Italien, um 1984
Rahmen: Stahl
Laufräder: vorne 26 Zoll, hinten 28 Zoll
Gewicht: 7,7 kg
Sammlung Stephan Dornhofer, Berlin

1981

Cinelli Laser track racing bike, 1981/84
Design: Antonio Colombo / Paolo Erzegovesi
Manufacturer: Cinelli, Caleppio di Settala (MI),
Italy, around 1984
Frame: Steel
Wheels: front 26", rear 28"
Weight: 7.7 kg
Collection Stephan Dornhofer, Berlin

40   130

Nicola Trussardi

Trussardi

Klapprad Trussardi, 1981/83
Entwurf: Nicola Trussardi (1942–1999)
Hersteller: Trussardi, Mailand, Italien
Rahmen: Stahl
Schaltung: Dreigang-Nabenschaltung
Laufräder: 26 Zoll
Gewicht: 19,1 kg
Die Neue Sammlung – The Design Museum

1981/83

Folding bicycle Trussardi, 1981–3
Design: Nicola Trussardi (1942–1999)
Manufacturer: Trussardi, Milan, Italy
Frame: Steel
Gears: Three-speed hub gear
Wheels: 26"
Weight: 19.1 kg
Die Neue Sammlung – The Design Museum

41   206

Odo Klose

Comfortable

Stadtfahrrad Comfortable, 1982
(Patentanmeldung 1983)
Entwurf: Odo Klose (1932–2020)
Hersteller: Sprick Fahrräder GmbH, Oelde,
Deutschland
Rahmen: Stahl, Kunststoff
Laufräder: 28 Zoll
Gewicht: 19,2 kg
Die Neue Sammlung – The Design Museum

1982

Comfortable city bike, 1982
(patent application 1983)
Design: Odo Klose (1932–2020)
Manufacturer: Sprick Fahrräder GmbH,
Oelde, Germany
Frame: Steel, plastic
Wheels: 28"
Weight: 19.2 kg
Die Neue Sammlung – The Design Museum

42   210

Wolfgang Taubmann / Paul Rinkowski

Textima

Bahnrad Textima, c. 1985
Entwurf: Wolfgang Taubmann / Paul Rinkowski
Hersteller: VEB Kombinat Textilmaschinenbau
Karl-Marx-Stadt, DDR
Rahmen: Stahl
Laufräder: vorne 26 Zoll, hinten 28 Zoll
Gewicht: 6,6 kg
Sammlung Stephan Dornhofer, Berlin

c. 1985

Textima track racing bike, c. 1985
Design: Wolfgang Taubmann / Paul Rinkowski
Manufacturer: VEB Kombinat
Textilmaschinenbau Karl-Marx-Stadt,
East Germany
Frame: Steel
Wheels: front 26", rear 28"
Weight: 6.6 kg
Collection Stephan Dornhofer, Berlin

43   214

Michael Conrad

AC 4

Rennrad AC 4, 1984/89
Entwurf: Michael Conrad (*1940)
Hersteller: CON-RAD-DESIGN (mit Hilfe des
Segelflugzeugbauers Streifeneder, Graben-
stetten), Leinfelden-Oberaichen, Deutschland
Rahmen: Karbon Monocoque
Schaltung: 14-Gang-Kettenschaltung Shimano
600
Laufräder: 28 Zoll, vorne Spinergy Karbon,
hinten Scheibenrad Karbon
Gewicht: 12 kg
Die Neue Sammlung – The Design Museum

1984/89

AC 4 racing bike, 1984–9
Design: Michael Conrad (*1940)
Manufacturer: CON-RAD-DESIGN (with
the help of glider builders Streifeneder,
Grabenstetten), Leinfelden-Oberaichen,
Germany
Frame: Carbon monocoque
Gears: 14-speed Shimano 600 derailleur
Wheels: 28", front Spinergy carbon, rear disc
wheel carbon
Weight: 12 kg
Die Neue Sammlung – The Design Museum

44   218

André Sablière

Sablière Perfection

Rennrad Sablière Perfection, 1985
Entwurf: André Sablière (*1946)
Hersteller: Cycles A. Sablière, Saint-Étienne,
Frankreich
Rahmen: Aluminium
Schaltung: 14-Gang-Kettenschaltung Huret
Laufräder: 27 Zoll, Aluminiumfelgen
Gewicht: 7,4 kg
Sammlung Stephan Dornhofer, Berlin

1985

Sablière Perfection racing bike, 1985
Design: André Sablière (*1946)
Manufacturer: Cycles A. Sablière,
Saint-Étienne, France
Frame: Aluminum
Gears: 14-speed Huret derailleur
Wheels: 27", aluminum rims
Weight: 7.4 kg
Collection Stephan Dornhofer, Berlin

45   222

Giorgetto Giugiaro

Blouson

Fahrrad Blouson, 1985
Entwurf: Giorgetto Giugiaro (*1938)
Hersteller: Bridgestone Cycle Co. Ltd.,
Tokio, Japan
Rahmen: Stahl
Schaltung: Sechsgang-Kettenschaltung
Shimano Exage 400 LX
Laufräder: 26 Zoll
Gewicht: 17 kg
Deutsches Fahrradmuseum, Bad Brückenau

1985

Bicycle Blouson, 1985
Design: Giorgetto Giugiaro (*1938)
Manufacturer: Bridgestone Cycle Co. Ltd.,
Tokyo, Japan
Frame: Steel
Gears: Six-speed Shimano Exage 400 LX
derailleur
Wheels: 26"
Weight: 17 kg
Deutsches Fahrradmuseum, Bad Brückenau

46   226

Mark Sanders

Strida 1

1985/1987

Faltrad Strida 1, 1985/87
Entwurf: Mark Sanders
Hersteller: Strida Ltd., Glasgow, UK
Rahmen: Aluminium
Laufräder: 16 Zoll
Gewicht: 9,7 kg
Deutsches Fahrradmuseum, Bad Brückenau

Strida 1 Folding bike, 1985–7
Design: Mark Sanders
Manufacturer: Strida Ltd., Glasgow, UK
Frame: Aluminum
Wheels: 16"
Weight: 9.7 kg
Deutsches Fahrradmuseum, Bad Brückenau

47   230

Mark Sanders

Strida 5

1985/2007

Faltrad Strida 5, 1985/2007
Entwurf: Mark Sanders
Hersteller: Strida Ltd., Ming, Taipee,
Taiwan
Rahmen: Aluminium
Laufräder: 16 Zoll
Gewicht: 9,7 kg
Die Neue Sammlung – The Design Museum

Strida 5 folding bike, 1985–2007
Design: Mark Sanders
Manufacturer: Strida Ltd., Ming, Taipei,
Taiwan
Frame: Aluminum
Wheels: 16"
Weight: 9.7 kg
Die Neue Sammlung – The Design Museum

48   232

Frank Kirk

Kirk Precision

1986

Rennrad Kirk Precision, 1986
Entwurf: Frank Kirk
Hersteller: Kirk Precision Ltd., Basildon,
Essex, England
Rahmen: Magnesium, gegossen
Schaltung: 14-Gang-Kettenschaltung
Shimano Dura-Ace
Laufräder: 27 Zoll
Gewicht: 10,4 kg
Sebastian Fischer

Kirk Precision racing bike, 1986
Design: Frank Kirk
Manufacturer: Kirk Precision Ltd.,
Basildon, Essex, England
Frame: Magnesium, cast
Gears: 14-speed Shimano Dura-Ace
derailleur
Wheels: 27"
Weight: 10.4 kg
Sebastian Fischer

49   236

Brent J. Trimble

Kestrel 4000

1986/87

Rennrad Kestrel 4000, 1986/87
Entwurf: Brent J. Trimble
Hersteller: Cycle Composites, Inc. (CCI),
Santa Cruz, USA
Rahmen: Karbon Monocoque
Schaltung: 14-Gang-Kettenschaltung
Campagnolo Chorus
Laufräder: 28 Zoll
Gewicht: 9,4 kg
Die Neue Sammlung – The Design Museum

Kestrel 4000 racing bike, 1986–7
Design: Brent J. Trimble
Manufacturer: Cycle Composites, Inc. (CCI),
Santa Cruz, USA
Frame: Carbon monocoque
Gears: 14-speed Campagnolo Chorus derailleur
Wheels: 28"
Weight: 9.4 kg
Die Neue Sammlung – The Design Museum

50   242

Bottecchia Cicli

Bottecchia Air

1987

Zeitfahrmaschine Bottecchia Air, 1987
Entwurf: Bottecchia Cicli
Hersteller: Bottecchia Cicli S.r.l.,
Vittorio Veneto, Italien
Rahmen: Stahl
Schaltung: 14-Gang-Kettenschaltung
Mavic
Laufräder: 27 Zoll
Gewicht: 11,1 kg
Sammlung Reiner Balke

Bottecchia Air time trial bike, 1987
Design: Bottecchia Cicli S.r.l.
Manufacturer: Bottecchia Cicli S.r.l.,
Vittorio Veneto, Italy
Frame: Steel
Gears: 14-speed Mavic derailleur
Wheels: 27"
Weight: 11.1 kg
Collection Reiner Balke

51   246

Togashi Engineering

Straßenrennrad

1989

Straßenrennrad, 1989
Entwurf: Togashi Engineering
Hersteller: Togashi Engineering Ltd., Japan
Rahmen: Karbon Monocoque
Schaltung: 14-Gang-Kettenschaltung Suntour
Superb Pro
Laufräder: vorne 26 Zoll, hinten 27 Zoll,
Scheibenräder
Gewicht: 12 kg
Sammlung Reiner Balke

Road racing bike, 1989
Design: Togashi Engineering
Manufacturer: Togashi Engineering Ltd., Japan
Frame: Carbon monocoque
Gears: 14-speed Suntour Superb Pro derailleur
Wheels: front 26", rear 27", disc wheels
Weight: 12 kg
Collection Reiner Balke

52   250

FES (Harald Schaale)

FES 89-1

Straßenrennrad FES 89-1, 1989
Entwurf: FES (Harald Schaale)
Hersteller: Institut für Forschung und
Entwicklung von Sportgeräten (FES) e.V.,
Berlin, DDR
Rahmen: Karbon Monocoque
Schaltung: 12-Gang-Kettenschaltung
Campagnolo Super Record
Laufräder: vorne 26 Zoll, hinten 28 Zoll,
Scheibenräder Karbon
Gewicht: 9,5 kg
Die Neue Sammlung – The Design Museum

1989

FES 89-1 road racing bike, 1989
Design: FES (Harald Schaale)
Manufacturer: Institute for Research and
Development of Sports Equipment (FES) e.V.,
Berlin, East Germany
Frame: Carbon monocoque
Gear stick: 12-speed Campagnolo Super
Record derailleur
Wheels: front 26", rear 28", carbon disc wheels
Weight: 9.5 kg
Die Neue Sammlung – The Design Museum

53   240

Kestrel

Kestrel 500SCi

Straßenrennrad Kestrel 500SCi, 1992
Entwurf: Kestrel
Hersteller: Cycle Composites, Inc. (CCI),
Santa Cruz, USA
Rahmen: Karbon Monocoque
Schaltung: 14-Gang-Kettenschaltung
Campagnolo Chorus
Laufräder: 28 Zoll, Karbon Trispoke
Gewicht: 9,5 kg
Heinz Fingerhut – Velo-Classic

1992

Kestrel 500SCi road racing bike, 1992
Design: Kestrel
Manufacturer: Cycle Composites, Inc. (CCI),
Santa Cruz, USA
Frame: Carbon monocoque
Gears: 14-speed Campagnolo Chorus derailleur
Wheels: 28", carbon tri-spoke
Weight: 9.5 kg
Heinz Fingerhut – Velo-Classic

54   254

Lotus

Lotus Sport 110

Straßenrennrad Lotus Sport 110, 1993/94
Entwurf: Lotus (Richard Hill)
Hersteller: Aerodyne Space Technology,
Südafrika, für Lotus Cars Limited, UK
Rahmen: Karbon
Schaltung: 18-Gang-Kettenschaltung Mavic
Mektronic
Laufräder: 27 Zoll, Karbon
Gewicht: 9,5 kg
Heinz Fingerhut – Velo-Classic

1993/94

Lotus Sport 110 road racing bike, 1993–4
Design: Lotus (Richard Hill)
Manufacturer: Aerodyne Space Technology,
South Africa, für Lotus Cars Limited, UK
Frame: Carbon
Gears: 18-speed Mavic Mektronic derailleur
Wheels: 27", carbon
Weight: 9.5 ckg
Heinz Fingerhut – Velo-Classic

55   258

Marco Bonfanti

C4 Joker

Straßenrennrad C4 Joker, 1993
Entwurf: Marco Bonfanti
Hersteller: C4 sas di Marco Bonfanti & C.,
Airuno, Italien
Rahmen: Karbon Monocoque
Schaltung: 16-Gang-Kettenschaltung
Campagnolo Chorus
Laufräder: 28 Zoll, Aluminiumfelgen
Gewicht: 10,3 kg
Die Neue Sammlung – The Design Museum

1993

C4 Joker road racing bike, 1993
Design: Marco Bonfanti
Manufacturer: C4 sas di Marco Bonfanti & C.,
Airuno, Italy
Frame: Carbon monocoque
Gears: 16-speed Campagnolo Chorus derailleur
Wheels: 28", aluminum rims
Weight: 10.3 kg
Die Neue Sammlung – The Design Museum

56   262

Ivan Lypa / Serhii Nytka

Antonov Enei

Bahnrad Antonov Enei, c. 1994
Entwurf: Ivan Lypa, Serhii Nytka
Hersteller: Antonov Aeronautical
Scientific-Technical Complex, Kiew,
Ukraine
Rahmen: Aramid, Monocoque
Laufräder: 26 Zoll, Dreispeichen-Felgen,
Aramid
Gewicht: 8,6 kg
C4 Collection, Schweiz

c. 1994

Antonov Enei track racing bike, c. 1994
Design: Ivan Lypa, Serhiy Nytka
Manufacturer: Antonov Aeronautical
Scientific-Technical Complex, Kyiv,
Ukraine
Frame: Aramid monocoque
Wheels: 26", tri-spoke rims, aramid
Weight: 8.6 kg
C4 Collection, Switzerland

57   268

Mike Burrows

Giant MCR 2

Straßenrennrad Giant MCR 2, 1994
Entwurf: Mike Burrows (1943–2022)
Hersteller: Giant Manufacturing Co. Ltd.,
Dajia, Taiwan
Rahmen: Karbon Monocoque
Schaltung: 18-Gang-Kettenschaltung
Shimano Ultegra 6500
Laufräder: 28 Zoll, Karbonspeichen
Gewicht: 9,9 kg
Deutsches Fahrradmuseum, Bad Brückenau

1994

Giant MCR 2 road racing bike, 1994
Design: Mike Burrows (1943–2022)
Manufacturer: Giant Manufacturing
Co. Ltd., Dajia, Taiwan
Frame: Carbon monocoque
Gears: 18-speed Shimano Ultegra 6500
derailleur
Wheels: 28", carbon spokes
Weight: 9.9 kg
Deutsches Fahrradmuseum, Bad Brückenau

58 272

TM-Design

Biria Unplugged

Mountainbike Biria Unplugged, 1996/98
Entwurf: TM-Design
Hersteller: Biria GmbH, Neukirch,
Deutschland
Rahmen: Karbon Monocoque
Schaltung: 27-Gang-Kettenschaltung Sachs
Quarz
Laufräder: 26 Zoll, Dreispeichen-Felgen,
Karbon
Gewicht: 13,3 kg
Die Neue Sammlung – The Design Museum

1996/98

Biria Unplugged mountain bike, 1996–8
Design: TM-Design
Manufacturer: Biria GmbH, Neukirch,
Germany
Frame: Carbon monocoque
Gears: 27-speed Sachs Quarz derailleur
Wheels: 26", tri-spoke rims, carbon
Weight: 13.3 kg
Die Neue Sammlung – The Design Museum

59 266

Ivan Lypa / Serhii Nytka

Antonov Elin 2

Bahnrad Antonov Elin 2, c. 1997
Entwurf: Ivan Lypa, Serhii Nytka
Hersteller: Antonov Aeronautical
Scientific-Technical Complex, Kiew,
Ukraine
Rahmen: Aramid Monocoque
Laufräder: 28 Zoll
Gewicht: 6,4 kg
Sammlung Reiner Balke

c. 1997

Antonov Elin 2 track racing bike, c. 1997
Design: Ivan Lypa, Serhii Nytka
Manufacturer: Antonov Aeronautical
Scientific-Technical Complex, Kyiv,
Ukraine
Frame: Aramid monocoque
Wheels: 28"
Weight: 6.4 kg
Collection Reiner Balke

60 276

BMW

BMW Super-Tech

Klappbares Mountainbike
BMW Super-Tech, 1997
Entwurf: BMW
Hersteller: BMW AG, München,
Deutschland
Rahmen: Aluminium
Schaltung: 27 Gang-Kettenschaltung
Shimano XTR
Laufräder: 26 Zoll
Gewicht: 13,5 kg
Monika Bock, München

1997

BMW Super-Tech folding
mountain bike,
1997
Design: BMW
Manufacturer: BMW AG, Munich,
Germany
Frame: Aluminum
Gears: 27-speed Shimano XTR derailleur
Wheels: 26"
Weight: 13.5 kg
Monika Bock, Munich

61 280

Richard Sapper / Francis Ferrain

Zoombike

1998/2000

Faltrad Zoombike, 1998/2000
Entwurf: Richard Sapper (1932–2015)/
Francis Ferrain
Hersteller: Elettromontaggi srl,
Massa Martana, Italien
Rahmen: Aluminium
Schaltung: Dreigang-Schaltung
Laufräder: 14 Zoll
Gewicht: 10 kg
Sammlung Sebastian Jacobi, Bad Ems

Zoombike folding bike, 1998–2000
Design: Richard Sapper (1932–2015)/
Francis Ferrain
Manufacturer: Elettromontaggi srl,
Massa Martana, Italy
Frame: Aluminum
Gears: Three-speed
Wheels: 14"
Weight: 10 kg
Collection Sebastian Jacobi, Bad Ems

62 284

Brady J. O'Hare / Michael G. Allsop /
James Allsop

Softride RocketWing

1998

Triathlon-/Straßenrennrad Softride
RocketWing, 1998
Entwurf: Brady J. O'Hare, Michael G. Allsop,
James Allsop
Hersteller: Softride Inc, Bellingham, USA
Rahmen: Aluminium
Schaltung: 18-Gang-Kettenschaltung Shimano
Dura-Ace
Laufräder: 26 Zoll
Gewicht: 8,3 kg
Die Neue Sammlung – The Design Museum

Softride RocketEing triathlon/road racing
bike, 1998
Design: Brady J. O'Hare, Michael G. Allsop,
James Allsop
Manufacturer: Softride Inc, Bellingham, USA
Frame: Aluminum
Gear shift: 18-speed Shimano Dura-Ace
derailleur
Wheels: 26"
Weight: 8.3 kg
Die Neue Sammlung – The Design Museum

63 288

Trek Bicycle Corporation

Trek Y-Foil

1998

Straßenrennrad Trek Y-Foil, 1998
Entwurf: Trek Bicycle Corporation
Hersteller: Trek Bicycle Corporation,
Waterloo (Wisconsin), USA
Rahmen: Karbon Monocoque
Schaltung: 27-Gang-Kettenschaltung
Campagnolo Racing Triple
Laufräder: 28 Zoll
Gewicht: 9,2 kg
Heinz Fingerhut – Velo-Classic

Trek Y-Foil road racing bike, 1998
Design: Trek Bicycle Corporation
Manufacturer: Trek Bicycle Corporation,
Waterloo (Wisconsin), USA
Frame: Carbon monocoque
Gears: 27-speed Campagnolo Racing
Triple derailleur
Wheels: 28"
Weight: 9.2 kg
Heinz Fingerhut – Velo-Classic

64   292

Marc Newson

MN02

Stadtfahrrad MN02, 2000
Entwurf: Marc Newson (*1963)
Hersteller: Biomega ApS, Hellerup,
Dänemark
Rahmen: Aluminium
Schaltung: Siebengang-Kettenschaltung
Shimano Deore
Laufräder: 26 Zoll
Gewicht: 13,9 kg
Die Neue Sammlung – The Design Museum

2000

MN02 city bike, 2000
Design: Marc Newson (*1963)
Manufacturer: Biomega ApS, Hellerup,
Denmark
Frame: Aluminum
Gears: seven-speed Shimano Deore
derailleur
Wheels: 26"
Weight: 13.9 kg
Die Neue Sammlung – The Design Museum

65   296

Ross Lovegrove

LDN/Biolove Carbon

Stadtfahrrad LDN/Biolove Carbon, 2003/2011
Entwurf: Ross Lovegrove (*1958)
Hersteller: Biomega ApS, Hellerup,
Dänemark
Rahmen: Karbon Monocoque
Schaltung: Achtgang-Nabenschaltung,
Kardanantrieb
Laufräder: 26 Zoll
Gewicht: 15,1 kg
Die Neue Sammlung – The Design Museum

2003/2011

LDN / Biolove Carbon city bike, 2003–11
Design: Ross Lovegrove (*1958)
Manufacturer: Biomega ApS, Hellerup,
Denmark
Frame: Carbon monocoque
Gears: Eight-speed hub gears, shaft drive
Wheels: 26"
Weight: 15.1 kg
Die Neue Sammlung – The Design Museum

66   300

Christian Zanzotti

Coren

Stadtfahrrad Coren, 2012
Entwurf: Christian Zanzotti (*1985)
Hersteller: UBC GmbH, Murr, Deutschland
Rahmen: Karbon T 1000
Schaltung: Gates Carbonriemen-Antrieb
Laufräder: 28 Zoll, Karbonfelgen
Gewicht: 7,7 kg
Zanzotti Industrial Design, München

2012

Coren city bike, 2012
Design: Christian Zanzotti (*1985)
Manufacturer: UBC GmbH, Murr, Germany
Frame: Carbon T 1000
Gear system: Gates carbon belt drive
Wheels: 28", carbon rims
Weight: 7.7 kg
Zanzotti Industrial Design, Munich

67   304

Paule Guérin / Till Breitfuss

Arvak

2014

Holzfahrrad Arvak, 2014
Entwurf: Paule Guérin / Till Breitfuss
Hersteller: Keim Cycles, Savonnière
(Indre-et-Loire), Frankreich
Rahmen: Eschenholz, 24 Lagen,
vakuumgeschichtet; Karbongabel
Laufräder: 28 Zoll, Karbon
Gewicht: 8,3 kg
Sammlung Reiner Balke

Arvak wooden bicycle, 2014
Design: Paule Guérin / Till Breitfuss
Manufacturer: Keim Cycles, Savonnière
(Indre-et-Loire), France
Frame: Ash wood, 24 layers, vacuum
laminated; carbon fork
Wheels: 28", carbon
Weight: 8.3 kg
Collection Reiner Balke

68   308

Nick Foley / Jacob Bouchard / Michael Liu

Jump, Mod. 5.6

2018

Elektrofahrrad Jump, Mod. 5.6, 2018
Entwurf: Nick Foley / Jacob Bouchard /
Michael Liu
Hersteller: Progear China Co. Ltd.,
Hongkong, China, für JUMP Bikes
(vormals Social Bicycles), San Francisco, USA
Rahmen: Aluminium
Schaltung / Motor: Dreigang-Nabenschaltung
Sturmey Archer / Bafang 250W 36V
Vorderrad-Nabenmotor
Laufräder: 26 Zoll
Gewicht: 33,7 kg
Die Neue Sammlung – The Design Museum

Jump electric bike, mod. 5.6, 2018
Design: Nick Foley / Jacob Bouchard /
Michael Liu
Manufacturer: Progear China Co. Ltd.,
Hong Kong, China for JUMP Bikes
(previously Social Bicycles), San Francisco, USA
Frame: Aluminum
Gears / Drive: Three-speed Sturmey Archer
hub gear / Bafang 250W 36V front hub motor
Wheels: 26"
Weight: 33.7 kg
Die Neue Sammlung – The Design Museum

69   312

Christian Zanzotti

Vässla Pedal

2021/22

Elektrofahrrad Vässla Pedal, 2021/22
Entwurf: Christian Zanzotti (*1985)
Hersteller: Vässla AB, Stockholm,
Schweden
Rahmen: Aluminium
Schaltung / Motor: Singlespeed, 250W,
Hinterrad-Nabenmotor, Riemenantrieb
Laufräder: 24 Zoll
Gewicht: 19 kg
Zanzotti Industrial Design, München

Vässla Pedal electric bike, 2021–2
Design: Christian Zanzotti (*1985)
Manufacturer: Vässla AB, Stockholm,
Sweden
Frame: Aluminum
Gearshift / motor: Singlespeed, 250W,
rear wheel hub motor, belt drive
Wheels: 24"
Weight: 19 kg
Zanzotti Industrial Design, Munich

70   316

Indexlab

New01bike

Stadtfahrrad New01bike, 2022
Entwurf: Indexlab (Pierpaolo Ruttico/
Francisco Martins Carabetta/Federico
Bordoni/Salvatore Urso)
Hersteller: eXgineering, Manno, Schweiz
Rahmen: Polycarbonat 3 D Druck
Laufräder: 27,5 x 1,50 Zoll
Gewicht: 13,2 kg
Indexlab, Lecco

2022

New01bike city bike, 2022
Design: Indexlab (Pierpaolo Ruttico/
Francisco Martins Carabetta/
Federico Bordoni/Salvatore Urso)
Manufacturer: eXgineering,
Manno, Switzerland
Frame: Polycarbonate 3 D print
Wheels: 27.5 x 1.50"
Weight: 13.2 kg
Indexlab, Lecco

Register / Index

Impressum / Imprint

Diese Publikation erscheint anlässlich der Ausstellung „Das Fahrrad – Designobjekt – Kultobjekt", Die Neue Sammlung – The Design Museum, Pinakothek der Moderne, München, 11.11.2022 – 22.09.2024

This catalogue is published on the occasion of the exhibition "The Bicycle: Designobject – Cultobject", Die Neue Sammlung – The Design Museum, Pinakothek der Moderne, Munich, November 10, 2022 – September 22, 2024.

© 2022 Die Neue Sammlung – The Design Museum, München, Buchhandlung und Verlag Walther und Franz Koenig, Köln, und Autor:innen / and the authors

Herausgeber
Published by
Angelika Nollert, Die Neue Sammlung – The Design Museum

Autor
Author
Josef Straßer

Redaktion
Editorial
Josef Straßer

Mitarbeit
Assistance
Polina Gedova
Linus Rapp
Michaela Klaube
Oliver Krug

Lektorat
Copy editing
Andrea Schaller

Gestaltung
Graphic design
wigel, Petra Lüer

Übersetzung
Translation
Jeremy Gaines

Fotografie
Photography
Kai Mewes

Bildbearbeitung
Plöckl Media Group GmbH
Franz Lichtenauer

Druckerei
Printing
Weber Offset, München

Bildnachweise
Image credits
© Die Neue Sammlung – The Design Museum (Kai Mewes)
© Brooklyn Museum, Marie Bernice Bitzer Fund, 2001. 36 (Abb. 4 / Fig. 4)
© 2020 Christie's Images Limited (Abb. 7 / Fig. 7)
© der abgebildeten Werke bei den Fotograf:innen, Urheber:innen, deren Erb:innen oder Rechtsnachfolger:innen
© photographers, authors, their heirs or legal successors of the works depicted

Verlag der Buchhandlung
Walther und Franz König
Ehrenstraße 4
D-50672 Köln
Tel.: +49 (0) 221 2 05 96-53
Fax: +49 (0) 221 2 05 96-60
verlag@buchhandlung-walther-koenig.de

Bibliografische Information der Deutschen Nationalbibliothek
Die Deutsche Nationalbibliothek verzeichnet diese Publikation in der Deutschen Nationalbibliografie; detaillierte bibliografische Daten sind über http://dnb.d-nb.de abrufbar.

Bibliographic information published by the Deutsche Nationalbibliothek
The Deutsche Nationalbibliothek lists this publication in the Deutsche Nationalbibliografie; detailed bibliographic data are available on the Internet at http://dnb.d-nb.de.

Printed in Germany

Vertrieb
Distribution
Germany, Austria, Switzerland / Europe
Buchhandlung Walther König
Ehrenstr. 4,
D – 50672 Köln
Tel.: +49 (0) 221 / 20 59 6 53
verlag@buchhandlung-walther-koenig.de

UK & Ireland
Cornerhouse Publications Ltd. – HOME
2 Tony Wilson Place
UK – Manchester M15 4FN
Tel.: +44 (0) 161 212 3466
publications@cornerhouse.org

Outside Europe
D.A.P. / Distributed Art Publishers, Inc.
75 Broad Street, Suite 630
USA – New York, NY 10004
Tel.: +1 (0) 212 627 1999
enadel@dapinc.com

ISBN 978-3-7533-0360-4

Eine Ausstellung der
Neuen Sammlung –
The Design Museum
An exhibition of
Die Neue Sammlung –
The Design Museum

Kurator
Curator
Josef Straßer

Ausstellungskonzept
Exhibition concept
Josef Straßer

Restauratorische Betreuung
Conservation department
Tim Bechthold, Julia Demeter, Helena Ernst,
Christian Huber

Registrar
Registrar
Waltraud Wiedenbauer

Museumstechnik
Technical department
Michael Daume, Cornelius von Heyking,
Florian Westphal

Beteiligte Firmen
Participating Firms
Büro für Gestaltung Wangler & Abele
Folienschriften Martin

Presse und Öffentlichkeitsarbeit
Press and public relations
Tine Nehler, Anika Koller

Online-Redaktion
Online editorial
Andrea Czermak

Online-Verwaltung
Online administration
Rainer Schmitzberger

Mit Dank an Leihgeber:innen
With thanks lenders
Deutsches Fahrradmuseum –
Ivan Sojc, Stefanie Faust
Reiner Balke
Monika Bock
Stephan Dornhofer
Dirk Eger
Adrien Elmiger
Sebastian Fischer
Heinz Fingerhut
Sebastian Jacobi
Eva Mayer

Gefördert
Sponsors